W9-BCS-483

3 0183 03103 5795

CHILDREN
OF THE
HOLOCAUST

CHILDREN
OF THE
HOLOCAUST

Conversations with
Sons and Daughters of Survivors

Helen Epstein

G.P. Putnam's Sons
New York

0040164/70
c. 1

Fourth Impression

Library of Congress Cataloging in Publication Data

Epstein, Helen, 1947-
   Children of the Holocaust.

   Bibliography
   1. Holocaust, Jewish (1939-1945)—Psychological aspects. I. Title.
D810.J4E62   940.53′1503′924   78-23429

ISBN 0-399-12316-4

PRINTED IN THE UNITED STATES OF AMERICA

ACKNOWLEDGMENTS

This book would not have been written without the cooperation and enthusiasm of the children of survivors whose names appear in this book, those whose names are disguised,* several hundred others with whom I spoke and corresponded over the last seven years, and many of our parents. I would particularly like to thank my mother for her moral support, patience and criticism.

I would also like to thank Dr. David M. Rubin and New York University for granting me a leave of absence from the Department of Journalism in order to write this book.

Four magazine editors worked with me on various aspects of my subject. They are: Charles Fenyvesi of *The National Jewish Monthly,* Murray Polner of *Present Tense,* Edward Klein and Holcomb Noble of the *New York Times Magazine.*

Several professionals took expensive time out to help me in my research. They are: Dr. Henry Krystal, Dr. William G. Niederland, Dr. Henry Fenigstein, Dr. Robert Jay Lifton, Eva Fogelman, Bella Savran, Henry Shaw and, particularly, Dr. Vivian Rakoff.

Many friends read parts of the manuscript, advised me, reassured me and kept me going. They are: Margo Jefferson, Pamela G. Hollie, Connie Shuman, Stephen Singular, Russ Patrick, Rosa Jordan, Jeff Swartz, Michael Rosenbluth, Moses Silverman, Allan Kaplan and Rochelle Rubinstein Kaplan.

Special thanks go to my agent Jim Brown, who is what every agent should be and more, and to my editors Barbara Wyden and Phyllis Grann for their consistent support, good sense and good taste.

*They are designated by an asterisk.

In memory of my father
and for my mother

CHILDREN
OF THE
HOLOCAUST

ONE

For years it lay in an iron box buried so deep inside me that I was never sure just what it was. I knew I carried slippery, combustible things more secret than sex and more dangerous than any shadow or ghost. Ghosts had shape and name. What lay inside my iron box had none. Whatever lived inside me was so potent that words crumbled before they could describe.

Sometimes I thought I carried a terrible bomb. I had caught glimpses of destruction. In school, when I had finished a test before time was up or was daydreaming on my way home, the safe world fell away and I saw things I knew no little girl should see. Blood and shattered glass. Piles of skeletons and blackened barbed wire with bits of flesh stuck to it the way flies stick to walls after they are swatted dead. Hills of suitcases, mountains of children's shoes. Whips, pistols, boots, knives and needles.

At night when my parents went out and my younger

brother and I sat watching television, our room, our very lives seemed unsafe and unguarded. Burglars and murderers might enter our apartment at any time and catch us unprepared. I made my brother my lieutenant and marched him off to the kitchen to be armed. I chose a potato masher, wooden spoons and two long knives from the drawer, and we stood vigil by the door until the scare paled or I was too tired to stand guard anymore.

Burglars and murderers—the words came in a pair—were always at large, liable to break up a party or disrupt my class in school or even take three thousand people out of Carnegie Hall. They would storm through the doors in their black boots and jackets, shoot their guns or just point them at people, shouting "Out! Quickly!" until everyone had filed out and the place was empty.

During the day, in the New York City streets, it was hard to imagine where these thousands of people would go. It was in the subways at rush hour that I saw them again. I stood, my face pressed to the glass in the first car beside the engineer's booth, watching the signals in the tunnel. The Seventh Avenue local became a train of cattle cars on its way to Poland. I closed my eyes as the train rumbled from station to station, willing the conductor to disregard the red signals, to rush ahead at full speed and crash the passengers to their deaths before they reached their destination. There would be no burial. The passengers would vanish.

In St. Patrick's Cathedral on Fifth Avenue there was a way of remembering people who were dead even if they didn't have graves. I would take a long thin taper from the rack beside the thick pillars and light a row of my own. I watched how the people prayed, how they dropped to their knees in the aisle, crossed the air with their fingers and then hurried out with their heads lowered. I did the same. I had to, or else that group of men in black boots and shiny jackets might turn up and take me away.

10

Sometimes I felt my iron box contained a tomb. The walls were stone, like those guarding the mummies in the Metropolitan Museum of Art and the air was cool. My grandmother Helena sat in one corner on a chair like a throne. Her brown hair was swept up above her ears and she looked stern although my father always said she had never hurt a soul. My grandfather Maximillian stood beside her, erect and tall like a military man. My grandfather Emil paced back and forth, arguing with himself in German, and my grandmother Josephine stood dreaming in a corner, dressed in shawls.

I did not know what the rest of them looked like: my uncle Erich and his wife and son; my uncle Bruno; my mother's first husband, Pepik, the one she had been married to before the war; and all the others, who were never even called by name. Our family tree had been burnt to a stump. Whole branches, great networks of leaves had disappeared into the sky and ground. There was no stone that marked their passage. All that was left were the fading photographs that my father kept in a yellow envelope underneath his desk.

Those photographs were not the usual kind of snapshots displayed in albums and shown to strangers. They were documents, evidence of our part in a history so powerful that whenever I tried to read about it in the books my father gave me or see it in the films he took me to, I could not take it in. The facts bounced like Ping-Pong balls inside my head, not only making no sense of their own but disordering whatever was already there.

The facts were these:

Just before the outbreak of the Second World War, there were nearly nine million Jews living in country villages, provincial towns, and large metropolitan centers throughout Europe. Seven years later, in Poland, Estonia, Latvia, Lithuania, Germany and Austria, 90 percent of them had

11

disappeared. In Czechoslovakia, where my father's family had lived for nearly five hundred years, more than 85 percent of the Jews were gone. In Greece, Holland, Hungary, White Russia, the Ukraine, Belgium, Yugoslavia, Rumania and Norway, half or more of the Jews who had been living there before the war had vanished by the time it was over.

Thirty-five million people had died in this war. Most of them were soldiers who had been killed in battle, and to whose memory hundreds of monuments and military cemeteries had been built all over the world. Five million of them were political prisoners, dissidents, anti-Fascists of various nationalities, homosexuals and gypsies who had been murdered by the Nazis. Six million—or two out of every three Jews in Europe—had also been murdered. For the murdered eleven million there were no graves. They had been gassed and then burned, like my grandmother Helena, my grandfather Maximillian and their sons, or shot into an open ditch like my grandmother Josephine and my grandfather Emil.

One third of the Jews escaped death at the hands of the Germans. Some died of natural causes. Some fled east to parts of Russia that remained unoccupied. Some went west to ports on the Atlantic or Mediterranean, ending up in the Americas, Australia, Israel, Shanghai. Some 400,000 to 500,-000 Jews who remained in Nazi-occupied Europe survived the war in labor camps; or in the forests fighting with small partisan groups; or in the forests hiding out on their own; or in the cities by passing as Christians with false papers; or confined for months and years to the constricted quarters of a secret pantry, attic or cellar. No more than 75,000 people outlived the Nazi concentration camps, and two of them were my parents.

The iron box contained a special room for my mother and father, warm and moist as a greenhouse. They lived there inside me, rare and separate from other beings. I did not need to know the statistics when I was a child: I knew my parents had crossed over a chasm, and that each of them had crossed it alone. I was their first companion, a new leaf, and I knew this leaf had to be pure life. This leaf was as different from death as good was from evil and the present from the past. It was evidence of the power of life over the power of destruction. It was proof that they had not died themselves. The door that led to that special room was secret; the place had to be protected.

I built my iron box carefully, the way we were taught in school that nuclear reactors were built. I conceived lead walls around the dangerous parts, concentric circles of water channels and air ducts that would soften and contain any kind of explosion. I enclosed it all with metal casing and buried the box far away from my brain toward the small of my back, in the part of my body that seemed least alive.

The box became a vault, collecting in darkness, always collecting, pictures, words, my parents' glances, becoming loaded with weight. It sank deeper as I grew older, so packed with undigested things that finally it became impossible to ignore. I knew the iron box would some day have to be dredged up into the light, opened, its contents sorted out, but I had built such fortifications that it had become inaccessible.

I needed tricks to get near it, strategies to cut through the belt of numbness that formed each time I made a move toward it. I needed company to look inside it, other voices to confirm that those things I carried inside me were real, that I had not made them up. My parents could not help me with this; they were part of it. Psychiatrists I distrusted; they had even more names to disguise things than I had already tried. There had to be other people like me, who shared what I carried, who had their own version of my iron box. There had to be, I thought, an invisible, silent family scattered about the world.

I began to look for them, to watch and listen, to collect their stories. I set out on a secret quest, so intimate I did not speak of it to anyone. I set out to find a group of people who, like me, were possessed by a history they had never lived. I wanted to ask them questions, so that I could reach the most elusive part of myself.

TWO

On a Sunday morning in the spring of 1977, in a blizzard that threatened to close down several airports, I flew to Toronto, Canada on the first leg of a journey that would take me into the homes and lives of several hundred children of Jewish survivors of the Second World War. I was twenty-nine years old, a New Yorker, a university professor, and a writer who had been reporting for newspapers and magazines since I was twenty. For nine years, I had been writing about other people's lives, learning to extract the essence of their experience and sensibility. Now, for the first time, I wanted to apply those skills to myself and to a group that had never before been the subject of journalistic inquiry—the children of the survivors of the Holocaust.

I had talked with other children of survivors before. Three of my closest childhood friends belonged to that quiet, invisible community, that peer group without a sign. After school, my friend Evelyn and I would often take our homework into Central Park and study Latin together, bound by a tacit affinity that we did not understand. Evelyn's parents, like mine, had insisted that she study Latin. They spoke English with thick accents; they had fled Vienna just as my parents had fled Prague. They read the newspapers as avidly as my own parents. A seemingly innocuous headline could plunge them into an hour-long debate. Like me, Evelyn did not have grandparents or any family besides her mother and father. Like my friend Jimmy, whose family had also fled Vienna, Evelyn never spoke about family, or history, or how her parents came to be living in New York City. But when I visited them, I felt at home. There was an intensity there, a kind of fierceness about living that was absent from the more casual, easygoing atmosphere of other homes. There was mystery of great consequence.

At my friend Mary's house, that mystery was sharpened by sadness. Her parents came from Poland and when they were alone they spoke Yiddish instead of German. They owned the small house in which they lived on West End Avenue and they rarely left it. Once Mary told me that they were afraid it would burn down or be looted if they left. I accepted that without question, as if it were a natural consideration. Neither did I wonder why they had given their only child a Christian name. All of our parents, the ones who had come to America after the war, were eccentric in my eyes. They were not like Americans, and we children were not like other American children. That fact was so obvious it did not require discussion and Mary, like Jimmy and Evelyn, never ventured to speculate on why that should be so. Friends, like family, are quick to shield each other from pain and although we all knew that a great deal of pain pervaded the households in which we were raised, we never addressed it by name.

At twenty-nine, I had decided to address it.

That was why I flew to Toronto. I was going to a strange city to meet a stranger as different from myself as another child of survivors who had grown up in the United States could possibly be. Her name was Deborah Schwartz*, and she had grown up in the South. She had been crowned her state's first Jewish beauty queen, and had spent a year behind the wheel of an official beauty pageant Oldsmobile that was turned in for a replacement every three thousand miles. Deborah had played the role of a Southern beauty queen to the hilt. She had visited county fairs, supermarkets and military bases. She had given dozens of gracious interviews to journalists representing city dailies, country weeklies, and even high school papers. She had addressed her state's legislature. She corresponded with hundreds of admirers on special stationery that had the imprint of her face and figure welded to the outline of her state. And she had walked down the runway in the Miss America Pageant in Atlantic City, a participant in one of the most American of rituals.

Her "talent" in the Miss America contest had been playing the piano and she had chosen Chopin's *Revolutionary Etude* because it had been played twenty-four hours a day over Polish radio when Adolf Hitler invaded Poland in 1939. The Second World War had greatly affected her family and, as a result, her own life, Deborah told the judges and newspaper reporters in Atlantic City. Her father, who came from a small town in Hungary, had spent the war in a labor camp and then in the underground. Her mother, who was also from a small town in Hungary, had celebrated her sixteenth birthday in the concentration camp of Auschwitz.

In the South, where the lives of local beauty queens are prime newspaper material, Deborah's story was published in dozens of versions. "OUT OF HORROR—LOVE AND BEAUTY" ran one headline. "NO NEGATIVE ATTITUDES FOR DEBORAH" proclaimed another. The newspaper accounts of her reign made much of her family history, largely because Deborah herself stressed its importance to her. "When I think of what my mother was going through at my age—do you realize

17

that her head was shaved completely?" she asked a newsman in Atlantic City. "She had nothing to eat. She was running around in the snow without shoes, and here I am, state queen at the Miss America contest—it's really unbelievable."

I felt utter bewilderment as I looked at the full-page features on Deborah Schwartz that appeared in Southern newspapers. It had never occurred to me that people like my parents could have emigrated to rural backwaters, places thick with tobacco fields, Baptist churches and trailer parks. I tried to imagine Hungarian accents softened by a Southern drawl, and what it was like to grow up rootless in a region which so clearly prized its history. I wondered at Deborah's unequivocal identification of herself as a child of survivors, the assurance of her voice.

I had often heard my own voice, sounding as if it belonged to someone else, explaining to people about the war. When I was small, the questions came from the other children: "Why does your Mommy wear that number on her arm?" I don't remember what I told them but none asked me a second time. It was later, in conversation with adults, that I remember how and what I replied. I no longer answered questions in the quick, unthinking way of a child. Discussion of the war split my being in two. My face remained calm, my voice matter-of-fact, but my feelings froze, keeping the conversation at bay, outside my body.

"You say you weren't born in New York?"

"No. In Prague. Czechoslovakia."

That part was easy. I was proud of being Czech.

"Your parents came here before the war then?"

"No. I was born in 1947."

"Oh, I see. So during the war they . . ."

"They were in concentration camp," I would say helpfully. "Each was the only survivor of the family."

The conversation usually died there. Few people questioned me further and those who did received flat, factual replies. *They were in concentration camp* was a warning. It meant don't step across this line I've drawn; watch the careless things you might otherwise say.

I had, by the time I was old enough to understand, heard what people said about survivors of the war: "Strange people. Crazy, some of them. You know, a human being can only take so much. Those people went through living hell. They went through things we can't imagine. It made them hard."

"I know a survivor," a woman had told me. "That man at the meat market with the blue number on his arm. Sweet man. Never raises his voice. Not like the others I've come across. You'd think they'd have learned something from their experience, wouldn't you? No. Those people seem to have learned nothing. Making money. That's all they're interested in."

I may have said *my parents were in concentration camp* calmly, smoothly, but in my ears the sentence rang like a declaration of loyalty. It put me squarely on the side of "those people," far away from the complacent, untouched Americans—Jews or Gentiles—who seemed to be so quick to make assumptions about things they did not understand. I answered their pity or embarrassment or confusion with pride. My parents were not particularly interested in money, they were not hard and they were not crazy, I told myself. They hadn't gotten divorced, like so many parents did. They never got drunk. They did not do illegal things. They were always home, unlike other parents who left their children behind and went on trips.

Although I thought these things to myself, I never said them out loud. I did not like talking about my parents or the war, because talk meant accepting that the war had happened and, more than anything else in the world, I wished it had not. The idea that my mother and my father had been forced out of their homes and made to live like animals—worse than animals—was too shameful to admit. To tell people that my parents had been in concentration camp in a cool, rational tone of voice was a kind of denial. Concentration camp became a location, not a prison or a death house or a human mill that turned free people into slaves. It became a badge of courage rather than a degradation. It became an untouchable standard of fortitude.

It suddenly occurred to me as I drove into Deborah's neighborhood, an upper-middle class Toronto suburb, that she might never have had any of those thoughts and reactions. It was six years since she had given interviews. In the interval, she had married a Canadian whose parents were also survivors and also came from small towns in Hungary; she had given birth to one child and was expecting another. Their house, a massive, split-level structure, stood at the end of a quiet street, frosted with snow. Its garage door was shut, all the curtains were drawn, and as I walked up the front steps with my tape recorder and suitcase I felt like an interloper, someone bringing unnecessary trouble.

I had had a hint of that feeling a week before in New York, when Deborah had telephoned me to confirm the date of my visit. In the first rush of excitement, we had agreed that I would stay with her in Toronto. Then came a cooler, more distanced telephone call. Perhaps it would be better if I found a hotel or made other arrangements? Her husband was studying for exams. It really wasn't a good time to have guests. There was a guardedness in Deborah's voice that had not been there the first time we spoke and it triggered a reserve of my own. We were strangers, after all, and I would be asking her questions that she was not accustomed to answering or even thinking about. A friend of mine, another child of survivors, who over the years had tried to talk me out of my plan to write about others like us, had told me that I was engaged in "stirring up shit to no good purpose." On that Sunday afternoon, as I knocked on Deborah's door, his words came back to me, and I waited, more than a little anxious, for her to appear.

The young woman who opened the door was eight

months pregnant and still moved like a beauty queen. For a moment her face looked blank and then she smiled—a full, unmistakably American smile brimming with self-possession. Deborah was accustomed to greeting strangers. Her poise and physical grace threw me into a confusion that I would spend the next few hours trying to shake.

Deborah prepared two cups of coffee. Her manner was leisurely. It was the only obviously Southern characteristic she had brought with her to Toronto. But reinforcing that unhurriedness was a reluctance to plunge too quickly into the topic that had led to our meeting. I sipped the coffee, thinking that it would not be easy to interview her. She was not an introspective person. She had spent a great deal of time presenting and living up to a Grace Kelly public image. The beauty pageant business had taught her to be careful, even suspicious. I had sent her some articles I had written and I had told her that a psychiatrist had found children of survivors severely traumatized by their parents' experiences. The very idea of psychiatric studies put her off.

"I became infuriated," she told me later. "I never felt abnormal in any way, shape or form. In fact, I always felt very much the opposite. I was living a very typical, normal, average life, playing the role of wife and mother to the best of my ability. I resented being talked about and categorized by anyone, especially by psychiatrists who were making strong negative remarks about my personality."

She was also wary of talking in depth to a stranger about her family even though she had done so many times before. "I was suspicious of your motives," she told me later. "I didn't know you and I wasn't sure how you would handle the whole thing. It seemed to me there were people trying to capitalize on the Holocaust and I object to seeing the memory of my family sensationalized."

But Deborah said nothing of the sort to me at the time. She was gracious. She asked me questions about myself. *Where had I been born? Where had my parents been during the war?*

21

Had any of my family survived? What did my parents do for a living? What had they done in Czechoslovakia? She was checking me out, with the peculiar brand of questions I would hear from many people before they would talk about themselves. Even after I had answered her questions, Deborah was reluctant to talk. "There're plenty of survivors in Toronto," she told me. "It was one of the cities they came to after the war. I called a couple of people I knew, because I thought this afternoon might be a good time to interview some of them. During the week, it will be harder."

Deborah looked at me over her coffee cup, her blue-gray eyes managing a combination of distance and cordiality. She wanted, I thought, to hear what kind of questions I intended to ask before answering them herself. She also wanted to watch me work and to decide whether I could be trusted. Many children of survivors whom I would encounter would do exactly what Deborah did that first day. I had to prove myself, make myself vulnerable before they would do the same.

A short time later, there was a knock on the front door and Deborah brought two young men into the living room. One was Irwin Diamond, a short, robust, extroverted man with a thick mustache under his nose and a small knitted skullcap on his head. Irwin was the first person Deborah had called when she knew I was arriving because he was active in the Jewish community. He was a teacher and vice-principal of one of its religious schools and the kind of guest who could always be relied on to keep a party lively. Irwin had brought along his close friend Eli Rubinstein who was, in perfect complement to Irwin, tall, thin and very shy. He was a doctoral student in philosophy who, I suspected, vastly preferred opening unfamiliar books to meeting strangers. Like Irwin, he was an observant Jew who lived within walking distance of *shul*, refrained from traveling, using electricity or answering the telephone on the Sabbath, and kept

22

a strictly kosher household. As Deborah ushered us all into the den and set about serving more coffee and cakes, I fiddled nervously with my tape recorder, as unconfident as though I were interviewing people for the first time in my life.

Stammering a little bit, I explained why I had come to Toronto, that I was interested in hearing the experiences of other children of survivors in order to clarify some things for myself, that I had no theories to prove. Irwin Diamond took this in with good humor and asked me a few questions about myself. Eli Rubinstein said nothing. His dark eyes seemed to be floating in his pale, fine-boned face and I had no clue as to what he was thinking.

Both men were twenty-nine years old, like me. Irwin had been born in Cheb, Czechoslovakia; Eli, in a Displaced Persons camp in Torino, Italy. Both had arrived in Canada as babies when their parents immigrated in 1948. They had attended religious schools, then university. Both had married daughters of Holocaust survivors and both were now enthusiastic fathers. "It isn't just the normal parental instinct," Eli Rubinstein said. "I really feel that my raising a family has cosmic significance. I feel I have a sacred duty to have children. I feel it's the only way to respond to the evil of the Holocaust and to assure that the death of my family and the Six Million was not in vain."

The import of his words and the clarity with which they were expressed startled me, Deborah, Irwin and even Eli himself. It was as if Eli had been waiting for years for an opportunity to say what he had just said.

"Are you named after someone who died in the war?" I asked him.

"Yes. My full name is Robert Eli Rubinstein," he replied, in the quiet voice that would not rise or fall very much for the next two hours. "But my Hebrew name is Eliahu Mordechai. I was named after both my grandfathers who were

23

murdered by the Germans. Although it's a weak substitute for not having grandparents, I've always felt that having their name enables something to live on in me."

A door slammed, and Joseph,* Deborah's younger brother, hurried in. He was twenty-two, red-haired, broad-shouldered and thoughtful, a sociology student. Without a word, he sat down in the circle. There were five of us now. All of us, like Eli, were named after people who had been murdered during the war, and as Eli continued speaking, his story merged with the stories each of us had heard at home, so much that the feelings he described became our own.

Eli's father, Béla Rubinstein, had been one of twelve children in a small town in Hungary before the war. Four survived; his father by working in a labor camp. Eli's mother, Judith, was one of four children. Only she and one brother were left of her family.

"I always had a feeling of something different in our house," Eli said, "but I couldn't ever really pin it down. I sensed there was something mysterious, something peculiar about the past, about the place where I was born but I didn't know what. I wondered about it: How did my parents end up here in Canada? It's obviously so difficult for them."

In 1948, I discovered later, representatives of the Canadian International Fur and Leather Workers Union, together with the Jewish Immigrants Aid Society and the Canadian government formed a commission to visit the Displaced Persons camps in Europe and bring back two hundred furriers and their families. When they arrived in Torino, Béla Rubinstein and his older brother claimed that their father had been a fur trader although, in fact, they knew nothing at all about furs. A few months later they were given the choice of emigrating to Montreal, Toronto or Winnipeg—all unfamiliar names. The Rubinsteins made inquiries. Winnipeg, people said, was very cold, and Montreal was a bilingual city. So they settled on Toronto where they knew not a soul. For the first three years, the men and their wives all worked as furriers, six days a week, at home as well as in the factory, from early in the morning until late into the night.

"I was aware that we lived in considerable poverty despite all this work," Eli said, "and that I had to do without a lot of things my friends had. Other children had grandparents and I didn't have a single one. When I asked my mother about that, she said that bad people had killed them. I didn't understand who these people were or why they would want to kill my grandparents. I wasn't aware of any connection between their being killed and their being Jewish.

"I knew there was this country, Hungary, far across the ocean, where my parents used to live. Somehow, something had happened, that world came to an end and now we were here in a new world. Their lives consisted of two parts: pre-War and post-War. That's how their calendar worked if they wanted to place an event. The war was such a turning point in their lives that they would constantly be referring to it without talking about it. So I was aware there had been a war with a capital 'W' which was very different from the kind of war I saw on TV with cowboys and Indians. But I didn't pursue the mystery. I just lived with it until one day when I was ten my cousin made the revelation to me."

The two boys were playing together when Eli's cousin began talking about a man named Hitler who had killed all their relatives because they were Jewish. Eli, as he recalled, could not make any sense of it. He had never heard of Hitler before. And what reason would he have had for killing all their relatives? His cousin could not elaborate. The Rubinstein family did not believe in talking to the children about the war, Eli's mother told me later. "Some of the kids still don't know anything about it," she said, "and their parents feel this is a good thing. They say, 'Why should they find out? It has nothing to do with them.' I waited to tell Eli. I waited until he was sixteen."

"My father to this day rarely says anything about the war," Eli said. "He gets jumpy, very edgy, when my mother starts talking about it. He tries to change the subject or shifts around in his chair or finds an excuse to leave the room. Once in a while, he'll blurt something out and then regret it afterwards. What I know of my father's experience I learned mainly from my mother."

Like my mother, and Deborah and Joseph's mother, Eli's mother would often drift into a memory of the war as she stood in the kitchen preparing dinner, or sat at the kitchen table afterwards. "I have a very difficult time recalling the stories she told me exactly. I couldn't tell you one and be sure I had the details right if my life depended on it," Eli said. "It was very painful to listen to. These were things that had happened to my mother and who's closer to me than my mother? Sometimes I cried but I was embarrassed to have her see me doing that. I certainly didn't want to hurt my mother further by upsetting her. I would feel the tears billowing up in my eyes and I would force myself not to cry. I would wipe my eyes so that she wouldn't see. I rarely asked a question, but I felt compelled to listen. I wanted to hear and I didn't want to hear. And I had extraordinary difficulty remembering what she told me. I have a pretty good memory and I usually recall the most basic trivia very well. But about this, my memory is very poor. I can't even remember the number on my mother's arm. I don't know what it is."

Eli glanced up at the four people watching him. His dark brown eyes shone against the pallor of his skin. No one said a word. None of the children of survivors I spoke with could recall the numbers, their order, or even the arm on which their parents bore a tattoo. Those whose parents had not been tattooed were relieved that they had escaped the procedure. It was an indelible brand, a constant reminder of suffering. The thought of it drew us together. I had the peculiar sensation of plasma flowing through the five of us.

An intimacy had settled in. Eli was no longer shy or tentative; he spoke fluently.

"By the time I began school, my mother had stopped working, to stay at home with me and my baby sister, Rochelle. My father still did not feel financially secure but the family had set up their own fur business and even employed a man or two. When I refused to speak Hungarian anymore, my parents cooperated. They had every intention of adapting to the new reality and my mother always said she learned along with me when she helped me with my schoolwork. My parents always said that a person can lose everything, but what's inside his head stays there. I had to acquire an education, they said, because our enemies could take everything away from us but that. Little by little, as I became aware of who the enemies were, I began to understand. Education is closely related to the idea of being self-sufficient."

Deborah looked up at him. She had been listening attentively, more than a little surprised. Like the rest of us, she was hearing Eli describe her own family.

"I was a fairly usual, though introverted, little boy. My parents were religious Jews and I was a dutiful child. I was never a rebel. I never violated the Sabbath or ate non-kosher food. But I wondered about things. I wondered about God. The standard question of how a merciful, beneficent God could allow millions of innocent men, women and children to perish. That was the question for me and it never, ever came up in school. It was taboo. In *yeshiva*, the religious high school I attended, the emphasis was on rabbinic texts. If you spend all your waking hours absorbed in them, you don't have any energy left for worrying about troublesome questions. In *yeshiva*, there is no such thing as free time. You go from early morning until night with prayer three times a day and required study sessions in the evening.

"We never touched upon the Holocaust in *yeshiva*. No one was competent; everyone was afraid. It could lead you into

27

dangerous territory. Only once, during the Eichmann trial, did we talk about it. We had a substitute teacher from Israel. He told us that Israeli agents had just apprehended a man called Eichmann in Argentina. I had never heard of Eichmann. The other kids hadn't either. So he told us. It gave me a nice feeling to know they had caught him. When you are twelve or thirteen, you're a bit bloodthirsty and after the teacher had explained what he had done, I identified him as one of the people responsible for killing my family. I had a certain satisfaction knowing that they were no doubt going to kill him.

"But we never got into the really weighty problems of the Holocaust with him or any other teacher. I don't know how many other boys were troubled by these things. Probably not many. But there just wasn't anyone to talk to about them. I admired and respected my teachers in *yeshiva*. I figured they're the experts. If they can't cope with these things, nobody can. So I just let it go at that. But privately, I continued to ask all kinds of questions, questions of good and evil and how it was possible that these things could have happened. I thought it was blasphemous to give the traditional answer that God in His wisdom knows what He's doing and it is not for us finite mortals to question His ways. That's the stock answer that's been given by Jewish thinkers throughout the ages to the various catastrophes that have befallen the Jewish people.

"I found that answer very hard to accept. I don't think that someone who lives in the twentieth century can be satisfied with it. What happened during the Holocaust is not merely quantitatively different from what happened to the Jews earlier but qualitatively different as well. There is something demonic about the goal of the Nazis to exterminate the Jewish people in their entirety, something that was totally lacking in all previous persecutions. For the first time in history, the murder of Jews became the national policy of a 'civilized' government, an end in itself. That idea is virtually impossible to relate to our experience in North America. My parents had come through that ordeal and I had boundless admiration for both of them, for surviving with dignity, for pulling the pieces together and succeeding so beautifully in their new life. I'm very proud of the fact that my father, my uncle, and my cousin, who arrived in this country as penniless refugees, managed to create a highly successful business instead of succumbing to despair. I never thought of my parents going through indignity or humiliation. I don't remember ever being angry at them or ashamed of them because of what they went through. But I always wanted to talk about it with someone. Talking about your experience legitimizes it in a way. It lets you know you are normal."

Eli's questions led him to philosophy. He entered the University of Toronto as a philosophy student, one of the only two graduates of his *yeshiva* ever to do so. His parents, who had always stressed the importance of acquiring skills as well as knowledge, were not pleased with their son's decision, but they put no obstacles in his way.

When he was twenty-one, Eli startled them, his friends and himself by suddenly emerging from reclusiveness and becoming a leader of the Toronto Student Committee for Soviet Jewry. "I still don't understand exactly how it happened," Eli said, "but I found myself making speeches at rallies, shouting into a megaphone outside the Soviet Embassy in Ottawa and even applying for a visa to go to Russia. That was in 1971, when there were no Soviet Jews in Canada and when there was not much public awareness of the problem. It was very much out of character for me. I had never done anything like that before, and my parents worried that something would happen to me."

They became even more alarmed the following year when Eli decided to go to Hungary to visit the town in which his family had lived. "It was a pilgrimage," Eli told us. "I just wanted to establish some sort of contact with my past. I wanted to stand in the place where all the lost people I never knew had lived. By standing there, by being among the people they had lived with, I thought I could come as close as possible. Otherwise, they would be just phantoms, names my parents mentioned.

"When my parents left Hungary they both vowed never to set foot in the country again. They couldn't understand what would drive their son, who had been born outside, to go back. They had nightmares about what might happen to me. I had to find a way of reporting back to them in Toronto every other day, to let them know I was okay.

"I didn't make it back to my mother's hometown but I did make it to where my father grew up. It is a little hamlet. Everyone came out to look me over. All the peasant women were chattering, gossiping among themselves until finally one of them came and asked me who I was. I said I was the son of Béla Rubinstein, who used to live there before the war. They were all very excited about that but seemed a bit nervous as well. Some of them were afraid I had come to reclaim my father's house and flour mill—which had long been nationalized anyway. I felt very, very uncomfortable. It was one of the lousiest feelings I had ever had in my life. It was as if I were a phoenix risen from the ashes and that I should not be there: I should be dead.

"And I think they felt, 'Where did this guy come from? You mean there are still Jews alive somewhere?'

"They were all very solicitous. They asked how my father was doing. Some of them said they had heard that all the Jews who had once lived in this village were alive in America and that they were all wealthy and happy. That was how they soothed their consciences, I guess. They talked among themselves about me, always referring to me as the Jew. I felt like an alien creature in that little village. All during my stay in Hungary I had the feeling of being in the presence of ghosts. It made me feel the events that had been so remote before."

Eli stopped talking for a moment and again no one said anything. I had made the same pilgrimage, only mine had been to Prague. I had wandered for hours in the cobblestoned streets, looking for the house in which my parents had lived, the hospital in which I was born, the grocery store where my mother bought food and the parks in which she had played as a child. Everything was gray in Prague, infused with a great brooding melancholy. I, too, had felt the presence of ghosts.

"You know," Eli continued, "when you live after the fact, you feel an impotent rage. You ask, even though you know the answer: Why didn't anyone do something to stop it? I fantasize about my being there and taking up arms. One of my fantasies today, something I still have at the age of twenty-nine, is getting my hands on a Nazi. I think of all of them as one person who killed my family. I would like to torture him and mutilate him. It scares me when I have thoughts like that. It shocks me because I am not a violent person. In normal circumstances I can't imagine myself doing violence to any other human being.

"There are other things as well. I am in awe of my parents. I often wonder if I could have survived myself and I doubt whether I could have. Being their child has given me a certain depth, a seriousness about life that most people can't possibly have. I'm aware of the evil in the world and I'm not complacent. I feel it requires an active struggle to prevent a revival of the sort of thing that led to the murder of my family. I'm especially sensitive to racism because I identify with the target. That brings out a certain activism in me that wouldn't be there otherwise.

"I'm also uneasy. I can't feel too secure. I can't take it for granted that I will live out my life in peace in Canada. My background has very much influenced my choices in life. Someone who doesn't have that background can't possibly understand me. When I chose my wife, I didn't go out looking for a child of Holocaust survivors, but I do know

31

that my parents-in-law understand me better than native American or Canadian parents could. Also, I've gone into the family business, although I do teach a course in Jewish philosophy. Had I chosen a purely academic career I would have had to move out of Toronto. I want to live where my parents and family are.

"As my parents get older, I'm beginning to sense that everything isn't quite in order, that what they went through just can't be suppressed. I have this fear that it's going to take its toll in a very terrible way. Physically, it's taken its toll on my mother already. She went through some terrible treatment in Auschwitz. She was young and resilient at the time. But the Holocaust is beginning to catch up with her. A few years ago she had an operation for what the doctors diagnosed as bursitis. It turned out when they operated that her shoulder bone was deformed. They questioned her about it and it was something she had blocked out of her memory. A guard had struck her very hard in Auschwitz. There was no care and the cold and the damp damaged it. Now she has trouble with the other arm and her inner ear. I never had the feeling she was maladjusted though. She was always her pleasant, charming self.

"The past comes through in subtle ways now. Uncertainty about the future, when on the surface things would appear very stable and secure. There's a reluctance to accept success and be smug about it. Canada has been very good to us. But my parents feel they can't be too secure, even though they are very rooted here. If you find yourself becoming too secure, you have to shake yourself up, to spare yourself the terrible feeling when someone does it to you."

Eli Rubinstein stopped talking and this time he did not continue. He appeared surprised, as surprised as his friend Irwin Diamond. "As I spoke," he told me later, "I began to realize things on a conscious level that I had known all along but had never put into words. Before, even with Irwin, it was a silent brotherhood. We felt a certain kinship but we

32

had never articulated it before. It was a revelation to him and to me too."

The five of us seated around the tape recorder in Deborah's den did not say much to each other then. We all had retreated into our own thoughts and memories which Eli's long monologue had set into motion. The two men rose to leave. It was late; their families were waiting. As they stood by the door getting into their coats, they appeared to me as different people than those who had come in early that afternoon. Something basic, something I still did not understand, had made us familiar to one another, something that overrode differences in temperament, religious belief, lifestyle, ambition, and personal priorities.

I felt excited. Eli had not only articulated some of his own feelings for the first time, but some of mine as well. A stranger in a strange city had confirmed the reality of my own experience. What Eli had spoken about was only a beginning, but it was a good one. I made arrangements to see Deborah again later on that week. I did not then know where this beginning would take me, that I would be coming back to Toronto, living there for months at a time. All I wanted was to get to a place where I could replay Eli's voice and put on paper what he had said. I wanted to read and reread it.

THREE

That night, when Eli Rubinstein returned home, he made a rare telephone call to his younger sister. The afternoon's events had startled him. He had been moved as much by the feelings he had found himself putting into words for the first time as by the reaction they had evoked. His friend, Irwin, who was always so outgoing, even tactless sometimes, had been curiously silent. "You've said it all," was his only comment when Eli had finished speaking. Joseph and his sister Deborah had also appeared subdued and Eli began to wonder how his own sister, Rochelle, would have reacted.

Although the two had never discussed the effects their parents' war experiences had had on them, he was convinced that his sister had been very much affected. That night, he told her to call me, and she did.

"It was an unusual thing for me to do," Rochelle Rubinstein Kaplan told me later. "I hate calling people on the telephone, particularly strangers. But I felt excited. I wanted to tell you a lot of things. I didn't exactly know what. I had hardly talked about the subject before and whenever I did, I never got anywhere."

Unlike her brother, who lived within walking distance of his parents' suburban home, Rochelle lived downtown. I made my way to her apartment through a metropolitan complex that housed a supermarket, several dozen expensive stores, two cinemas, eight sets of escalators and fifty floors of residential units. It was plush, shiny, antiseptically clean, and as far removed from her family's community as one could find in the city.

In Downsview, where Eli and Rochelle's parents lived, life had been reconstructed after the European model. Families had reputations to maintain. Success was measured not only in property but in the continued adhesion of children to tradition. Much of the community life centered around *shul*, and a rich pattern of weddings, engagement parties, circumcisions, and religious festivals. The men worked in business. Their wives shopped, kept house, planned social events, exchanged menus and conducted far-flung, lively gossip over the telephone. There were close ties between the religious community in Downsview and other North American religious communities, which provided an enormous pool of people to talk about. They discussed new matches for the young people, wayward children, unsuccessful husbands, neglectful wives. Most of their children attended Jewish schools. Young women were expected to marry before they were twenty, and to begin shopping for maternity clothes within a year.

At its best, it was a warm, cohesive society, which maintained tradition and took care of its own. At its worst, it was like a fishbowl, where it was difficult to keep secrets, where men and women competed in religious one-upmanship and where some people did not speak to others because they had been left off the guest list of a social event three years before.

Since adolescence, Rochelle had been struggling to leave.

"She was a little bit revolutionary," her father told me indulgently. "She never said much," her mother told me, "and she didn't argue. But she never wanted to do what other people did." When she turned seventeen, Rochelle had taken to bed until her parents consented to allow her to attend college in New York City. She had attended a religious school, Stern College for Women. She also took classes at the New York School of Visual Arts, shopped at Bloomingdale's, wandered happily in Manhattan and enjoyed anonymity for the first time in her life. Up to that time she had rarely visited downtown Toronto or eaten in a restaurant since her family observed strict dietary law. New York, with its many kosher restaurants and less parochial Jewish community made her feel free. She was drawn to museums, rock concerts, and theater. Nevertheless, at twenty-one, she married Allan Kaplan, the son of an American rabbi and a student at Yeshiva University. They were married in Toronto, at a lavish wedding with five hundred guests.

Allan had been accepted at several medical schools in the United States and had decided upon New York University, where he had been offered a generous scholarship. The couple had already found an apartment in Manhattan and Rochelle had made plans to enter art school when Allan was accepted at the University of Toronto as well. When Rochelle's father learned that the couple had considered the option of Toronto and rejected it, he urged them to reconsider. He became ill at the prospect of his only daughter living in New York for four years, so ill that Rochelle flew to Toronto to see him. When she arrived he told her, for the first and only time, that he had been married before the war. He had lost two sons to the Nazis and he could not bear the thought of being separated from his daughter for so long a time. Then, his eyes full of tears, he had left the room.

The couple settled in Toronto, but downtown, where Rochelle felt she would have more breathing space. Now

36

twenty-three, Rochelle looked as though she had never lived anywhere else but the center of a large city. She was wearing jeans. Her long, dark-blond hair fell loosely over her shoulders. There was a modesty in her manner, a reserve she shared with her brother Eli, but there was nothing I could see in her or her apartment that offered an indication of her background. The walls were hung with small, vivid watercolors she had painted. The shelves held music boxes, piles of paperback books and magazines. The stereo played rock music. The dining room table was cluttered with paints, paper and other artist supplies.

Her parents had resigned themselves to this lifestyle so different from their own. They were relieved she was living in Toronto and that she had married a good and religious man. Like most survivors, their most pressing concern was that their children be healthy and, above all, safe. They were reasonable people and open-minded to a degree that was unusual in their tightly circumscribed community. Yet, when it came to their children, a certain fear invariably colored their behavior. Every evening when Béla Rubinstein came home from work, he asked his wife whether she had heard from Rochelle. Perhaps they should give her a call?

"My relationship with my parents has always been a serious one," Rochelle told me when we met. "It's not casual. I think a lot of other kids took their parents for granted. They were there to serve them mostly. We had to be gentle with our parents. Terrible things had happened, so terrible they didn't want us to know about them. I thought a lot about my parents. It was not as if they were the parents and we were the children. We became the parents sometimes and I didn't like that. I would throw tantrums and rebel against the idea of protecting them, unlike my brother, who was always their protector. We often try to protect each other, even now. It's a very tender relationship in that way. There's this deep, deep love that transcends everything. We're always trying to shield each other from pain."

Rochelle hesitated. She talked in stops and starts, in scattered bursts of words that flew out of her mouth, accompanied by quick movements of her small, clean hands. She looked like an artist's model with her long hair falling in wisps over her face. She was slim, yet not boyishly so. A pale-blue work shirt brought out the same color in her half-absent eyes. There was a tentativeness in her speech, a self-effacing quality, that drew me close to her, that made me want to assure her that what she had to say was important. Once a week she conducted art therapy with prisoners at a minimal security institution in Brampton. I imagined that the men she worked with regarded her as some sort of spirit that had wandered into their prison by mistake.

"I was always quiet. I was scared and extremely quiet as a child. It was a very quiet house. My father was always away, working hard, and my mother was in the kitchen, wearing her apron. Eli was five years older than me, always trying to lecture me, being more of a father than my father was. But I remember hearing things in the air. Tensions. I was always expecting some kind of explosion. I think I had some strange idea that it was because of me, that it was because I wasn't good. If I wasn't good, something terrible would happen.

"My mother had the number on her arm," Rochelle said, and the tone of her voice made me see, with perfect clarity, the blue imprint on my mother's arm. "I never asked her about the number or about anything else related to the war. My brother talked about it with her and hearing that made me aware of it. My brother used to ask my mother all kinds of questions. He was like a journalist. It seemed to me that he pretended he was interested in collecting facts. It would be in the evening, my mother would be clearing up and Eli would be at the table in the kitchen and I'd be hovering in the background. I'd want to tell them to stop. I was curious about it but the feeling of anger always overtook me. I was kind of mortified when Eli asked questions. I was envious that he could talk about it. I was never able to talk about it. There was too much feeling there. He seemed to be pulling

38

things out of my mother and then just leaving them there, exposed. He was breaking my rules."

Rochelle smiled. "I had this magic system of rules when I was a child. There were things you could do and couldn't do and certain things were not allowed to be touched and if you touched them it would be like a grenade that would explode. I think I felt these things inside me. I was very careful not to let them out, which is probably why I was so quiet and watchful.

"I can't remember specifically what they talked about but I can remember what they were *like* when they talked about the war. My father's face got pale and he withdrew completely. He would never talk about the war himself and on Friday nights at the dinner table if my mother did, he'd start singing. My mother got very sentimental and sometimes she cried and I hated that. I didn't know what to do. She'd get this faraway look in her eyes and she'd start dreaming. She really romanticized a lot about the past, about her parents when she was growing up. She idealized her father. And the people during the war—they were all saints! I didn't hear about bad Germans. I just heard about wonderful people. I remember her talking about the friends she was with in Auschwitz and how they took care of each other and when they shaved their heads they started laughing, they thought it was so funny.

"I was horrified; I couldn't understand how they could laugh. There were all kinds of stories like that. Someone had a baby that they hid. Close calls. Once they saw some berries in the forest and wanted to eat them. The Germans thought they wanted to escape and ordered them to be executed the next day. But the guard who was supposed to be watching them got them out because he didn't want to get into trouble. My mother never said anything bad about anyone and that really confused me. She would tell me about terrible things and she would make them almost into a nice fairy tale with a happy ending. She was so lucky to have come out, and look what she has now in Canada!

What a nice family! I never heard her blame anyone for anything."

A note of distress had come into Rochelle's voice but her face retained the same slightly embarrassed expression it had taken on at the beginning of our conversation. It seemed to me that she was just beginning to feel what she was saying and the feeling impinged on her voice, making it smaller.

"One Friday night when I was thirteen years old, my mother called me into the living room. She said, 'Your father doesn't know I'm telling you this, but he was married and he had two lovely children and they were killed during the war. He never wanted to talk about it but I think you should know.'

"I didn't say anything. I just sat there. I didn't even look at her. It was a strange feeling, not being able to ask questions when there were so many I wanted to ask. I never heard anything about it again until that time Allan was accepted by the medical school in Toronto. My father told Allan that he has a picture of them which he looks at sometimes but no one else sees it, not even my mother. I have two dresses that belonged to my father's first wife. I found them a few years after my mother told me and I was so excited I made my mother alter them for me. I wore each once. Now I keep them in my closet and look at them."

Much later, Rochelle showed me the dresses, clean, freshly pressed, and clearly forty years old. They hung among her capes and shawls and blue jeans in the closet of her bedroom. As a teen-ager, her mother told me, Rochelle had been the trend-setter of her class. She had always wanted to dress in men's suits, shirts and ties, provoking community gossip and endless fights at home.

"My parents would always give me the same silly arguments about clothing. They wanted me to be something I could never be. They screened whoever I went out with and after a while I stopped bringing anyone home. Every year, they threatened to send me to a more religious school. I didn't like religion and religious people. I blamed them for

40

not having the answers. I couldn't believe in this God that I read about all the time. I saw no indication of Him anywhere. How could He have let all of this happen? I asked. I wanted to say: How could He have let all these terrible things happen to *you?* I didn't understand all this business of the Chosen People. It seemed we had been chosen for suffering and not for anything nice."

In school, in Hebrew class, Rochelle remembered talk of the Holocaust but she did not relate it to her own family. "I thought it happened in another world in another time. Way back in history. They talked a great deal about it but it seemed to have no effect on me. I used to feel guilty about not feeling anything. I thought there was something wrong with me. I couldn't figure it out. I would see people start to cry when they heard about the six million Jews and here I was, the child of survivors, and I didn't feel anything.

"I had my own theories about the Holocaust. I saw a face that was Sophia Loren's face: skin stretched tight and blazing eyes, a very dignified lady. She was suffering silently, trying to preserve her dignity, and because she was so noble and dignified, she had to be saved, because a person like that can come to no harm. What she was suffering was that people did not understand her. People were thinking she was something she wasn't. That was *my* way of suffering as a child. That was one thing I could identify with. When I thought of torture, it was a psychological terror more than a physical one. Being forced over and over again to feel exposed, to have your qualities perverted and twisted and turned into a handicap.

"I don't think my parents ever told me about being hit or tortured. The most important message was that they had suffered and they were fragile. They appeared to be very strong people but we had to be gentle with them because they could shatter very easily. I had no right to get angry at them—and they were the *only* people I ever remember feeling angry at. I felt they had imposed a burden on me and I had a right to feel a little resentful."

41

"What was the burden?" I asked, knowing the answer.

"I had to be happy in order to make up for everything that had happened," Rochelle said. "It was a tremendous responsibility. I didn't know if I could do it. It was as if each of us was making up for a lost person.

"I was taught that the most terrible thing is to be selfish. To put yourself first. I equated that with being happy, so my conclusion was that I didn't *deserve* to be happy even if I was expected to be. My parents always said they wanted me to be happy. They wanted me to have a good life and a peaceful life with no tragedy in it. But when I indulged myself and did something I really enjoyed, I used to think: I should be suffering.

"Somewhere I got the idea that suffering was a noble thing. All our relatives who were so brave and noble had suffered. I thought if I wanted to be a special, noble person, I had to suffer too. And I tried. Children suffer. I *wanted* to suffer. Sometimes, I wanted to be dead. Death was never scary to me. Ghosts were scary, torture was scary, but not death. Death was like a blanket, soft, like being held in someone's arms."

Death had never frightened me either, I thought. Everyone in my family besides my parents had been there, in death, when I was born. It was the only place where we could hold a reunion.

"The whole thing was something I was trying constantly to keep out of my mind. I find history very hard to read. My mind just rebels. Especially about the war or about Israel. I wanted always just to escape from the whole thing. I wanted to be a special kind of Jew, a Jew who wasn't too Jewish. I stayed observant but I didn't want to be conspicuous. I had this theory if people knew I'd be one of the first to be taken away. I had very blond hair when I was young and I got very upset when it began to turn dark. When people would say *you don't look Jewish*, it made me happy. I thought I was safe. And when it turned darker I thought I'd never escape.

"I was forced to confront it for the first time when I went

42

to Israel on a Yeshiva University tour. I was sixteen. We visited the Yad VaShem memorial in Jerusalem. I saw a photograph there of two children and all of a sudden I had this absolutely positive feeling that these children were my father's two sons. I felt so terrible for being there, standing there and looking at it. Finally I was feeling something and it was very strong. I wanted to talk. I tried to explain to this guy I was with but he didn't respond, he just changed the subject. And it was so important to me, seeing that photograph, that I didn't want to ruin the experience. So I forgot it.

"I always thought when I was growing up that it was not good to talk about your personal feelings. Sexual feelings for sure you didn't talk about, but it was the same with very private things. I guess that's why I never talked about this subject before. I thought I wasn't allowed to. It's very unusual for someone in the religious community to see a psychiatrist and, if they do, they don't discuss it. There's a stigma attached. I wasn't ready to see a psychiatrist. But I think I felt a need for some kind of help. I first heard about art therapy when I was at school and it seemed a perfect solution. I would be *studying* art therapy. I'd be learning to be an art therapist. The emphasis when I talked to my family was on the art, not the therapy.

"I was twenty-two, the youngest and the only Jewish person in a class of English middle-class Toronto ladies. In the first class, I thought I was being very creative and open. I work very easily and there were all kinds of ideas. Light, pretty, airy stuff. The second session the therapist said to try to get in touch with a feeling and not to think about it, just to do it. I was feeling a feeling that I often get. I felt something like a heavy black object weighing me down. Sometimes it's in my gut but other times it's almost weighing my brain down so that I can't think straight. My head's fogged up, I don't know what I'm feeling and all I want to do is go to sleep.

"So I set out to draw this. I got very excited. I didn't

know what I was doing. I got very involved. When I finished and put it up on the wall, I was very moved by what I had done. I was also a little bit scared. For the first time in my life, my ugly feelings came out . My ugly and hateful feelings. The painting was just one big symbol. It was about two feet by one and a half. It was mostly black and red. Blood and barbed wire. There was one little yellow star of David in it. Ghostly figures. As I was drawing I had no idea what I was drawing but that black thing I had always felt was released from my shoulders, like a cape.

"Then those English Toronto ladies asked me to explain what it was all about. They didn't know much about the war. I told them that my parents had been in concentration camps, that a large part of my family had been killed in them, including my father's first wife and his sons and my mother's fiancé and her parents and brothers. They had never had any experience with someone like me. They asked all kinds of questions and I was happy they asked. It gave me a chance to answer.

"I guess because these people weren't Jewish themselves, they didn't feel guilty. That's the reaction I've found among a lot of Jews who didn't go through it or whose parents didn't. I felt true sympathy from these women and a pretty objective understanding of what I was saying. I felt they were really trying to understand me and it was a great feeling. I felt really free. So lightheaded. Very clear and clean. That foggy feeling was gone. I guess I was trying so hard not to feel all the time that half my emotions had been lost to me. I saw a thousand images at once. All these images I had imagined or heard about when I was young. They all came together. Strong feelings, violent feelings that I never thought I was allowed to express.

"It was the first time I ever felt any real kind of emotion about the whole thing."

Rochelle and I sat looking at each other. In the back of my mind, as if in a cloud, I saw a line of women standing in formation near a barracks. Rochelle's mother and my mother were standing close to each other. I was suddenly and absolutely sure that they had been in Auschwitz together and that Rochelle and I were thereby sisters. But the thought struck me as so mawkish that I shook it off. It was only a year later when our mothers met that we discovered that they had arrived in Auschwitz within two days of one another, that they were the same age, the same height and build, that they had in all probability passed each other in the multitude of bodies in the women's camp.

Of all the children of survivors I had met, Rochelle struck the most responsive chord in me. I, too, had never been able to feel what I imagined other people felt when they spoke of the war. I, too, had watched other people cry at memorial services and at films about the Holocaust. I never could. All I felt was a numbness, a cold, deadening blanket which covered me like a fog. I felt it creeping over me again as I sat in Rochelle's living room. But beneath it, deep down, I felt something give way, like a bank of sand crumbling under an ocean wave. That night, as I sat bent over my typewriter, listening to Rochelle's soft, hesitant voice coming out of my tape recorder, I began to cry. I typed with tears blurring my view of the paper on which I was transcribing her words, and I began to remember things I had never allowed myself to remember before.

FOUR

At five-thirty, when her girls had swept up and gone home, my mother sat alone in her workroom and lit the sixteenth or seventeenth cigarette of the day. She leaned her head on her open palm and stared out at the dim stone apartment houses on either side of 67th Street; a few moments in the only corner of our apartment that was her own. Shelves of old shoe boxes formed the boundary with the living room where she and my father slept at night. They were filled with buttons and zippers, sequins, elastic bands, metal snaps and artificial flowers, all labeled in my mother's illegible script. Beside them was fabric: satins, wools, organzas and glittering brocade for the customers from Palm Beach. Her dummy stood in the center of the room near the old Singer sewing machine that had been her first big purchase in the United States. Some of her Prague customers had preceded her to New York. She had started working right away.

46

My mother looked up at the portrait she had framed in leather and hung over her cutting table. It was an old photograph, sepia-toned, of a woman's face. A dark fur collar rested against her cheek and made her skin seem very white. She had dark hair, firm eyebrows and sad, glistening eyes.

"Who's that?" I asked when I was three.

"That's Pepi," said my mother. "Grandmother Pepi."

"Where is she?"

"She died. She was killed."

"Was she bad?"

My mother was startled. "No. It was the Germans who were bad. Very bad."

"Where is she?"

"I told you she died," my mother said. "I don't know where she died. The Germans didn't tell me. Now let me do some work."

My mother's eyes were like my grandmother's: dark brown, so deep with secrets that they seemed to have no bottom when you looked into them. They were seductive eyes that drew you in and made you want to know who she was.

"Why did the Germans kill her?"

My mother did not know how to answer me. How did other parents explain? Why did this child never stop asking questions? One after another: Who put the number on your arm? Why do you keep it? Why won't it come off? Did it hurt when they put it on? Why doesn't Daddy have one?

My mother worried about the questions and, with my father, about the answers. My parents had determined not to frighten me with their recollections, yet they did not want to lie. They had not anticipated the extent of a child's curiosity, just as they had not expected the commotion that my younger brother and I could make.

"*Mommy!*" I would scream into the workroom. "Tommy's hitting me!"

47

"I am not!" my brother called in after me.

My mother sighed, put out her cigarette, and stood up as the two of us ran into the workroom. She worried about our constant squabbling almost as much as about my questions. She did not know much about children. She herself had been an only child, whose closest friend had been my grandmother Pepi. At the age of fifteen, after French and German schools, she had quit to join her mother's business. It was a salon for *haute couture* in the center of Prague, with thirty girls in the workroom and a cosmopolitan clientele. My mother remembered railway carriages, seasonal trips to Paris and Berlin to purchase fabrics and view the new collections. There were long walks with her mother and afternoon tea dances in smart hotels.

In New York, my mother chose styles and fabrics from the pages of *Vogue, L'Officiel* and *Bazaar.* Only two girls sewed in her workroom and in summer, when her customers went off to Connecticut or Long Island, my mother sat in her workroom alone.

By five-thirty, her features were slack, her eyes bleary from following the movements of her needle. Although her hair was a deep brown and her cheeks dimpled girlishly when she smiled, my mother looked older than thirty-five. She often sat alone, in the half-dark room, sewing; that is my earliest memory of her. She appeared stunned by solitude. As I looked up at her, she seemed to be behind a pane of glass.

When she wasn't working, my mother would read or spend three hours listening to the Saturday afternoon Texaco Opera House, but I rarely saw my mother having fun. My father was chronically unemployed so, most of the time, she sewed. She made coats and suits for Mrs. Lewis, Mrs. Chauncey, Mrs. Glucken and the other women who sat down on my parents' beds in the living room, flipping the pages of glossy magazines, weighing the possibilities of necklines and hemlines, for the most part uncurious about who she was and where she came from. For them, she was a great find, a refugee, a good dressmaker with hands, they said, of gold.

Her customers in Prague, my mother said, had been cultured people. In America they were, for the most part, neither aristocratic nor gracious. Most paid their bills in due course—although one woman had run off to the Yucatán owing my mother eight hundred dollars—but few appreciated her patience with them. They prattled on about their husbands and lovers, the deteriorating quality of help in St. Thomas, the difficulties of finding hats and shoes to match their dresses. Occasionally, they forgot who my mother was and complained that New York was being "overrun by refugees" or that a certain stockbroker had attempted to "Jew us down." My mother would remain impassive. We would hear about it at dinner. The next day, there would be a telephone apology or perhaps a pair of gloves from Saks. My mother did not allow what she called "scenes" to develop between herself and her customers. She let them play patron, and when they invited her to the theater or to the opera, she went. The customers' checks paid our rent. The customer, however self-indulgent, troublesome or offensive, was life.

By five-thirty though, when my brother and I came tearing into the workroom, her reserves of patience were spent. She threatened, and sometimes delivered, quick slaps that stung. Then she dispatched my brother to his room and me to the kitchen. Dinner was at six and could not be delayed. The notion that one might take a nap beforehand, or drink cocktails, or simply do nothing for an hour had no currency with my parents. As six o'clock approached, a tension was palpable in our household. It was like the anxiety of travelers on their way to an airport or railway station. If they are late, if their watches have stopped or if they have misread the schedule, they will be left behind.

While I set the kitchen table, my mother stood beside the

49

stove, cutting up potatoes and preparing meat. She lit more cigarettes, stopped to touch a hand to the small of her back, or gasped slightly when she left her weight on one leg for too long and it froze into a cramp beneath her. She had been injured in concentration camp when a roof collapsed on her back and since then she complained of a slipped disk. Sometimes, when she moved uncomfortably around the kitchen, my mother said she had colitis. Or a migraine. Or a muscle spasm. Or melancholia. The women in our family had all suffered from that, she said. My great-grandmother had jumped from a third-story window and died.

Her pain was visible. It drained the blood from her skin, making her appear even paler than she normally was, and the blue numbers tattooed on her forearm almost seemed to blaze. I watched her as I folded napkins, brought out glasses and silverware and plates. I could see the pain creep through her body, trapped, moving from place to place, eluding a list of specialists which grew longer each year. Internists, neurologists, osteopaths, chiropractors, even hypnotists had treated my mother. They put her in traction, prescribed lotions, pills, injections, exercises, diets. But the pain would not go away. At times, when she read or listened to music or when we were in the country and my father and she relaxed together, it would ebb. But then, without warning, triggered by an innocent motion of an arm or leg, it would return. "Don't just stand there like an idiot! Help me sit down!" she would order, in a tense, distorted voice. Or worse, she would say nothing. She would gasp and remain in the position in which pain had cast her, her eyes like wounds.

I would stop what I was doing, offer my arm, draw up something on which she could sit. I had no idea what was happening to her when she became stuck in space, unable to budge. I was seven years old, loud, impertinent, active, all the things my parents meant when they said, "American child." The fact that my mother, who had lost her menstrual period for three years during the war, could produce such a healthy child still seemed somewhat of a miracle to her. Cousins in America had sent monthly packages of powdered milk for me to Prague like deposits in a bank of new life. In New York, I was plied with food, books, art, music and dancing lessons; I was taken skating, skiing, bicycle riding; to the opera, to concerts, to the theater—all on a budget that barely sufficed to pay the rent. Her child was more than a leaf in the future for my mother. I could recapture the best of her past.

We talked as I set the table. That is, I chattered on about my penmanship and arithmetic grades, our class spelling bees, our trips to museums and candy factories. I told jokes: "Mommy? Why did the moron salute the refrigerator?"

"Why did the moron salute ... " my mother repeated in her sharply accented English. "I don't know. Why?"

"Because it was General Electric!" I sang out. "Why did the moron throw the clock from the Empire State Building?"

"I don't know."

"Because he wanted to see time *fly!*"

"*Hhhhmmpphh!*" said my mother.

"Do you want to hear another one?"

"Later," she told me in Czech, going about her business with an intentness I never saw in other mothers. Her motions were measured, intensely concentrated. Sometimes, if she had had a good day, she laughed at my stories from school but mostly she told me to quit fooling around or else the table wouldn't be ready when my father got home.

My father came home ravenous, as if he had not eaten in several days when, in fact, he ate three big meals every day without fail. He was fifty-one years old, a tall, strong, optimistic man with the broad shoulders and tapered hips of a swimmer. His forehead was high, his eyes lively under tangled brows. In Prague, he had been a water polo player and a long-standing member of the Czechoslovak National

51

Olympic Committee. He had retained the carriage of a man who lived an athlete's regimen long after retiring from competition. *In mens sana in corpore sano,* he intoned in the mornings when he woke us up at seven, wet from his cold shower, a towel wrapped loosely around his waist. He was sixteen years older than my mother, a man who had commanded the best tables in Prague restaurants, who now could not find a job.

Upon their arrival in New York in 1948, my father had walked over to the New York Athletic Club on Central Park South. He believed firmly in the equality conferred by sport. He had participated in the Berlin Olympics in 1936 where "the American Negro Jesse Owens," as he called him, had won a gold medal. The New York Athletic Club would surely help him find work as a swim coach, he thought. My mother and he were invited to view one water polo game there but the reception they received was markedly cool. My father spoke little English and it was only after a few days that someone explained to him that the club was restricted, closed to Jews.

My father moved from job to job. He worked as a shipping clerk, a salesman, a bookkeeper. Finally, a neighbor whose husband had died taught him how to use the cutting machine that the couple had used in their T-shirt business. He became a cutter in the garment center, working for other refugees. Each evening he came home tired from the scrap-strewn factories of Seventh Avenue, irritated by the filth and rudeness of the subways. He strode into the apartment with a mangled copy of the *New York Post* under his arm, kissed my mother good evening, and then stood for a moment, tying up traffic in the small kitchen.

"What's for dinner?" he asked in Czech and, without waiting for an answer, pulled open the refrigerator door, found an open can of sardines or an end of salami and wolfed down the food, using a piece of bread as a fork. He stood this way, hunched over the kitchen counter in his overcoat, for several moments. Then, sated, he turned to us with one of his daily garment center anecdotes, offering me a taste of salami.

"For heaven's sake, Kurt," my mother interrupted him. "Dinner will be on the table in a few minutes."

"I'm hungry. I worked all day," replied my father, chewing hard, as if to intimate that were he deprived of this snack he might very well drop dead right there on the kitchen floor, famished.

My mother said nothing. She lit another cigarette, pushed the rings of salami that lay strewn about the kitchen counter into a small pile, and threw them into the garbage pail. My father asked me what I had done in school, whether I had done well in the spelling bee. We were learning to spell together: I at school, he in the night classes he attended to learn English. He came home with passages from Shakespeare, homilies and proverbs which he recited with one hand on his chest like Napoleon, chin thrust forward. His pronunciation of the syllables was so distorted that the sense of what he was saying got lost. *"Ehr-*ly to *bed,"* he intoned, *"Ehr-*ly to *rise.* Makes the man *heal-*thy, *weal-*thy and *wise."*

"Tommy! Are you washing your hands?" called my mother.

"Was there any mail?" asked my father. He meant: had any checks from a customer come in?

My mother shook her head and took out the meat. We ate cold cuts for breakfast, leftover meat for lunch and roast or stew or chops for dinner. When I asked why we never had tuna casserole like other people, my mother said they had gone three years without meat and that was enough. The kind in the supermarket did not pass muster. My mother shopped at the Nevada Meat Market whose owners had noted her blue tattoo and extended credit when she had no money to pay for her purchases.

Her tattoo was like a mysterious flag. It made some people blush, turn their eyes aside, mumble odd, garbled things.

53

Others acted as if my mother was a species of saint. I watched her respond to both groups with a fierce pride. Her manner, always abrupt, became distant. She threw up a wall between herself and them.

"Tommy! Dinner!" she called now, like a train conductor.

My brother was preoccupied with trucks, trains and elevators. He was four years old, thin and unenthusiastic about meals. He fidgeted in his chair and pushed his food in circles around a central morsel on his plate, making my mother even more nervous. In a small voice, he asked for chocolate milk, but most of the time he kept quiet, especially at mealtimes when tensions were high.

My father was already at the table, hunched, head down. He swallowed his food so quickly that he seemed not to chew, looking up only to see what my mother was doing, why she hadn't sat down to the table herself.

"Daddy didn't always eat this way," my mother sometimes told me. "His family had manners. They had a cook and servants." My father himself did not acknowledge any peculiarity in his eating habits. "When someone sits down to eat, he should eat and do nothing else," he said. "That's the trouble in America. Everyone wants to sit with one fanny on three stools. They want to watch television while they eat. They want to read a book. They want to conduct a debate!" By the time my mother had finished dressing the salad and sat down with us, his plate was clean. He never left a trace of food, not even a streak of gravy.

My mother sat down and served herself.

"Daddy?" I said.

"What?" He wiped his chin.

"You're finished and nobody else has started yet."

He glanced at my mother.

"Don't be fresh to your father," she said automatically. She took my brother's plate and began to cut up the meat on it in brisk strokes. Her face looked swollen, the way it did before she started to cry. My brother looked down at the table top. There was silence in the kitchen.

54

My father took another helping of meat but we could sense an explosion coming. It did not take much for my father to be drawn into conflict. Almost every evening when he came home from work, he announced that he had severed relations with someone in the garment district. A waiter had served him lukewarm soup. A fellow cutter had made an insulting remark about refugees. "And you, Izzy?" my father replied. "Was your father an Indian chief?"

Even his boss was not exempt from my father's chronic rages. Also a refugee, who had escaped from the Warsaw Ghetto, this man capitalized on my father's status. He paid substandard wages and could offer no guarantee of employment, but he understood that my father needed to be left alone to do his work, that he had difficulty accepting authority. My father carted fabric, rolled it out on long narrow tables until it was six or seven inches thick and then sliced through the wad with a two-inch, razor-sharp blade. There were times when his thoughts strayed from the blouse and apron pieces beneath him to the Olympic Games or to the small town where he was born when Franz Josef was still Emperor, and the blade sheared off a piece of his skin and flesh with the cheap cloth. He came home with a bandage enlarging his hand. After dinner, he took it off to show us that he had not lost his finger, that it had stopped bleeding, that he was all right.

The garment center was a relatively safe place for my father. He could lose his temper daily, rail in broken English at his colleagues and risk nothing more than a harangue in return. In the Seventh Avenue luncheonettes near his place of work, he was known to the waitresses as Mr. Epstein, the gentleman from Prague. He saluted the elevator operator in the morning and greeted the receptionist with a deference he had learned from his father. His style was Austro-Hungarian, circa 1910.

Although we had no sense, not even a sketch, of where he came from, my father expected that we behave as children did in Roudnice-nad-Labem. That meant waiting at the door when he came home from work, our hair brushed behind our ears, hands and faces clean, attitude smiling but subdued. We would say, "Good evening, Daddy," eat our dinners, have our baths, and go off to bed. The fact that my mother, who did not enjoy the services of servants as his mother had, was exhausted by dinnertime was a mystery to him.

Since he had been separated from his family in the Terezin Ghetto, he had idealized his mother as well as the general tenor of family life. He had named me after her and when I did not conform to this model I had never seen, he was perplexed and, sometimes, sad. "How *can* you whistle before breakfast?" he would ask me. "Grandmother Helena never did that. Don't you know young ladies don't whistle? You'll marry a crazy husband!"

His expectations, the frustrations of his life in a closed-in, poorly ventilated factory, and our behavior often collided. When he was tired, when his optimism was worn down by worries about money or my mother's health, a terrible anger erupted from him. His face grew dark and when he began to shout, his fury was like a sudden hailstorm.

It was utterly silent at the dinner table. My mother began to eat. I ate. But my brother let the food sit on his plate. His mouth, which was not as clean as my father would have wished, hung open as he looked at the ceiling, then down at the floor between his legs. He played with his fork and when the fork hit his glass of chocolate milk, it made a small *ping!*

My father looked up. He took a breath and his chest grew even larger than it was; his shoulders loomed over the table. "Tell me, what are you waiting for?" he demanded. "You think food stays warm forever? Or you are too fine to eat this kind of meat? Perhaps you would like some filet mignon?"

My brother's eyes grew larger as the volume of my father's voice rose, the Czech interspersed with a coarse German whose meaning we deduced rather than understood.

"Hajzel!" he shouted. *"Svine!"* The words meant "toilet" and "swine." He seemed to be in another world, raging at people we could not see. Our misbehavior was just a trigger that released a rage which was there all the time, locked inside like my mother's pain. Once unlocked, it spurted out of him lavalike and furious, impossible to restrain.

"Don't stare at me like an idiot! Eat!"

"Kurt, *stop* it," came my mother's voice, also in Czech, terribly low and yet sharp.

"Spoiled brats!" my father muttered and there was a second of quiet.

My brother dropped his fork, splattering gravy on the table.

"Pigs! You eat like pigs in a pigsty—not like children from a good family! You should be grateful you have meat to eat and instead you poke around your plate. Brats! Miserable brats! Do you know what we would have given for a meal like this! Seven hundred calories a day we were given! And we didn't spend the day in school!"

"Kurt!" my mother said.

"Don't interrupt me. When—"

"I can't *stand* this anymore," my mother shouted over his voice. *"Always* at dinner! We cannot have *one* peaceful dinner in this household! We *have* to have a scene. You can't live a day of your life without getting mad!"

She too looked gripped by something that had nothing to do with us at the dinner table in our kitchen in New York. Her jaw went rigid, her eyes were rimmed with red. She gasped as a pain caught her back. Then she burst into sobs and ran out of the kitchen.

My brother and I sat still. We listened to the shuffle of my mother's steps as she ran into the bathroom, closed the door and locked it. My father went to the sink for a glass of water. He drank it there, then began to pace between the table and the stove.

"Eat!" he ordered. "Or do you want a slap in the face?"

My father found nothing incongruous in this demand, just as he found it perfectly natural to become angry whenever my brother or I hurt ourselves. Anything that endangered the health of his children was a personal threat and the fact that we were not eating was no exception. But I did not understand this then. I hated my father when he lost his temper. He spoiled dinner, he made my mother cry, he insulted us with ugly names. He was a bully.

I did not say this out loud. I was afraid he would hit me and also, I knew that when he was in this state he understood nothing one told him. The only thing to do was wait until my father's rage had run its course. My brother retreated whenever this was happening. His pale eyes and face, his blond hair, seemed to melt into the yellow wall behind him. His expression was bleak and closed. I never knew what he was thinking. Unlike me, he could not even pretend to eat.

"To your room!" my father ordered.

My brother froze, fork in hand, like a small, stunned animal. Then he slipped down from his chair and out of the kitchen, glad to have escaped a thrashing.

My father too left the kitchen. He walked to his desk in the living room and switched on the small lamp over his work space. Within minutes he was absorbed in the large black ledger of my mother's business, paying bills, writing out sums in his fine, graceful hand. He made small, deft marks in the book, furrowing his forehead so that it became a steeplechase of lines. If you had asked him then why the house was so quiet, why everyone had taken refuge, he would have been unable to say. For him, the storm was over.

For me, the frightening part had just begun. The silence was like a great big open hole I could fall into if I wasn't careful. My father often got lost this way. He would stop in the middle of a sentence and his eyes would go vague. His lower lip dropped and he was unreachable. I'd tap his shoul-

58

der or call his name without success. I was sure he was in that brown-toned world of photographs, among all the people who lived in the yellow envelope in his desk.

My mother did not move from world to world so easily. Her exits and entrances were theatrical, jarring and full of suppressed feeling. All the rage my father spent on taxicab drivers, bank tellers and other people who did not treat him with appropriate respect, my mother turned inward. It festered inside her and came out only when she barricaded herself in the bathroom for hours, carrying on a broken conversation with me through the closed door.

That was where I stationed myself after an explosion, with excuses for opening a conversation, disguises for my need of reassurance.

"Mommy? I need someone to test me for the social studies quiz tomorrow," or "Mommy? The refrigerator's leaking." My mother was the parent who fixed things. In Auschwitz, during the selection of prisoners for work or death, she had identified herself as an electrician rather than a dressmaker. She had survived by pretending to know how to repair faulty wiring, and had become so good at it that now she rarely needed to call a repairman.

"Mommy?"

She did not answer. There was no sound behind the locked door. Behind it was a medicine cabinet. It was crammed full of pill bottles, tubes, yellowing prescription labels and a few hypodermic needles that a doctor had given her. My mother knew her pills by sight. I knew them as well as I knew the candy bars at the pharmacy where I was sent every week. There was Darvon. Morphine. Butazolidin. The pharmacist, like our butcher, extended us credit.

"Mommy?" I touched the door with my knuckles.

"Leave me alone. I want to be alone."

"Are you okay?"

My mother was crying. "I don't want to go on anymore. I can't stand it."

59

I listened hard. I thought I could somehow leach the pain from her by listening. It would leave her body, enter mine, and be lessened by sharing. Otherwise, I thought, it would one day kill my mother. She could kill herself easily behind the locked door. She could give herself an injection or swallow a bottleful of pills as I stood waiting outside.

"Mommy!"

No reply.

It was nearly eight o'clock by now and I went into the living room where my father had dozed off. Sometimes when my mother locked herself in the bathroom, he insisted that he needed to use it. Once he had threatened to call the Fire Department to get her out of there. But when he figured that the situation was under control, he simply went to sleep. I did not understand that then. All I knew was that my mother was gone, and that she might disappear the way she said her own parents had, without notice, without any noise.

"Mommy!" I banged on the door.

"What? What do you want?"

It was not a real question but it was all I needed for the moment. My brother was inside the hall closet, playing elevator with its sliding doors.

"Going up?" he asked quietly. "Fifth floor?"

Then he closed the closet door, waited, and let the people out.

I went into my mother's workroom where I could make believe that behind the shoeboxes of ribbons and zippers were secret panels, doors and cupboards. In that room, in the dark, I could be Nancy Drew or the Hardy Boys. Her workroom was my attic and it contained secret messages from the past to be discovered in treasure chests, old hats and tablecloths. Downstairs, in their prim sitting room, would be my grandparents. My grandfather would sit in his socks and smoke a pipe and say what my father had really been like when he was small. My grandmother Helena

60

would tell me it was all right, sometimes, to whistle. But I could not imagine very well what they wore, how they talked, or how they would act toward me. The brown-colored photographs distanced them in time, and the one-line phrases in which my father described them were so general that I had no idea what they were really like.

My grandmother Pepi was different. Her photograph over my mother's cutting table was even prettier at night. Her eyes glowed. I did not believe she was dead. She did not look old enough to die and it made no sense, what my mother said, that the Germans had shot her. She was never tired like my mother or likely to flare into a rage. Her eyes were like a caress. Her lips looked about to form a word. I wondered where she was and when she would come back. My mother said she was not buried. No one had been buried. One day, I thought, my grandmother Pepi would step out of her photograph and into the room, like the fairy godmothers in storybooks. She would come live with us and my mother would not be so lonely then.

I went back to the bathroom and knocked.

"What is it?" My mother's voice was clear now, not muffled with crying.

"Are you okay?"

"I'm okay. I'm just depressed."

"Are you coming out?"

"I'll be out in a little while. Go get ready for bed. Help Tommy undress."

I did not move away.

"Don't worry. I'm okay. I just want to be alone a little bit more."

I pulled my little brother out of the hall closet and told him to get ready for bed. Then I went into the kitchen and cleared the table. Putting things in order was my way of pretending that nothing was wrong. It was the tactic I often used to ward away pain. There was no way I could shout back at my father; no way I could reproach my mother.

How could I not be a happy, healthy, good girl after all they had been through? My father got angry when he saw me listless or unhappy, just as he got angry when my brother or I fell down and scraped our knees. "After the war I put three things what were most important to me," my father would tell people. "First freedom. Then health. And the third thing, contentment. I wanted that my child will live in a free country without any experience what I had to suffer."

I did not like to hear my father say these things. He said them all the time, to anyone who would listen. He talked in a loud, emphatic voice, in an English so queerly cadenced that it sounded as though he were speaking Czech. I did not want to know that my father had been in prison, that other men had spit on him, kicked him, beat him. He did not mention these things but we knew them nonetheless. The way his feet looked, the toes yellowing, the nails deformed; the way he ate meals; the way he reacted to demands on him—all said more than words. How could my father, so tall, so strong, let that happen? And how could he tell people about it?

"When we came to Auschwitz," my father would say, "we went out of the trains and I was marching toward Dr. Mengele, who was making a selection. He asked sometimes questions and said, 'right,' 'left,' but we didn't know what it meant. When I stood before him, he asked me a question: *'Sind Sie wirklich gesund?'* Are you really healthy? Because I was after a sickness and I was looking in bad shape, especially I was not shaven for three days. I said, *'Jawohl!'* Yes! and he sent me to the good side. From fifteen hundred people were saved three hundred. So I passed the first test. After twenty minutes we went to a barrack where a young SS officer came and asked people who wanted to volunteer for work. Most of my friends joined these groups. I also, but in the last second something came to my mind and I stepped aside. There were three groups. The first went to the mines and nobody came back. The third group nobody came back. The second group, what I joined, ninety-six people came back. So you see . . ."

My father would smile, showing teeth that also reflected the years of the war. "I was thinking all my life what was it, was this a sixth sense, was this God, was this a providence? Because the fact that I am here and can give you this report is a matter of one fraction of a second what I decided."

I went into the living room to kiss my father good night, and then joined my brother in the bedroom we shared. I lay awake listening for the sound of the bathroom door. The apartment was silent. Outside, there was a long wail of police sirens.

By the time my mother finally came in to say good night, I pretended to be sleeping. I could throw up my own walls. I could make her wait.

"Are you awake?" she asked.

I did not answer.

"You know Daddy doesn't really mean anything when he shouts like that," she said. "You know he loves you."

She did not volunteer any explanation of her own behavior, as if there were nothing at all peculiar about locking herself in the bathroom for two hours. Nothing she said acknowledged that she had, in fact, done so. Any reference I might make to it would be a reproach and I could not reproach my mother. I knew the stories. She was doing the best she could. Even to compare her to other mothers was treason.

But when she left the bedroom, I did. I imagined other mothers, other dinner tables with white tablecloths and decorum, where families conversed quietly and nothing went wrong. I imagined other fathers, who had offices where they were doctors or lawyers, who did not feel compelled to challenge every parking attendant who told them where to leave their car. At their homes, I was sure, these things did not happen. Children misbehaved, mothers and fathers quarreled but there was no extra presence in the air like there was in our home.

In our home words ricocheted between worlds, their meaning uncertain. My parents told stories but the stories never explained. They talked about people, but the people were all gone. Simple facts required long explanations. Few things could be taken for granted starting with the fact that we were, all of us, alive.

I could hear my mother in the living room getting ready for bed. My father was already asleep; every few minutes I could hear him snore. After a while, the light in the living room went out. The apartment was completely dark. I fell asleep.

In the morning, my father was wet from his shower, dripping water on the floor, his eyes fresh and happy. If he was feeling especially cheerful, he whistled Reveille and if my brother and I did not have our feet on the floor right away he left and came back with a wet washcloth which he wrung gleefully over our heads. There was struggling and laughter, a scrambling to start a new day.

In the kitchen, my mother had already prepared breakfast. She was brisk and efficient in the morning, despite the stiffness in her back. She wrapped sandwiches in wax paper, sorted out our clothing and hauled me off to brush and plait my hair into two sturdy braids. She was better than other mothers because she did five things at once as if they were nothing. Her face was so vivid, her eyes so busy with thoughts of the day ahead that I forgot the emptiness that had been in them the night before. There was nothing wrong with my mother in the morning. She did not need help. She did not question her right to be alive.

In the mornings when I went to school I had no questions either. I did not wonder why good people got killed or were put in prison when they had done nothing wrong. I did not wonder why we had no money when, before, my parents had had plenty of it. I did not wonder about the place they had come from or why they had had to leave it.

I kissed my mother good-bye, clutched my Lone Ranger lunchbox and set off for school. I ran races during recess and sang songs from Broadway musicals during show-and-tell. I was Peter Pan and Cinderella and a Mickey Mouse Club mouseketeer. In school, we learned about government and science, things which had reasons and unshakeable order. In arithmetic, grammar and gym, it was easy to push away the things I saw and heard and imagined the night before. I must have imagined it all, I thought. No one else talked about such things. They were not in the books I read or in the world I lived in. They had not happened. I refused to believe they had happened at all.

FIVE

On the morning of April 15, 1945, my mother Franci Solar woke up in the concentration camp of Bergen-Belsen, one among thousands of people still breathing and ten thousand others who lay dead among them. She was twenty-five years old then and her cousin Kitty was twenty-three. The two had managed to stay together since they were first deported from Prague in 1942. The first train had taken them to Terezin, the concentration camp located less than an hour's journey from the city in which they were raised. A second train had taken them to Auschwitz, in Poland; and a third train had brought them to the north of Germany, to a factory in Hamburg. A fourth train had brought them to Bergen-Belsen three weeks earlier. In Belsen, thousands of men and women lay dying of typhus. There was no food. The few communal water pipes dribbled water. My mother and her cousin were no longer aware of the cold or the stench or the hardness of the bare floor or the lice which had colonized it. They wondered which would come first: death or the British Army.

A little after daybreak on April 15, a woman lying near the door of the barracks said she saw a line of tanks coming down the road.

No one believed her. No one even stirred.

But then a second voice confirmed the approach of a tank with a white star, and then a third. No one cheered. No one had the strength to be glad. Those who could stood up and straggled outside to see.

The bright red, white and blue of the Union Jack fluttered against the sky now as tank after tank appeared, stretching back in a long column as far as the cousins could see. Men in khaki stood on top of the tanks, their arms extended above their heads, their fingers forming wide Vs for Victory. As the first tanks neared the fence of barbed wire that surrounded the compound, a few women straggled past my mother and her cousin toward the tanks. For a long moment, the men moving by and the women standing unsteadily on the ground seemed to lock eyes. The faces of the soldiers changed. The Victory signs disappeared as their hands dug into pockets, pouches, knapsacks. Suddenly, chocolate bars, cigarettes, cans of food came hurtling over the barbed wire. The women chased after the scraps like dogs, biting, scratching, tearing at each other to reach food.

The two cousins watched, restraining each other, telling each other there would soon be plenty more to eat. The war had made them equals. Before 1942, in Prague, Kitty had been the compliant cousin, a pink, blond, happy girl, my mother said, who had learned to flirt before she could walk. My mother, two years older, had been more practical, boyish, dark-haired and decisive. Now there was little to tell them apart. Both women were listless and encrusted with a grayish filth. Their hair, matted and dingy brown, broke off at chin level. Kitty's body was skeletal and covered with boils and open sores. My mother was swollen from retaining

67

water. She looked several kilos heavier than she was. Only their eyes, the deep brown striking feature they shared, seemed alive.

The drama they watched unfold before them, which my mother recalls watching without emotion, as if it were a movie, was repeated in the spring of 1945 in Nazi concentration and labor camps throughout Europe. In the East, where my father was a prisoner, the Russian Army was the liberator. The Russians had come through the small camp of Frydland, he said, mounted on horses. They carried bottles of vodka, sides of bacon and collected wristwatches which they wore up the length of their sleeves like Egyptian bracelets. They had moved through Maidanek, Auschwitz, Chelmno, Belzec, Treblinka, Sobibor and smaller, lesser-known camps, had told the prisoners that they were free to leave, and had moved on. In the West, the armies of the United States and Britain applied administrative know-how to the chaos they discovered. In Dachau and Bergen-Belsen, the liberators dispensed food, registered the prisoners, organized the burial of the dead, and hospitalized as many of the sick as they could.

Seven days after the British Army first appeared at the end of the compound road at Bergen-Belsen, my mother and Kitty were taken in a jeep to the former German military camp of Celle, which had been converted to a British administrative center. Both women spoke fluent English and French as well as Czech and German. They had volunteered, along with several other ex-prisoners, to serve as interpreters.

They drove past the gates of Belsen dressed in old but clean mechanics' overalls. Their hair had been washed, cut, and blown through with DDT, as part of the general delousing procedure. They had been fed regular rations and Kitty's face and body had already begun to show signs of healing. My mother, though, showed no such change. Her legs and arms were still bloated, the flesh puffed up away from the bone, tender to the touch. The smell of food nauseated her. Her body rejected it: she could not chew or swallow. She felt feverish as the jeep moved past the gates of Belsen. A haze seemed to form around the concentration camp as it receded into the landscape. Once or twice, as the jeep turned a corner, the lieutenant at the wheel had to grasp her shoulder to prevent her from falling out the open side.

The officer pulled up to a large building in the central square of Celle, then stepped out to help the women alight. My mother looked up at the glass windows of the administrative center, then down at the lieutenant offering his hand. The ground seemed to move up toward her.

"This girl is very sick," she heard someone say.

Then she pitched forward, unconscious.

"What's your name? You must remember your name!"

When my mother next remembered opening her eyes, she saw a tiny woman in a white coat bending over her bed. Behind her were white walls, white beds, and other white figures.

"Your name. Don't you remember your name?" the woman in white repeated. "Where were you born?"

My mother closed her eyes and tried to remember. Nothing came to mind. She fell back into sleep. She too had contracted typhus.

For three weeks, as she lay semi-conscious in the hospital at Celle, my mother's only identity was the small blue number tattooed on her forearm, the number I can never bring myself to remember. In the confusion that followed her arrival in Celle, she had been placed in a ward filled with Hungarian women, quarantined from the rest of the camp, and her name had been lost in the process.

On May 8, 1945, she suddenly sat up in bed, wakened by the noise of shooting.

"Help me!" she screamed into the ward. "Open the window! Somebody please!"

Two women in white came to her side, unable to understand the language she was speaking.

"That's not the Germans shooting," one of them explained in slow German. "It's Armistice Day. They're shooting to celebrate. It's the British who are shooting."

My mother stared at them skeptically. Then she listened to the cannons going off, it seemed, just outside the hospital window.

"Armistice Day," she repeated. "Armistice Day."

When she awoke the next day, she remembers that a British soldier was pushing a teacart down the hospital ward. He had curly hair and blue eyes, and he stopped by her bed.

"Would you like anything?" he asked pleasantly, and my mother remembered the actor Leslie Howard, in the movies she had loved as a girl in Prague.

She surveyed the cart piled with books, newspapers, candy bars, toothbrushes and soap. The profusion of items and colors confused her. It was the first time in three years that she had been invited to choose a gift for herself.

"May I have a package of Players, please?" she asked.

The soldier looked down at her doubtfully. "Are you permitted to smoke?" he asked.

"I don't think so," she conceded. "But I like the picture on the box."

The soldier smiled and handed her the cigarettes.

"Would you like anything else?"

"What else?"

"How about some nice soap?" he offered, placing another small packet into her hands. Then he told her he would be back the next day.

My mother put the two gifts under her pillow. From time to time she reached her hand behind her head and took out the package of cigarettes. The Players trademark, a bearded sailor encircled by a life preserver, seemed to her a masterpiece of art. She studied it for long periods of time, seeing nothing else, hearing nothing in the large white room. Something had happened to her hearing, she noticed. Sounds entered her ears only intermittently.

In the afternoon another pushcart stopped by her bed.

"Would you like some pajamas?" another soldier asked.

She did not quite understand but nodded, and he placed on her bed a pair of white cotton pajamas with red rosebuds printed on the fabric. The label said: *Made in Canada.* She read and reread those words without losing interest until a nurse came to help her put the pajamas on. Some time later, my mother does not remember when, she sat up in bed and tried to talk to her neighbors.

It was impossible. Both were Hungarians who spoke no other language. All the women in the ward were Hungarian, and after a few days of smiling and gesturing, of learning to say good morning and thank you and please in Hungarian, my mother grew restless. She now could walk from her bed to the hallway, and sit up in bed for several hours without tiring. She could eat small meals. She began to wonder what had happened to Kitty. How could her cousin have abandoned her like this?

"We have no telephone service," one of the nurses explained to her. "This section is still under quarantine."

Every day, it seemed to my mother, a liaison officer from a different country passed through the ward. A representative of the French came, and of the Dutch, the Poles, the Hungarians. Although my mother was still far from recovery, her mind was no longer appeased by the sailor's picture on her box of Players cigarettes. She wanted to know what was happening outside the hospital. She wanted to have conversation. When finally one morning a woman came into the ward and asked whether anyone there was from Czechoslovakia, my mother shouted, "*I* am!"

An hour later, Kitty breezed past the hospital guards and into the room, wearing a summer dress and white high-heeled sandals. Her mouth was red with lipstick and her hair streaked shining blond. My mother thought she looked like Ginger Rogers. Everything that she saw now seemed to be happening in a movie. Kitty acknowledged the nurses and patients with a toss of her head and sat down.

"We've got to get you out of here. That much is clear," she told my mother. "I just don't understand how this could have happened that you got stuck here. Why didn't you tell them you were my cousin? I thought you had died. You're sure to die if you stay here. I'm going to get you out right now."

My mother stared at her. Her ears were not working properly again. She could barely understand what Kitty was saying.

"Don't worry. I'll handle everything. I'm the liaison officer of the Czechoslovak Repatriation Committee and I have a car waiting for me downstairs. I'll have you out in half an hour. Believe me, it will be no problem at all."

Kitty breezed out of the ward, leaving my mother staring at the place she had been sitting. Since the time they had been children in Prague, my mother had been the one who gave orders and Kitty had carried them out. In the games they played, my mother had always been the Empress and Kitty the lady-in-waiting. Now Kitty had become a liaison officer. The words even seemed absurd. She gave orders to other people. As if there had been no war and no concentration camp. Kitty's bearing had changed. Her eyes were clear and sharp. Authority seemed to suit her.

When Kitty returned, she had a tiny doctor in tow.

"I can't let her go," the doctor argued. "You don't understand medicine. She can't just be let go. She can't eat properly. She needs to be fed bite by bite, ounce by ounce. Every day, a bit more. She needs to be watched carefully. When a patient has a relapse of typhus it's nearly always fatal. She's still dizzy. She's half deaf. She can't even stand properly. She should remain at least another week."

"She's *my* cousin. She's my responsibility," Kitty answered. "I'll sign an affidavit. I'll bring you a voucher from the Czechoslovak Repatriation Committee if you insist."

The doctor shook her head and retreated. Kitty dug into the straw bag she was carrying and brought out a summer dress, a pair of high-heeled sandals like her own, and pair of nylon stockings.

"Get out of that garbage," she ordered, giving the sleeve of my mother's pajamas a tug. "You can leave those here."

My mother pulled back. "But I want them."

"You can't. They're quarantined. They stay here."

"Oh no," said my mother, moving back under the sheet. "I want them. They were a present from a British soldier. They're made in Canada."

Kitty grabbed the sheet with a firm hand and sat her cousin up in bed. "Don't be an idiot. I'll buy you half a dozen of those if you like."

Buy? my mother thought. How could Kitty buy half a dozen of anything? Suddenly she was frightened of leaving the ward in which she had been for nearly one month.

"I'm taking my cigarettes," she said defiantly. "And my soap. And my toothbrush."

"All right. Just get dressed and let's go."

Kitty helped my mother into a wheelchair and rolled her out of the hospital to a waiting jeep. A red-haired Englishman called Sunshine lifted her up into the seat. She could see his mouth moving as he drove but could not understand anything he said. He was a Cockney, Kitty told her, laughing. My mother tried to make sense of what he was saying but it all sounded like gibberish. She wondered if her illness had affected her mind.

They stopped in Celle's central square, where she had passed out one month before. Kitty and Sunshine made a seat of their crossed hands, and with her arms around their necks, my mother was carried into Kitty's room, a room which had once belonged to a German officer. Her bed was covered with a white feather quilt. A nightstand stood be-

73

side it. There was a large table in the room, with four chairs, and two tall armoires. Sunshine left them there with a parting phrase that she missed entirely. Then Kitty took a nightgown out of one of the armoires and tucked her into bed.

"I have a couple of things to finish up at the office," she said. "There's a chamber pot inside the nightstand. Don't try to go to the bathroom. It's too far. Try to get some sleep and I'll be back as soon as I can."

For the first time in three years, my mother was alone.

She lay still, enjoying the clean smell of the starched sheet and the sight of small feathers escaping in tufts from the seams of her quilt. She felt warm, incredibly warm and cozy. The nylon stockings that had felt so smooth on her legs lay over the back of a nearby chair where she could look at them. She was in an officer's room, she thought again and again, before she dozed off to sleep.

When she awoke, Kitty had still not returned. She surveyed the room inch by inch several times until there was nothing she had left unexamined. Suddenly her eyes focused on what appeared to be a large bowl set back on top of one of the armoires. It was the kind of bowl she remembered from Prague, the kind Kitty might use for cake dough.

She sat up in bed, then stood and pulled a chair over to the armoire. Then she took down the bowl, filled to the brim with sauerkraut and pork goulash. In her whole life nothing had smelled so delicious. There seemed to be enough for twelve people. No one would notice there was a bit less. She began to eat but could not stop. She ate until the bowl was empty. Only then did she feel the nausea flooding her chest and throat. She clamped her mouth shut and glanced about. Then she walked out the doorway, down the corridor, accelerating blindly until she finally collapsed spitting and gagging on her knees over the toilet bowl, where Kitty found her one hour later.

Her cousin could not be left alone for a minute, Kitty decided, and organized a rotating system of babysitters. Former concentration camp inmates, British foot soldiers and even Kitty's officer friends sat with my mother. Whenever she awoke, someone was there with a cup of tea and a summary of the last newspaper. Her color was still poor and her hair was falling out in thick tufts but the men who sat beside her bed behaved as though she were a beautiful woman. Throughout the war, she had thought of herself as a soldier. She had learned to melt into a group, to make herself unremarkable and as anonymous as the blue number on her forearm. The softness of her hair, the sensation of putting on lipstick, the blunt ache of menstruation were all memories to her. Only now did she begin to take an interest in manicuring her fingernails, putting dabs of cologne behind her ears and cream on her face. Kitty's officer friends took her on rides through the countryside. It was June and everything was green. Kitty had taken up with a British physician and before long the gossip was that her older cousin was involved with a captain.

My mother refused to discuss it. There was something vulgar, she thought, in supposing that anyone could form an attachment so soon. She was not Kitty, who had from birth been disinclined to take things seriously. Besides, unlike Kitty, she was a married woman. At least, before the war, she had had a husband.

Each morning she walked to the center of the Celle garrison to the Red Cross bulletin board. She searched the long lists of the dead for his name but it did not appear. She did not look for the names of her parents for she knew they were dead. A friend, a former prisoner, had taken one of the first repatriation buses back to Prague and had returned with sobering news: my mother's parents were dead; Kitty's parents were dead; my mother's husband was missing and Kitty's fiancé had married another girl two months before the end of the war.

This news did not hasten their return to Prague. Whenever a repatriation bus was scheduled to depart, Kitty would tell her cousin, "You're not yet strong enough to travel," or "It's out of the question while there's still a danger of a relapse." One cousin would say to the other, "Let's take the next bus," with a nonchalance that belied their deep fear of return. They lived from day to day, refusing to consider the future. During the day, my mother made skirts from the English wool blankets she and Kitty had received as gifts. At night, there were Red Cross dances, films and small parties in the officers' rooms. There was no rent to pay, no food to buy. As liaison aides to the British Army, they had delayed the prospect of facing what remained of home. But Kitty's doctor friend began to urge the two cousins to think about returning to Prague. He and his entire company were due to return to Britain soon and a new occupation force would replace them. Those soldiers would not have seen the liberation of Belsen, he told them. "A soldier in an occupied country feels free to take what he wants. He won't know the difference between a Czech former prisoner and a German *fraulein.*"

But the two cousins ignored the advice until one night, when my mother was dancing with a newly arrived Scottish major.

"Bizarre, this practice of writing your telephone number on your arm," he told her as they turned on the dance floor, and my mother looked up at him, uncertain whether this was not one of the dry jokes Britishers made.

Then she said, "You know, this is not my telephone number. They gave me this in Auschwitz. Have you heard of it?"

"Oh yes," he said. "Saw a film about it the other day. Mind you, if I try to imagine my wife or daughters in such a place, I shouldn't think they'd live two days."

My mother, accustomed since liberation to the unfailing sensitivity of the British officers she met, dropped her arm and left the Scottish major standing alone in the middle of the dance floor. She brushed off the soldiers and other women who asked her what was wrong and went to her room where she lay down on her bed. It was time to go home. It was nearly four months after liberation. One could not go on pretending that home was in a British administrative center. In the first week of August, 1945, the two cousins set out by bus and truck, with eleven pieces of luggage, for Prague. They traveled slowly, from the British into the American war zone, and then into the Russian zone, across the country in ruins that was Germany.

They arrived in Prague one week later at four in the morning. Their driver honked the truck horn in the dark, empty street in front of the house where a former classmate of Kitty's lived. The apartments both my mother and Kitty had lived in before the war were now occupied by strangers and Kitty's friend had kindly invited them to stay with him. He came down to greet them now, followed by a group of neighbors who helped the two cousins unload their baggage and plied them with pastries and coffee until my mother felt paralyzed by solicitousness.

"I don't know what I was expecting," she told me when I was older. "But whatever I had expected, whatever I had dreamed it would be like, it was different. I kept thinking that I had come home to strangers. That I was in Prague, the place I had lived all my life, and I was staying with strangers."

Later that morning, my mother and Kitty went downtown. They walked to the back of the streetcars and remained standing there although they saw seats vacant. They had not had time to accustom themselves to the fact that the Nazi transportation regulations concerning Jews had been rescinded. As the red streetcar clattered through the morning streets, my mother grew gloomy. It seemed to her that the war had bypassed the people around her. She compared the cloth of their suits and dresses to the flimsy cotton sundress she wore, the one that had seemed a miracle just four months before. The conversations she overheard around her seemed peppered with new Czech expressions which had not been fashionable three years before. There were small changes in the shop windows and street signs of the city. Life had gone on here, she saw, while for her it had stopped for three years.

Kitty, standing beside her in the tram, seemed oblivious to any of these things. She was busy taking in old sights, chattering on about the changes in a bright, happy voice. When they reached the center of town, the two women went their separate ways. My mother had an appointment with Max, who had been her parents' friend. It was at his home that her family had planned a reunion when the war was over. She walked to the café where they had agreed to meet, her dark eyes following the faces in the street, searching for one that was familiar. She imagined her mother's figure, small, elegant and soft, each time she turned a corner. She was twenty-five now, a woman who had survived Hitler and even typhus, she told herself. But her feet dragged on the pavement and she felt like a lost child.

"Franci?" a man asked as she walked into the café.

She sat down with Max and neither knew what to say. Then he told her that her husband, Pepik Solar, was dead. He returned to my mother a letter she had written her husband in the belief he had survived. She held the unopened envelope between her fingers and felt nothing. Numbness was becoming part of her nature. She had first noticed the loss of feeling in Auschwitz, after they had given her the blue number. She had been sitting in a bunk watching a Jewish *kapo* deride some fellow prisoners. *A striped S.S.*, she had thought to herself. *How strange to see.* She had stared at her forearm then and the forearm became two arms, one that belonged to her, Franci Solar, and one that belonged to that other woman, the one that looked exactly like her but had a number on her arm. From that moment on, she had become two people: one who acted and one who watched. She watched herself now, holding the unopened envelope between her fingers. And she watched Max.

"Vera told me to ask you to dinner tonight," he said. "That is, if you have no other plans."

"I have no other plans," she replied, staring into his face and finding it terribly stupid. What other plans could she possibly have? She wanted to hear that Max was happy to see her back, that he was glad she had survived. But Max seemed tongue-tied. Why did he not understand that she did not need this silence, this embarrassment, this awkwardness? She had wanted warmth.

Max thrust his hand toward her. It was filled with bills. "Just to tide you over," he said, blushing so that his summer tan showed even more prominently. "It's not really as much as it looks. The currency's been devalued so many times. I'll see you tonight."

My mother sat with the devalued bills in her hand for several minutes after he left. Then she walked in the direction of the Jewish Community Center, where Jews returning to Prague were issued documents to replace those confiscated by the Gestapo three years before. At that moment, had she been stopped by a policeman or accused of a crime, my mother could not have proved who she was. She did not possess a single document. Her birth certificate, her passport, working papers, and health records had been taken from her in 1942. She watched herself waiting her turn, answering questions in a monotone, filling out forms.

"Where can I find a room?" she asked a clerk.

"Are you married?"

"My husband is dead."

"Children?"

"None."

"There's a terrible housing shortage," the clerk told her patiently. "It's a difficult situation. We give preference to families. Then, married couples."

That made sense, my mother told herself. It was only fair. But a terrible anger burned inside her as she walked the streets to kill time before dinner at Max's house. By what right were strangers living in her parents' house? Was this what they called repatriation, to be sent home only to find no roof to live under? Why hadn't she stayed in Celle? Or

79

married one of the Englishmen like some of the girls had? She wandered past the bookstores that she had spent hours in before the war, seeing nothing, aimless and blank. When she stopped, she found herself standing before the door of what had been her mother's dress salon. Without thinking, she rang the bell and Marie, the Czechoslovak woman who had been her mother's assistant, came to the door.

"Franci. You're back."

The tone of her voice was not happy or welcoming, just surprised, my mother thought. She imagined her former employee was thinking: *What does she want? How did she get back? What did she do to survive?*

"Come in. Please come in." Marie recovered quickly. She took my mother into the workroom where Franci had, as a teen-ager, learned to cut and baste and finish the dresses and coats that her mother designed.

"Almost nothing that was yours is here any longer," Marie said. "I put everything in storage. I didn't want the authorities to make trouble for us. I mean, we had to protect ourselves against the charge of enriching ourselves with Jewish property. Do you see what I mean?"

My mother nodded and understood nothing. Marie seemed to be talking gibberish. Nothing was in its proper place in the workroom. Her favorite sewing machine was gone. There were fewer tables. The room was poorly swept. There was grime on the windows.

"Business is off," Marie continued. "The old customers, the ones who came to your mother? They don't come here anymore. Some of them emigrated, I've heard. At any rate, I don't see them. We refurnished the place, you see. And the lease came up for renewal last year. Of course we had no idea where you were. We took it out in our own name."

"Yes," my mother said.

Something in her face seemed to frighten Marie.

"There was nothing else to do," she said loudly. "We didn't know that you would be coming back. We didn't know that you were alive."

My mother's mouth had swelled and her jaw thrust out as it had when she had been a child affecting indifference.

"Your mother . . ."

"She's dead."

"I'm so sorry," Marie said and that part of my mother that was observing the scene observed that Marie seemed sincerely distressed.

"Thank you," my mother said mechanically, and then wondered what she was thanking Marie for.

"You should have the address of the warehouse where your mother's things are stored. There should be no problem requisitioning them. Not now. It's been very hard these past few years but it's easier now." She gave my mother a slip of paper with the name of the warehouse written on it. "I'm sure we will be seeing one another now that you're back. We're in the same business after all, no?"

The door closed and my mother wandered through the streets again. A hazy August light had settled over the city, warming the gray stone buildings and sending glints of gold off the tips of church spires. People hurried home with packages of bread or potatoes. Prague had been bombed less than other major European cities during the war. Most of it was intact, just as my mother remembered it. Only she was different.

At seven, she presented herself at Max and Vera Bocek's house. Her mother had very much liked the couple. They were people to be trusted. They had two teen-age boys whom she had watched grow from babies into adolescents. The Boceks were old family friends. It would be all right.

When Vera Bocek opened the front door, her face showed a prepared smile. She served dinner almost immediately after my mother arrived and then busied herself so effectively with the ladling of soup and the cutting of bread that she was able to disregard the dearth of conversation.

As soon as she sat down at the table my mother had seen the "R" on the tablecloth. It stood for Rabinek and it came from the linen closet in her parents' home. The heavy silver

81

knife and fork at the sides of her plate were part of the set of silverware my mother had, as a small child, helped her polish. The crystal wine glass which she held between her fingers was from the dark wood cupboard that had stood in the dining room. She had helped her mother pack the glasses carefully and brought them over to the Boceks for safekeeping until the war was over. Vera Bocek said nothing about the pale-blue tablecloth, the silverware, the glasses, or anything else. At first my mother thought these things had been brought out of storage in her honor. But as the meal drew to a close without mention of them, she understood that Vera Bocek had forgotten, or had made herself forget, that they were not her own.

My mother caught herself staring at the "R" in the tablecloth so fixedly that she became embarrassed. She wanted to change the subject that claimed her mind, so she asked about the Bocek children. How old were they? What were they doing?

At the time my mother and her parents were deported to Terezin in 1942, Pavel and Edvard Bocek were twelve and thirteen.

"You won't recognize either of them, they've grown so," said Vera Bocek, and as she spoke Pavel walked in, taller and skinnier than my mother had remembered him. He was wearing one of Pepik Solar's suits, one of the many items of clothing my mother had carried over to the Boceks' house for safekeeping.

But for reasons that my mother did not understand, it was she—not Vera Bocek—who was embarrassed by the sight of her dead husband's suit on Pavel. Her embarrassment grew as they finished dinner and sat down in the living room for coffee. Max had said little. Conversation was stilted and my mother saw no smooth way to pose the question she had to ask. Finally, she took a breath and asked it.

"You know the jewelry my mother left with you," she asked Vera Bocek. "I thought maybe I'd sell one of the rings. I don't have a place to live. Or a job. All I own is a couple of suitcases."

Vera exchanged glances with her husband. "I'm terribly sorry," she said, "but we were very hard up the last year of the war. We had the same idea. We sold your mother's jewelry. It's gone."

My mother felt the way she had in the Jewish Community Center that afternoon looking for a place to live. There was nothing to say, nothing to do. She could hardly haul Vera Bocek to court for stealing her family's possessions. She didn't even have an address of her own or a piece of paper proving she was a Czech citizen. Besides, they had been close friends of her parents. The war had been hard for them too. They had not expected she would come back.

The encounter with the Boceks was typical of several reunions my mother was to have in the following weeks and months. The gist of the conversations and the embarrassment of things left unsaid were repeated so many times that my mother came to expect them. Soon she only wanted to see people she had known in prison. Or entirely new people, people she had never seen before the war, people who could not compare her to the person she had been before. During the day, she walked through Prague, turning the corners with the impossible hope of seeing her parents walking toward her arm in arm, the way they had walked away from her in Terezin, on their way to the transport which took them to Poland. At night she saw Kitty or sat in small rooms rented by other survivors who drank ersatz coffee and argued politics. Only Communism could prevent another Fascist regime in Czechoslovakia, some said. Others argued that only a strong Socialist party could prevent the Communists from becoming new Fascists. She sat listlessly, uninterested in politics, and then went home with one of the debaters. Neither she nor Kitty had been able to find a room of their own. They moved from one place into an-

83

other, always on the understanding that it was temporary. There were no apartments to be had.

Autumn came to Prague, bringing bad weather and another currency devaluation. My mother had retrieved small amounts of cash she had left with friends but the devaluation reduced them to one-tenth their value. The rain put an end to her walks, and she needed money so badly that she accepted a job as assistant to a former competitor of her mother.

"Franci Solar!" old clients would exclaim when they saw her buying in the fabric shops. "You're back! Have you opened the business?"

My mother shook her head. "I need a license," she would say. "There's too much red tape. I need documents I don't have. I need a place to work. I have no equipment. I'd have to buy everything from scratch."

What she did not say was that the long lines at the Community Center, the questions the clerks asked her and the forms she had to fill out terrified her. She was frightened by any form of authority. How could she run a business? She would have to give orders to her employees and she was incapable of giving orders to anyone. She could barely take care of herself.

Autumn became winter. There were fewer people on the streets. Many of the ex-prisoners who had returned to Prague along with my mother married and emigrated to England or America, propelled by the fear that the Russians would take over Eastern Europe bit by bit, just as Hitler had done not even a decade before. My mother spent long evenings alone. For a time, she had a puppy, a terrier who reminded her of the puppy she had before the war. During the last few months before she was deported, when it was too dangerous for her to continue appearing in the workroom, she had spent hours sewing fancy covers for his collar. Once she had made him a yellow Star of David. "Take that off him!" her mother had warned as they set out for a walk far from the center of the city. In a meadow filled with wildflowers and rabbits, the puppy had disappeared. That evening someone had found him. He had been shot dead. My mother became certain that if she kept the second puppy, he would die too, and one day she gave him away.

On New Year's Eve of 1946, my mother lay in a lukewarm bath, listening to the shouts and songs coming in through the window from the street. She had been invited to several parties but did not feel like going. She was too lonely. Her documents were still not in order. She still did not have her own place to live. She had lost all interest in men. She had decided never to marry again. Every day she imagined that she heard her mother's voice correcting her as she pinned dresses to headless dummies. She wanted all the noise in her head, all the images that passed through it day and night, to stop.

My mother got out of the tub, got dressed and walked to the Vltava River, which runs through Prague. She passed partygoers bundled up against the cold and a few drunks who wished her a Happy New Year. But apart from them, the streets were deserted. Once, as a child walking home from school with her governess, my mother had seen a dead man dredged up out of the Vltava. His body was tinged with green and reeked of dead fish. For several nights after that, she had dreamed about the mythical Water Man of Czech folklore who was said to lure young girls into the water. The servants had always told her that the Water Man would take her away if she misbehaved. My mother remembered those stories now. She kept looking at the river in the darkness, thinking how peaceful it would be to sink down into the water and forget everything.

She walked along the river until a policeman stopped her. It was one o'clock, he said. Not the best time to be walking alone by the side of a half-frozen river. He smiled at her, then offered to walk her home. It was the first day of the new year, 1946, eight and a half months after the British tanks had rumbled into Bergen-Belsen.

That February, my mother turned twenty-six. It was difficult for strangers to believe that she had ever been a concentration camp inmate. Her face was smooth and round. She wore lipstick and applied mascara to her large dark eyes. She dressed fashionably. But when she looked into her mirror in the mornings before leaving for work, my mother saw a shell, a mannequin who moved and spoke but who bore only a superficial resemblance to her real self. The people closest to her had vanished. She had no proof that they were truly dead. No eyewitnesses had survived to vouch for her husband's death. There was no one living who had seen her parents die. The lack of confirmation haunted her. At night before she went to sleep and during the day as she stood pinning dresses she wondered if, by some chance, her parents had gotten past the Germans or had crawled out of the mass grave into which they had been shot and were living, old and helpless, somewhere in Poland. What if only one of them had died? What if they had survived and had died of cold or hunger after she had been liberated, while she was in Celle dancing with British officers?

She did not talk to anyone about these things. No one, she thought, wanted to hear them. She woke up in the mornings, went to work, bought groceries, went to the Jewish Community Center and to the housing office like a robot.

One afternoon when she left the housing office emptyhanded as usual, a tall man across the street called her name, hurrying toward her with a smile so wide that his whole face seemed to radiate joy.

At the sight of him, her childhood spread out before her. She had been thirteen, and Kitty had been eleven, when they first met Kurt Epstein. Twice each week, after school, they had taken the streetcar to the swim club dreading the cold water and anticipating the severity of their swimming teacher. Kurt Epstein, one of the top swimming coaches, was there when he was not abroad playing water polo. "Good morning, Mr. Epstein," the two cousins would murmur politely as they passed him on the clammy tiles. He would grunt acknowledgment without breaking his stride. He had been twenty-nine then, over six feet tall, and unapproachable. "He thinks he's such a bigshot," Kitty would whisper to Franci. During their lessons, Kurt Epstein would often stroll over to the pool for no discernible reason. He would criticize their form and then tell their teacher to have them do ten or fifteen more lengths than usual.

"I'm so glad to see you," Epstein said now.

He was far thinner than she remembered. The shoulders of his suit stood up by themselves. There were long gray hollows in his cheeks. He kept his weight on one leg. The other was still healing from an abscess that had formed while he was in concentration camp. He wanted to know why he had not seen my mother swimming. It was May, he informed her, as if she had not noticed. Surely she was not waiting for the weather to get any warmer. My mother told him that she was wary of returning to places she had frequented before the war. She was not sure what kind of welcome she would receive.

"Are you crazy?" Kurt Epstein demanded. "Everyone will be happy to see you. We're having races tomorrow. You should be there."

"Maybe," my mother told him. "Maybe I'll come."

The next day was sunny and warm. My mother bought a bag of plums and took the streetcar to the swimming club. Kurt Epstein was busy organizing the afternoon's races and immediately put her to work selling tickets. During the races, he seated her with the functionaries of the club. All the men who had been coaches when she was a child remembered and welcomed her. Kurt Epstein moved from the bleachers to the pool, stopping every few minutes to take a plum from her brown bag. The sun was shining. An odd sensation made itself felt to my mother. She was happy.

After the races, Epstein and a fellow coach sat on the lawn playing chess. She sat with them, studying their faces. Kurt Epstein was forty-two but he looked younger. He had not aged as much as other survivors. He had retained his athlete's body and an easy camaraderie with his teammates, mostly Gentiles who had not been in the camps. She did not know many sportsmen. But they exuded an exuberance and a solidity that made my mother want to stay near them. They were simpler than the men she was accustomed to, and shyer. They seemed to live for the water, oblivious to politics or the intellectual society of the cafés, and when Kurt came home they had taken him back into their circle with little fuss.

The shadows of the trees had grown long on the lawn when the chess game was over. His partner stood up and left, leaving Kurt Epstein alone with the young woman he remembered as a child. He was a reserved, courteous man, with a reputation for puritanism. He had been in the first transport sent to Terezin and even there, where gossips were quick to malign fellow prisoners, he had been known as a fair, principled man. But he had no talent with women and my mother grew impatient.

"What are you doing tonight?" she finally asked.

"Me?" he said, blushing in surprise. "Why? Would you like to have dinner?"

My mother enjoyed herself at dinner and her contentment puzzled her. Her escort came from Roudnice, from the provinces. She had had to advise him on their choice of wine. Yet she liked the man. When he said, "I just found an apartment, would you like to have a look at it?" she forgot it was the oldest line in the world. Coming from Kurt Epstein, who had always lectured the other swim coaches when he caught them flirting with her girl friends, it had to be genuine.

"All right," she said. "Let's go."

His apartment faced the river. It contained a bookcase empty of books, a coffee table and two easy chairs, a dining table, a couch, and an upright piano. There were dirty coffee cups in the bathroom sink. Otherwise there was no sign that anyone lived there. Kurt uncorked the bottle of wine they had taken with them from the restaurant, and my mother stayed the night.

"I don't want you to think I just seduced you," she heard him saying as she opened her eyes the next morning. "I want to get married and start a family."

My mother looked up him, wet from his morning shower. He had to be joking, she thought. People did not decide to get married after one night! She tried to remember what had transpired between them. Dimly, she remembered complaining of bedbugs in the couch. They had moved to the floor with hardly a break in Epstein's monologue. He had talked to her all night. He had talked about Roudnice and his parents and two brothers. He had talked about his time in Terezin and about Frydland, where he had been liberated by the Russians. He had said that he mourned his family for one year and that now he was through with mourning. He was forty-two years old and ready to start a family of his own. Her back and legs ached. It was not even eight o'clock. It was Sunday.

"You'll feel better after a swim," Epstein said, and helped her to her feet.

Less than an hour later they were riding on the streetcar back to the swimming club.

"All right," he said. "When are we getting married?"

"I don't know," she said in confusion. The man who had seemed so protective the night before suddenly seemed a stranger. How could he want to marry her after only twenty-four hours? And how could he say he had done with mourning? Did he think he could simply shut the door on the past five years? Did he know of a way to keep the past out of his dreams at night? What kind of a future did he foresee?

He was not a subtle man, she thought. He would be stubborn, opinionated, authoritarian. He was sixteen years older than she. He had been born when Franz Josef was still

Emperor. His values were those of another age. But, my mother thought, those values had survived the war. They were stronger than anything that had been pitted against them. At that moment, riding to the swimming club, Kurt Epstein seemed an anchor to her, someone who would put an end to drifting.

"If you take care of getting the papers," she said, "we'll get married."

It took him until December to assemble them, but life changed for Franci Solar so quickly that documents lost their importance and their former power of definition. The days that had seemed so interminably long were now not long enough to manage a household, and to organize the reopening of her couture salon. The couple was invited out to dinner. There was furniture to be bought, sports events to attend. They planned a small wedding ceremony to be held just before Christmas, and they planned for children.

At first when he talked about children, she said nothing at all. Pregnancy had always frightened her. She could not imagine herself, a woman who ran a business, as a mother. She had not the slightest idea of what one did with children. As a child, she herself had spent most of her time with adults. Often now, when she showered or while she prepared for bed, she examined her body for a bent toward motherhood, but saw none. The body which she had watched turn into two bodies when she sat on her bunk in Auschwitz could not have children, she thought. Any child it produced would be deficient in calcium, in vitamins. Her baby would be born with soft bones, or no arms, or blind. Or she would be like some of the women who had been in Terezin and Belsen. She would be pregnant for a few weeks and then begin to bleed, and the baby would be lost. Another loss. Her body refused another loss: she did not become pregnant.

But my father was a stubborn man. He persisted in talking about children. He had already decided that the first of their children would be a girl whom they would name

90

Helena after his mother. Children were life. Children were the future, he told my mother. They had both survived the war for reasons that were beyond his understanding, but surely their purpose was, in part, to rebuild a family. My father had gone into business with a friend, a man with whom he had survived the camps, and business was good. They had a new apartment. My mother's business was flourishing. What reason was there not to have children?

Cautiously, my mother began to question her friends who had already given birth. They scolded her. Was she crazy? they asked. Every woman who could was having children. Not every woman was able to. Even those who had been told it was hopeless were trying special diets and pills, greasing the palms of quack doctors in exchange for the promise of fertility. Slowly, my mother began to want a child.

My parents were married four days before Christmas in 1946, and as soon as they returned from their honeymoon, my mother's employees began to watch for signs of pregnancy.

"How are you feeling?" they would ask hopefully, and my mother would be brusque in her reply. It seemed to her that every woman she knew was expecting a baby and that she alone had been singled out for sterility. Nights when my father was at one of his sportsmen's meetings, she often walked through their apartment to the room which had been designated as a nursery. All the anxiety she had previously turned to the question of having children was now directed toward the possibility that she might not be able to conceive. Even women who had miscarriages were better off, my mother thought. They, at least, had succeeded in becoming pregnant. She could not even manage that. Often she would stare down at the blue number on her arm and wonder if the camps had taken away her capacity to bear children. Other times she worried that she had been with too many men after returning to Prague and had contracted some rare, undiagnosed venereal disease.

A few days after her twenty-seventh birthday, my mother

felt a twinge of nausea, and immediately made an appointment with her obstetrician.

"What makes you think you're pregnant?" he asked.

"My period is two days late," my mother told him.

He sighed.

"It's really far too early to tell," he continued after examining her.

"Are you sure?"

"No." He shook his head. "I've learned to trust the instinct of my patients. If you think you're pregnant, Mrs. Epstein, let's assume you are."

My mother left the doctor's office with her stomach stuck out as far as it would go. She went straight to a bookstore to buy a baby book and that evening she and my father began a regimen of evening strolls. Kitty began to appear at the apartment with lemons and oranges she bought on the black market. The butcher put away calves brains, then deemed beneficial for pregnancy.

Six weeks after the doctor's examination my mother awoke to find the insides of her thighs sticky with blood. "It will probably stop in a day or two," the obstetrician told her. "Just go to bed and keep still."

She lay motionless in bed. The next morning the bleeding was stronger. "Be reasonable," my father said, but my mother would not stop crying.

"I want my mother," she said, in a voice sodden with repetition. "I want my baby and I'm going to lose her like I lost everyone else."

My father paced up and down beside her. He was not good with words. "If we lose this one, we'll have another," he told my mother. "We have time. There's no rush."

"But I want *this* one," my mother repeated.

The doctor came again. This time with a new drug from America, but he also said that perhaps it was for the best that she lose this baby. She had been undernourished for three years. She had suffered a severe bout of typhus. She had undergone severe emotional strain. "It's possible that your body is simply not strong enough yet," he said.

On the fifth day, the bleeding stopped. My mother moved about the apartment cautiously, ready to lie down at the slightest irregularity. But the bleeding did not start again and the following week she was busy in her dress salon. At the start of her eighth month, in October of 1947, she weighed 190 pounds, almost double her weight at the end of the war. The only place she felt comfortable was standing by her work table, cutting a dress. One night, about two weeks before time, she was working there when she felt liquid running down her legs and saw a small puddle forming on the floor.

My mother telephoned for a taxi. My father was at another of his sportsmen's meetings. Her friend Margot, with whom she had shared a bunk in Auschwitz and who was staying with my parents, helped her get to the hospital. There was no time for anesthesia. There was barely time for the doctor to arrive and wash his hands. My mother lay on a table watching the clock that showed it was nearly two in the morning.

"Doctor, come," she heard the midwife's voice above her.

My mother groaned, and with her final, heaving thrust I came head first into the world.

SIX

By the end of 1947, thousands of Holocaust survivors had given birth to a new generation. During the summer months of 1945, they had made their way back to the homes they had left in Hungary, Poland, Czechoslovakia, Austria, Yugoslavia and Rumania. Most found a far less hospitable reception than my parents had found in Prague. Their homes, too, were inhabited by strangers, and their possessions had been stolen or confiscated or lost. They had no place to live or work. But, in addition, many of their communities had been totally destroyed, their cemeteries and shuls desecrated. In Poland, particularly, survivors came home to open enmity. Hundreds of men and women returning from the concentration camps were shot by Poles. In July of 1946, the scattered, random killing turned into a full-scale pogrom in Kielce, Poland, where nearly fifty Jews were slaughtered.

Word of that pogrom spread through the surviving Jewish

communities of Eastern Europe. Most of the survivors who had returned to the East packed up their few belongings again and made their way West to the parts of Europe occupied by the Allies. Stateless and penniless, 250,000 of them congregated in new kinds of camps, waiting for the opportunity to emigrate. Some waited nearly ten years for visas. The last Displaced Persons camp—Foehrenwald in Bavaria—remained in operation until 1957.

The plight of Holocaust survivors, many of whom had been homeless since 1940, became known in the press as "the refugee question." In the United States, President Harry S. Truman dispatched a commission to study the situation in the DP camps. It concluded that at least 100,-000 of them should be allowed to enter Palestine. In a letter to Clement Attlee, head of the new Labour government in Great Britain, President Truman wrote, "The main solution appears to lie in the quick evacuation of as many as possible of the non-repatriable Jews, who wish it, to Palestine. If it is to be effective, such action should not be delayed." Attlee replied that there was no evidence that Jewish displaced persons had suffered any more than non-Jewish victims of Nazism and proposed that the survivors be shipped to camps in North Africa. At the end of 1945, an Anglo-American Committee of Inquiry was formed to study the situation. Their report was published in Washington on May 1, 1946, and President Truman publicly endorsed its recommendation for admitting 100,000 Jews into Palestine. British Foreign Secretary Ernest Bevin replied that the Americans' recommendation was prompted by the fact that "they did not want too many of them in New York," and London rejected the committee's report.

Meanwhile, the Jewish Agency had grasped the plight of the refugees as a potent political tool to dramatize the need for a Jewish State. A massive, illegal immigration effort began. Groups of Jewish displaced persons were taken out of camps in the American zone of Germany, transported to the coasts of France and Italy, and shipped in obsolete sailing vessels toward Palestine. The British, who had blockaded the shores of that country, intercepted the boats and took their passengers to yet another type of camp—internment camp— in Cyprus. All but five of sixty-three ships carrying illegal immigrants to Palestine were intercepted between 1945 and 1948, and 26,000 Jews were interned in Cyprus.

Holocaust survivors were therefore squarely in the public eye for at least five years after the war. Photographs from the Middle East showed them on ships, surrounded by British soldiers, holding up banners such as "We survived Hitler. Death is no stranger to us." In the United States, Australia and Canada, the newspapers ran a different kind of local story. "Mr. and Mrs. Motel Fiszman and their two-year-old daughter Miriam arrived here aboard the S.S. *Marine Flasher* today and will get a fresh start on life at the home of Max Keiter, Clark Avenue, Chelsea," reads a clip from the Boston *Herald-Traveler* of February 9, 1949. "Mr. Fiszman spent three years in Buchenwald and his wife endured six years of hard labor in Siberia before they met and married in Landsberg, Germany."

The Fiszmans were among more than 92,000 survivors who emigrated to the United States. America was, in some cases, the only country where survivors had a remnant of family. It was a symbol of freedom and security, two conditions they had lived without during the war, and which had gained unparalleled importance for them since. That initial postwar immigration was augmented throughout the fifties as Polish and Hungarian Jews left their countries in 1953 and 1956.

More than 25,000 survivors went to Canada. Several thousand made their way to South America and to Australia, determined to get as far away from Europe as possible. Others—French, Dutch, Belgian, Czech, Hungarian, and even Germans—chose to remain in their country of origin.

The largest group of survivors, estimated at 250,000, emigrated to the newly established state of Israel. Between September, 1948, and August, 1949, fifty-two refugee centers in Europe were closed down and the survivors were shipped to the Middle East. The 26,000 survivors who had been living in Cyprus were also transported there, making up in total nearly 70 percent of the immigrants who arrived in the country for the first eighteen months after the War of Independence. They arrived in an Israel ravaged by war and barely capable of feeding and housing its instant citizenry. Many of the same people who had been through the concentration camps, the Displaced Persons camps, and the British internment camps on Cyprus were now placed in *ma'abarot*, temporary immigrant camps in Israel. By 1952, nearly 40,000 new immigrants had left Israel, among them a large proportion of survivors.

By 1952, however, Holocaust survivors and their difficulties had been largely forgotten by the press, the public and even large sections of the Jewish community. In the United States, the Hebrew Immigrant Aid Society, which had originally brought the great majority of them over, kept in close contact with survivors, assisting them in finding work and housing. In Canada, the Jewish Immigrant Aid Society performed the same function. But, for the most part, Holocaust survivors dropped out of sight.

Some arrived in their new countries, changed their names and sent their children to Protestant Sunday schools. One couple who settled in southern Ontario, like others who did not wish to pass on a stigma to their children, refused to have their son circumcised, and only told him he was Jewish when he turned thirteen. Some, like the survivors who swelled the populations of Williamsburg, Crown Heights, Flatbush and Boro Park in Brooklyn, New York, formed strong survivor communities where several of their children grew up thinking that "everyone's parents had been in concentration camps."

Some arrived in a new place, put down roots and never moved out of their neighborhood again. Others emigrated, stayed a while, then moved on to another city or country. Many trekked from Europe to Israel to North or South America, unsettled until the late fifties.

The survivors were perhaps the most heterogeneous group that had ever made a mass migration. Some had come from Eastern Europe *shtetls* and had never lived among Christians before. Others had been so assimilated into their national cultures that it had taken the war to make them recognize that they were Jews. Some had come from wealthy, educated families; others had never finished elementary school. Some were well-established professionals or craftspeople; others had no talent or training on which to build a livelihood. There were, among them, young children, teenagers, young adults, and middle-aged men and women. Some—the German and Polish Jews—had lived in ghettos or camps for seven years; others, like the Hungarian Jews, less than one.

The communities in which they settled, however, did regard them as one, clearly identifiable group. They were *greeners,* New Americans, New Australians—Jews without money, social position or security. In England, the United States and Canada, where Jews had been living for several generations, the newcomers were often perceived as a threat and living evidence of an event most people preferred to forget. In some cases, survivors were a financial burden to their relatives. More generally, they were regarded with ambivalence, a mixture of respect and suspicion. People wondered how they had survived. They speculated on possibilities like collaboration with the Nazis, unfair play, prostitution. Some people asked these questions out loud while others did so silently. Neither course was conducive to trust.

The survivors themselves did not take the initiative, for the most part, in establishing close relations with people who were not refugees. They did not want to be seen as a burden. Also, they were busy learning new languages, finding jobs and raising the children that the overwhelming majority of them had wanted as soon as possible.

Few sought additional help once they had jobs and a home. They wanted to shut the door on their past. Neither they nor anyone else realized that they needed anything but material assistance. "It seems altogether incredible today that when the first plans for the rehabilitation of Europe's surviving Jews were outlined, the psychiatric aspect of the problem was overlooked entirely," wrote Paul Friedman in the *American Journal of Psychiatry* in 1949. "Everyone engaged in directing the relief work thought solely in terms of material assistance."

Nonetheless, it was the psychiatrists and a small number of lawyers who remained in close contact with survivors during the first decade of their relocation. The reason for this was the Luxembourg Agreement of September 10, 1952. Under the terms of this agreement, the Federal Republic of Germany assumed the obligation to provide partial recompense for material damage to the Jewish people under Nazism. The first part of the agreement provided that Germany pay some $714 million in goods and services to the State of Israel, and the deliveries included power-generating plants, locomotives, teletype equipment, machinery and raw materials. In addition, $107 million was pledged to a "Claims Conference" acting on behalf of various Jewish organizations. Another provision pledged the enactment of far-reaching German legislative measures providing indemnification to individual victims.

The Federal Restitution Law, enacted in 1957, provided Nazi victims with compensation for household furnishings, jewelry, precious metals, bank accounts, securities and other movable objects which Nazi authorities had confiscated. The compensation payments were intended to replace the restitution of the properties themselves. The Federal Indemnification Law, enacted in 1953 and overhauled in 1956, was to redress "personal wrongs" suffered by survivors. Included among these wrongs were injuries to health, loss of liberty, damage to property, damage to professional or economic advancement and other hardship.

The provisions of these two laws were so complicated that an entire sub-group of lawyers came into being to untangle them, and litigation on some cases is still being carried out today. The survivors themselves differed greatly in response to the German legislation which was termed *Wiedergutmachung* or "to make reparations." This term infuriated many survivors. Some refused to accept what they called "blood money," pointing out that no amount of cash could restore their families or right the wrong which had been done to them. Others, particularly those who were in sore need of financial help, decided to press their claims, particularly claims of damage to health. To do so, they were obliged to undergo medical and psychiatric examinations to establish a link between the physical and mental disabilities they suffered at present, and the abuse they had sustained during the war.

Through this process, which began in the fifties and dragged on for more than two decades, a sub-group of psychiatrists was created. So many survivors had to be examined that some individual practitioners had soon compiled more than one thousand case histories. At a time when Holocaust survivors had dropped out of public sight, this psychiatric material provided the only comprehensive account of survivors as a group. Through professional journals and the first-hand accounts of survival by psychiatrists like Viktor Frankl and Bruno Bettelheim, and novelists like Elie Wiesel and Josef Bor, a body of literature on Holocaust survivors began to grow.

The psychiatric studies were problem-ridden from the start. Psychiatry had never before been faced with such a complex mass problem. Many of the examiners, who had been schooled in strict Freudian tradition, were unprepared to accept the notion of mass, adult trauma and refused to believe that the Holocaust and its aftereffects might cause permanent psychological or physical change. According to their textbooks, "Traumatic Neurosis," the term they used to describe what survivors had undergone, was a short-term, self-limited syndrome. Survivors were expected to display clearly defined and consistent symptoms which would eventually disappear.

Reality looked nothing like the textbook. Instead, psychiatrists found a bewildering variety of people and problems, scattered throughout the world. A small percentage of survivors had been hospitalized for severe psychiatric disturbances after they had resettled. Others were relatively well adapted but prone to chronic periods of difficulty. Some were marked by striking changes in personality. Others appeared to have resumed, more or less, the lives they had led before the war. Moreover, the problems they presented to the examiners in the late 1950s had not troubled them greatly in the period immediately following liberation. They had been suppressed and began to surface as much as ten years later.

The dimensions of the "trauma" also staggered researchers. The people they were seeing had been yanked out of a routine existence and placed into a protracted period of terror as well as, for many, total helplessness. Many had been systematically starved, living on 1,000 calories per day while performing ten to twelve hours of hard physical labor. In a study of 227 survivors, Leo Eitinger found that 184 had lost more than a third of their body weight and that over seventy had lost more than 40 percent. Over half of the survivors he saw had suffered head injuries with attendant loss of consciousness and almost as many had suffered back injuries.

All the survivors the psychiatrists saw had experienced

intense forms of psychological degradation. All had been witness to recurrent selections for death. All had experienced partial or total loss of family. All had undergone the transition from the camps to their homes to emigration and readjustment. The condition that the British had called "the refugee problem" was now renamed by the psychiatric profession. They referred to it as "the Survivor Syndrome," a term coined by Dr. William G. Niederland, a psychiatrist who worked with hundreds of survivors and had himself left Munich just before the war.

The psychiatrists confronting this problem were themselves a heterogeneous group, perhaps even more heterogeneous than the survivors themselves. Some were Jews who had been in the camps; others, Germans who had served in Hitler's army; others were people for whom the war had been a story to be read in the newspapers. The psychiatrists found it difficult to pretend to professional distance from the issues the survivors raised by their very presence. Many confessed to extreme emotional difficulty in relating to the problems the survivors presented.

"One case per week was about the maximum I could stand," said Robert Gronner, a psychiatrist in Illinois. "It was only after my own working through succeeded and I could gain some perspective of it, that I was able to do more." Some psychiatrists protected themselves by a facade of harshness. The Central Park West psychiatrist who examined my mother, among over 1,000 other survivors, was known for his stern, almost martial conduct of interviews. In 1961, he concluded, publicly, that Holocaust survivors, as a group, had a lower rate of mental illness than New Yorkers. "We are confronted with the illogical conclusion," one of his colleagues observed drily, "that people's mental health is improved by persecution."

Some examiners were so averse to obtaining details of their patients' experience that their reports glossed over the

102

war and concentrated on early childhood. Others used the restitution interviews to discuss their own suffering under Nazism. Dutch psychiatrist Joost A. M. Meerloo was told by several patients that their examiner had "played a dual role. On the one hand he identified with the enemy, whose financial interests he had to defend, but on the other he also had to defend himself against his own inner emotional turmoil." Some psychiatrists identified so much with their patients that they were unable to function as therapists.

The ambivalence of the examiners was dwarfed by that of the survivors themselves. Most of them did not want to be in a psychiatrist's office at all. They went under duress to claim a right, not to request treatment. They resented the doctor for representing an authority whose opinion would validate their experience. They perceived him as a judge and a prosecutor, an official paid by the government of the country that was responsible for causing their pain.

Few survivors requested treatment, for that implied that liberation had not put an end to Hitler, that Nazism had achieved a posthumous victory. Moreover, many survivors had developed a profound distrust of words, of the futility of trying to communicate their experience to anyone who had not participated in it. In 1968, Dr. Henry Krystal, a survivor himself and a psychiatrist in Detroit, reported that of 697 survivors in the Detroit area receiving pensions from Germany and eligible for fully paid-for psychiatric care, only thirty-one had requested treatment.

By 1968, psychiatrists had become interested in the phenomenon of massive psychic trauma. They began to look at entire populations—American Blacks and Indians, Japanese victims of the atomic bomb, survivors of great fires or floods—that had outlived disaster. They began to speculate that extreme circumstances of traumatization effect marked changes in people and often leave them with lifelong psychological problems. Holocaust survivors were an ideal group on which to test this thesis. Their case records were available by the thousands, and many studies based on them had already been published.

The components of the "Survivor Syndrome" as set forth by Dr. Niederland are complex and multifold. "The syndrome appears to be characterized by the persistence of multiple symptoms among which chronic depressive and anxiety reactions, insomnia, nightmares, personality changes, and far-reaching somatization prevail," he wrote in 1968. "More specifically, clinical observation of about eight hundred survivors of Nazi persecution revealed that the Survivor Syndrome is composed of the following manifestations: anxiety; disturbances of cognition and memory; chronic depressive states; tendency to isolation, withdrawal and brooding seclusion; alterations of personal identity; psychosomatic conditions and a 'living corpse' appearance."

Niederland cited anxiety as the predominant complaint, associated with fear of renewed persecutions, sleep disturbances, multiple phobias and nightmares. "The most prevalent manifestation of the Survivor Syndrome is a chronic state of anxious, bland depression," he wrote. "When first seen, the patient often appears pale-faced, sallow, sitting huddled and silent in the waiting room chair. He demonstrates little or no spontaneous activity. There are usually vague, nonspecific physical complaints such as localized aching, gastrointestinal disfunction, and rheumatic or neuralgic symptoms. Complaints of fatigue, lassitude and feelings of heaviness or emptiness are common. Depressive fatigue is characterized by a feeling of intense unpleasantness and is unrelieved by rest or relaxation. Sleep disorders are extraordinarily frequent and include early morning awakening as well as the fear of falling asleep at night because of the dread of tormenting nocturnal experiences such as nightmares, awakening in terror, hallucinatory or semi-hallucinatory reliving of the past. Restrictive social or asocial behavior, accompanied by withdrawal from human contact, seclusiveness, brooding preoccupation with the past, chronic apathy alternating with short-lived outbursts of rage, flattening and blunting of affect and the like are common. Another important characteristic of such patients is their inability to verbalize the traumatic events. In fact, the experience is of such a nature that it frequently cannot be communicated at all."

Niederland's portrait of the survivor as patient complements the profile of the survivor in the novels of Elie Wiesel. "You must look at them carefully," he wrote in *The Accident*. "Their appearance is deceptive ... They look like the others. They eat, they laugh, they love. They seek money, fame, love. Like the others. But it isn't true: they are playing, sometimes without even knowing it. Anyone who has seen what they have seen cannot be like the others, cannot laugh, love, pray, bargain, suffer, have fun or forget. Like the others. You have to watch them carefully when they pass by an innocent-looking smokestack, or when they lift a piece of bread to their mouths. Something in them shudders and makes you turn your eyes away. These people have been amputated; they haven't lost their legs or eyes but their will and their taste for life. The things that they have seen will come to the surface again sooner or later. And then the world will be frightened and won't dare look these spiritual cripples in the eye ... they aren't normal human beings. A spring snapped inside them from the shock."

At the Wayne State Conference on Massive Psychic Trauma held in 1968, this picture of the Holocaust survivor was reinforced by testimony from fifty specialists who reiterated that they were describing a "clinical" picture of Holocaust survivors but whose conclusions came to be ascribed to the whole group.

"When some of these patients hear a knock on the door," noted Dr. Gustav Bychowski of New York, "this seems to them a dangerous portent. When they see a black limousine coming up and stopping before the door, this evokes terror. When they see a man in uniform, they respond in panic because all this brings back memories of past horrors."

"One common problem in the survivors of the Holocaust," noted Israeli psychiatrist Hillel Klein, "is a profound fear of getting to love someone. Having lost most, if not all, of their early love objects, they now fear that to love anyone means to lose them and go through the pain all over again. Since they have not been able to work through their losses, such a situation threatens overwhelming depression."

At the same time, many survivors held on to a belief that, despite all odds, members of their families who had disappeared during the war would return. Some waited for them. Others saw their return in the form of children born after the war. "In such situations," noted Dr. Niederland, "the children represent the new versions of parents, close relatives, or offspring lost in the holocaust. Therefore, when a survivor's child suffers an illness or injury, the parent has to deal with the revival of all of his psychological reactions which had remained repressed up to the time of this new misfortune."

The depression almost all survivors suffered was a more complex phenomenon. "If we try to approach the structure of this depression," observed Dr. Bychowski about one of his patients, "we see a picture characterized by the destruction of his world, the destruction of the basic landmarks on which the world of human beings in our civilization is based, i.e., basic trust in human worth, basic confidence, basic hope. Here, there is no trust, there is no confidence, everything has been shattered to pieces."

One major component of the depression was repressed mourning. While prisoners or fugitives, Holocaust survivors had had neither the opportunity to bury their dead nor the luxury of time and freedom to mourn. Some psychiatrists were astonished to hear from their patients that of all the deprivations they had suffered, this absence of a mourning ritual had been the most difficult to bear.

A second component was what the psychiatrists called "survival guilt," an unusual form of mourning where the survivor remained "stuck in a magnification of the guilt which is present in every bereaved person." Dr. Robert J. Lifton, who had studied both Hiroshima and Holocaust survivors, found this guilt prevalent in both groups. Other researchers, who had worked with war veterans, described similar findings. *Why did my buddy die?* asked former soldiers. *He was better than me.* Holocaust survivors often fell into prolonged, exacerbated depressions whenever friends or relatives in their new surroundings died, or when a public figure like President John F. Kennedy was assassinated.

A third and striking component was what Dr. Lifton called "psychic closing off" and what other psychiatrists termed "lack of affect," an inability to feel or project emotion in the ways survivors had been able to do prior to their war experience. In the camps or forests, "psychic closing off" had been a survival skill, a way to get from one day to the next without losing one's life or mind. When the war was over, however, and the wartime adaptation remained, it became an impediment rather than an advantage. Researchers spoke of survivors who seemed to have built walls around themselves, who could no longer relate to the idea of "fun," who saw themselves as having conquered death but also living it. Many seemed to remain closed off or emotionally constricted for the rest of their lives.

Because the Wayne State conference focused on psychological effects of persecution, few researchers made mention of the physical disabilities many survivors grappled with long after the war was over. These aftereffects included broken bones or spine injuries that had not received appropriate care during the war, scars, and deformities of the hands and

107

feet that had never fully healed. Some researchers found evidence of permanent damage to the central nervous system, the result of numerous beatings.

"We see individuals with healthy psychophysical constitutions and a good former background and history develop at much too early an age symptoms of hypertension, arteriosclerosis and premature senility," noted Dr. Bychowski. "I would postulate that the extreme stress lasting for years has resulted in this premature senility, premature arteriosclerosis, or even some changes in cardiac function; *secondarily,* this affects the cerebral substance, which is the most vulnerable tissue we have ... We see an individual who is depressed, but we are also dealing with a person whose memory is faulty, whose orientation is defective."

Survivors complained of a variety of physical problems: headaches, muscle tension, joint pain, gastrointestinal disorders. But many researchers felt that the combination of circumstances they had been through—starvation, typhoid or typhus, beating and general stress—were so complex that cause and effect could not be sorted out.

What they were certain of, however, was that as the survivors began to raise families, their problems did not work themselves out. On the contrary, as the children of survivors began to reach their teens, coming closer to the age at which their parents were imprisoned, new problems appeared.

"We now see increasing numbers of children of survivors suffering from problems of depression and inhibition of their own function," reported Dr. Henry Krystal in Detroit. "This is a clear example of social pathology being transmitted to the next generation."

Other researchers were not so quick to call what had apparently happened "social pathology." Instead, they identified "disturbances in the parent-child relationship" in the families of survivors. They were puzzled by numerous contradictions in survivor families. Many had become extremely successful in real estate, construction or manufacturing, building mammoth businesses. Others worked in the most menial positions, sweeping floors or cleaning other people's homes. Some were vibrant and optimistic; others listless and depressed. No psychiatrist undertook to study what survivors were like as parents, and little was known about family dynamics in survivor families. The children seemed to be as averse to psychotherapy as their parents. If they had anything to say, they had not said it publicly.

Only a very few psychiatrists, psychologists and psychoanalysts were interested enough to follow up that problem. For most of the psychiatric profession, as well as the world at large, the Holocaust was history.

SEVEN

Sara* and Aviva,* whose parents were among the 250,000 Holocaust survivors who emigrated to Israel, both asked that I keep their identities secret. Like many young Israelis I had met, they were of two minds about the war. They were accustomed to public discussion of the Holocaust, for they had been raised in a country which had institutionalized it, made it part and parcel of everyday life. Every year, Sara and Aviva, along with the rest of the population, had observed a day of national mourning for the six million Jews who had been murdered under Nazi supervision. In school, they had been among the thousands of children who were taken on class trips to museums and monuments built to commemorate the dead. References to the Holocaust were frequent in political and military debates within Israel. They were implicit in the names of settlements, like Kibbutz *Lochamei Ha'Ghetta'ot*, the kibbutz of the Fighters of the Ghettos. There was probably not a soul in Israel who did not come into personal contact with a survivor, if not as a friend, then as a grocer, lawyer, taxi driver or dressmaker. The Holocaust had been integrated into the nation's consciousness as the most massive, but certainly not the last instance of persecution of the Jews.

But while both Aviva and Sara could discuss details of the war with an ease that was uncharacteristic of children of survivors who had grown up elsewhere, neither was comfortable with relating those details to her own life. Their reluctance was typical of the Israelis I encountered. Although Holocaust survivors in the early fifties made up more than 20 percent of the national population, their problems of adjustment received scant attention. They were only one of several groups of new immigrants to a country beset by severe economic and military difficulties. In addition to being *greeners,* they were a reminder of the ghetto past, out of keeping with the pioneer mythology that the new state had created in its art, music and literature. Israel, even in the fifties, had already developed a special hierarchy. Many of its established members were natives of Palestine or Zionists who had left Europe in the twenties; others had foreseen danger in the thirties and had left Europe then at great cost or peril. They, like many established Jews in the United States and Canada, exhibited a number of contradictory attitudes toward the newcomers: smugness for their own initiative in getting out before it was too late; guilt for not helping more people to leave; a desire to forget the lives they had led before.

Israel had forged a new prototype of the Jew—a soldier, farmer, citizen of his own country—in which the Diaspora Jew had no place. Some Holocaust survivors embraced this image and made it their own. They came to Israel "to build and to be rebuilt," in the words of a popular folksong, while others found themselves unable to make the leap from one life into the other.

Aviva's parents had apparently done so; Sara's parents

111

had not. Both families arrived in Israel in 1948. Both women had lived there until their late teens, when they came to the United States. Both had married American men and both lived in American suburbs. But apart from their strongly accented English and the forceful, direct manner of speaking that was a carryover from the Hebrew, they had little in common.

Aviva was a musician, tall, composed and immaculately groomed. She had played with many major orchestras in the world and enjoyed a fine reputation among musicians as well as the general public. Aviva was known, as well, for her dislike of theatrics, on stage or off. She was a straight-forward, highly disciplined woman who drew a clear-cut line between her private and public life. She had a number of old and close friends with whom she relaxed; she was not one for cocktail party acquaintances and small talk.

Aviva had begun her musical studies at age eight, encouraged by her mother who taught piano. Before reaching her teens, she was winning music competitions and performing in public concerts. Her family lived in Herzliya, a pleasant, bustling town near Tel Aviv and its music conservatory. Aviva graduated from the conservatory and received her high school diploma at sixteen, then had gone abroad to pursue her career, becoming part of the small coterie of young performing artists on their way up. Although she lived in the middle of America now, she maintained close contact with her parents and younger sister, who remained in Herzliya. Theirs was a happy family and Aviva often referred to her mother as her closest friend.

The musical circles in which Aviva moved were international in character. Their members—Koreans, Israelis, expatriate Russians, Americans—traveled from country to country to earn their living. A foreign accent was almost a badge of belonging. Most of the older musicians had fled either the Nazis or the Bolsheviks. Migration and escape from repressive political regimes were facts of life for many of them. Aviva knew that several of her colleagues were children of survivors but that did not impress her one way or another. "I never thought of my parents as survivors," she told me with some impatience. "It was part of their life and not necessarily the most significant part as far as my conception of it."

Yet my interest in tracking down other children of survivors piqued Aviva's curiosity. She herself did not believe there was anything special about the group but she was willing to answer questions. "I will always finish an article about the Holocaust even though I may find it uninteresting—just as I will always finish an article about Israel or about music," she told me. "But I have an emotional reaction when people try to make it sensational, when they say that survivors or their children are disturbed. I don't think I'm disturbed at all. Nor do I think my sister is disturbed.

"Psychologists find five people who fit a certain mold and then formulate a theory about them. I think the attempt to generalize is false. It's wrong. I don't recognize anyone I know in these studies and I know quite a few survivors. Let's say, for argument's sake, that out of those 75,000 people who survived concentration camp, you find 5,000 who are disturbed. Does that mean it's a general situation resulting from the war? *I* don't think so. I'd have to make a study to be sure but I don't think so."

Despite the negligible importance she placed on any effect her parents' experience might have had on her, Aviva insisted on anonymity. She did not want neighbors or concertgoers broaching the subject to her. It was not a topic for social conversation. It was not something she would be inclined to discuss with strangers.

Sara's reasons for anonymity were quite different from Aviva's just as their lives had been different. She was short and indifferently dressed; she had been a high school dropout and, as she put it, a "drifter." Sara had been at war

113

with her parents ever since she could remember. She had left her family as soon as possible because she could not cope with what she saw as constant abuse and manipulation. Two years before I met her, Sara's mother had become very ill and had asked Sara and her husband of a few months to leave what they were doing and move to where she was. Sara had done so grudgingly, feeling more "like a parent than a child." She lived in a comfortable apartment house, had graduated from university far later than her contemporaries and now worked as a teacher. She took an interest in psychology, had read several of the studies on Holocaust survivors and, when she learned that I was interviewing their children, immediately found out where I was and rang me up.

Unlike Aviva, Sara recognized many of the characteristics described in the studies all too clearly, and was worried about passing on her problems to her newborn son. She wanted to talk, she said, but I would have to change her name, her place of birth, anything that might identify her. When I pointed out that one-quarter of a million survivors had emigrated to Israel, that they had produced at least that number of children and that it was unlikely for anyone to cause trouble for her more than thirty years after the war, Sara shrugged but remained firm. "It's an effort for me to trust you," she said. "It doesn't come to me naturally. I'm very suspicious, even though it's not nice to say. I don't want my name in it. It's too personal."

While Aviva's parents had moved from a small town in Rumania to the modest but decidedly middle-class surroundings of Herzliya, Sara's parents had came from a Displaced Persons camp in Germany to an Israeli slum. "There were a lot of Arabs, Moroccans, Iraqis and Poles in our neighborhood," she told me, in a sharp, incisive voice that quickened as she described the particulars. "Lots of prostitutes and pimps and drugs. Lots of fighting and drinking in the street. And I was a street kid. All the time in the streets. I didn't like to be at home.

"We lived in an old Arab house where the walls were damp and there were a lot of bugs. The toilet was a hole in the floor. One room was a storage room and you couldn't sleep there because the walls were too wet. We all slept in one room: my parents in a double bed, my brother in his bed, me in mine. We didn't have pillows. Even today, when I lie down in bed, I'm excited that I have pillows. I was very ashamed of our house because we stayed there as I grew older, and that meant we didn't make it. Every time I saw somebody I knew go by my house, I would hide. I think it wasn't the money. I was ashamed of living in that neighborhood."

Sara pushed her lank, blond-streaked hair from her face.

"My parents often had nightmares. Either she cried and woke my father up or else he started screaming and woke her. In the middle of the night he'd scream: *Germans!* My father was a very passive man and he never did anything with us children. He tried to make a go of it as a grocer and failed. Then he worked as a porter and that must have been very demeaning. He was always trying to please my mother and she was always putting him down because the grocery store had failed, because he wasn't capable.

"My mother came from a wealthy, educated family in Poland. She was going to go to university in Russia before the war broke out and finished that. She had the mentality of the *shtetl* in a very negative way: showing off and being somebody, respecting things instead of people. She was very bitter because her sisters were married to *vatikim,* old settlers in Israel, and here she was at the prime of her life, so gorgeous and so bright, and she was with a man who made no money and whom she really didn't love. They met in the forest in Poland. My father found her there, alone, sick, and without shoes. He brought her back to the partisans and that's how they got married."

She smiled a quick, bitter smile that seemed to sum up her parents' marriage.

"It's true we did not have so much to eat, but that was

true for everybody in Israel at the time. It was *tsena*, austerity. I remember one time we went to the beach and my mother saw, a very long distance away, an apple that must have fallen from a boat. She swam all the way out for this apple and when she got there she discovered the apple was rotten inside. I remember her telling my brother and me: *This is what life is. Everything looks so beautiful, so nice on the outside and you touch it and see how rotten it is inside.* I was about eight years old then but I still remember that.

"My father had a wife before the war and two sons who were killed before his eyes. We heard this from the time we were children. He was always talking about them ... my son would be this old now ... my son would have done this ... It didn't seem real to me that he had had other children and they were shot in front of his eyes. I don't remember feeling sad. I don't remember feeling anything. That's one thing I have never understood.

"My mother talked about her father. She said they wrapped him in a Torah and burned him alive. The people in the village put all the children in a hole. My mother crawled out and hid in the barn of some Polish Christians, in the hay. She said that the Germans came and urinated on the hay and she had to remain in it for three days. Then one day she was discovered there and she ran into the forest and they were shooting after her. That's when she met my father. I never could follow their stories all the way through. I think they must have changed them. Each time they were different. My father said he ran away from labor camp eleven times. He was badly beaten up. I always had the impression that my mother was sexually abused. But who knows the truth? After a while, you give up. I didn't ask any questions. I don't remember having conversation with my parents."

Sara pulled on her hair. She was uncomfortable.

"I don't know if you can understand this, but my family never did anything together. We never sat down at a table together; we never ate together; nothing ever as a family. Food was eaten alone. In the store, my mother would always be the first one. My father always used to say that even in the forest she always took food for herself instead of thinking of other people. She always talked about how hungry she was. They eat like horses on Yom Kippur."

Something in my expression, an involuntary shutting off, a resistance to what she was saying, made Sara stop talking. Then, as if understanding my difficulty, she went back over it.

"Try to imagine the kind of bitterness, the kind of depression I'm talking about. There was never a happy moment that I can remember at home. Never a period of time when you could put your guard down and relax. My mother didn't teach me to be proud of myself. She didn't teach me how to take care of a household, she never told me about my body, she never *talked* to me, can you understand that? We were not a family that touched. I never felt that we were loved: I felt we were there to be used. I think that they used on their kids the techniques for survival that they had learned in the forest. The order of normal life was so confused for them during the war that abnormalities became normalities. People were capable of everything. Anything was permissible in order to live. Their needs became the center of their universe. My mother was like that. I think when I was a child she ate more than she gave us. We were there to fill her needs, not the other way around.

"I was very smart and mischievous as a child. Nobody could control me, even when I was four and five. By the time I was twelve, I pulled myself out of the slums and joined the youth group in the better part of the city. I was the only one who made it. My parents never gave me anything, so as a reaction I was very independent. I had friends in this youth movement, I had things going for me and my mother was very jealous of my life. I didn't want to be at home. When I stayed away, they used to call me a pros-

117

titute, a thief, a *meshugah*, a *stoup*—which means idiot in Polish. We were hit as children. And when they treat you like this all the time, you start thinking that maybe you are an idiot, maybe you are a *stoup*, maybe you are a prostitute. Even if you are only thirteen years old."

Sara took a deep breath.

"It made me angry. It made me *so* angry. I was put down very much as a child. I was not smart enough. I was not pretty. I was a slut. I was a lesbian. I had too many boyfriends. My mother always said this when I came home late at night. She would hit me and I would hit her back. I guess I was really bad, a super rebel. My brother was obedient and studious. He will not talk about any of this, even today. He gives my parents a blank check for behaving as they like because of what they went through. I accepted all of that treatment then for the same reason. I felt so lucky I didn't have to go through the war. I thought I could not judge them, that I had to accept them the way they were. I wanted them to like me, I wanted to be treated with respect but neither of my parents had a basic respect for human beings. I don't know if they were that way before the war, but they were simply not fine people.

"I lived in that house with them until I was fourteen. Then my teachers became very concerned about me. They thought I was terribly bright and here I was failing everything. So they sent me away to an agricultural school. My parents made some monkey business with my papers. They changed the date and place of my birth and got money for me somehow. I don't want to go into details; it might cause them trouble. At any rate, I got out of that house and lived at the agricultural school."

Sara asked for a cup of tea. Her shoulders had slumped, her long hair had become disheveled from repeated movements of her fingers through it, and her eyes, which had been hard and shrewd when she began to talk had softened.

She no longer looked like a street corner bad girl. She looked sad and somewhat lost.

As I fixed tea for us both, I realized that I was glad for a break. I felt angry at Sara for answering my questions in such pungent detail. Like Aviva, I was prone to be skeptical of psychiatric studies. I did not find their method scientific or humane; I was astonished by the carelessness with which many of the professionals whose work I had read gathered and interpreted data. But reinforcing these reservations was my wish to deny that the kinds of things Sara described had, in fact, occurred. I found myself refusing to take in her words. I did not want to believe her: it was simply too painful, too humiliating. It was easier to reflect on Aviva's busy, successful life in the same country at the same time. I could count on Aviva to downplay disagreeable things. Dignity was very important to her. She insisted upon it.

"In our family," Aviva had said flatly, "this was not a subject that we discussed. My parents are people who talk very little about the past in general. When they do, it's about particular people. Whenever the subject of the war came up, my father said, 'That's enough,' and I think he was right. I don't know how I first found out about it. I would imagine that it came from asking why she had that number on her arm but I don't know. I suppose it was strange to have a number tattooed on your arm but it wasn't unusual. It seemed to me that there were quite a few people who had them. It's just part of the heritage in Israel. There's no escaping it. I mean, the official policy is that it should not be forgotten and I'm all for it. Not in terms of revenge but to make sure it doesn't happen again. Because it's possible. It could happen in a lot of other places.

"My father doesn't talk about it much and when my mother does, on occasion, it doesn't become a very melodramatic issue at all. From what I understand, the Germans arrived in Rumania relatively late. My father was in what

119

they call a work camp for three years. I have no idea where, I really am ashamed to say. Somehow, we always minimized my father's experiences. In work camps, where he was, people did not get killed. They just worked, like prisoners of war in so-called 'normal circumstances.' "

Aviva had laughed a peculiar, ironic laugh.

"My mother and her family were taken to Auschwitz the last years of the war. She would recall certain incidents of stealing food and trying to cheat the system, things like that. But it never really got out of hand at all. I had the impression she survived because she was young and strong and she worked. If I didn't ask questions it was because I didn't want to hurt them. The only time my mother ever gets emotional about the war is when we go to a memorial like Yad VaShem or the museum at *Lochamei Ha'Ghetta'ot*, where we have relatives, or when we were in Paris together and she wanted to go to the war memorial near Notre-Dame. She insists on going and then it upsets her. Otherwise, she is a calm, logical, warm person. She doesn't have complexes. There is no hysterical trait in either of my parents. Both my sister and I are far more explosive. I always knew my grandparents were killed in the war but I don't think that was especially traumatic. I didn't know anyone who had four living grandparents. Not anyone."

Aviva fixed her large brown eyes on my face and spoke firmly.

"I think my parents and I have a very close relationship, certainly closer than most families I see in America. I never rebelled against them. I would not want to do anything that might hurt them. For example, I had always assumed that my parents wouldn't want me to perform in Germany, although they never said so. When I was invited there some years ago, I told my manager I wouldn't go because I thought my parents wouldn't like it. It wasn't important enough for me to go if it was going to hurt their feelings. My manager said, 'Why don't you ask them?' That seemed like the logical thing to do, so I did. My father said that he himself wouldn't go but that he wouldn't stop anyone else from going. My mother said it would be silly not to go. So I went."

Did she ever think her parents were overprotective? I asked.

"Overprotective? I don't know if that is the word for my parents. Yes, I suppose that would be the word. They're worriers. They always perceive the worst possible outcome for things. Little things. Like when I was in elementary school, all the excursions we made were in trucks, not buses. They wouldn't let me go because they thought it was dangerous, because there had been two accidents in the last ten years where children were on trucks. It's a kind of family joke. You can't go into the next room without my father saying, 'Be careful!' I think it's become an automatic reflex with him. He doesn't even think of what he says. If my mother goes to the grocery which is literally across the street, he will say, 'Be careful!'

"I remember that they followed the Eichmann trial very closely, and that my mother was pretty upset by it. I remember her crying during the testimony. I kind of walked away from it. I didn't know what to do. I resented the Eichmann trial for that reason and I just wished it would be over quickly. I couldn't deal with it. What could I do? It was there and she was upset because she had lots of reasons to be upset. If I would talk to her it wasn't going to do any good; she'd still be upset.

"Around the time of the Eichmann trial there was also a lot of discussion at school. We were allowed to bring in transistors and would spend hours listening to testimony. We talked about why it happened and why the Jews reacted the way they did. The monuments were integrated into what I would suppose you'd call sightseeing. . . ."

Again, Aviva laughed an ironic laugh.

"When our class made a trip to Jerusalem, we saw Herzl's

121

tomb, we saw Mt. Zion and we went to *Martef Ha'shoa* (The Cellar of the Holocaust.) I was maybe twelve. Thirteen? And I remember most that there was a lampshade made out of—what was it?—skin or something ... and there was soap ... and something made out of hair ... a broom, a brush, something. That's all I remember. I had *not* known that they had made soap out of human fat and I don't know how necessary it is for someone to see this. The teacher had not prepared us for that trip more than for any other. It's just revolting to think that anyone would come up with such an idea. It's just not human at all. It was the result of hatred to the point of sickness. I don't want to understand it. It made me mad. Furious."

Aviva paused but she did not elaborate on her reaction then or now. Although she read a great deal and impressed one as a thoughtful person, she had not been an introspective teen-ager. She had not read newspapers when she was in high school; she had always been busy practicing and doing her schoolwork. What was there to talk about?

"There was a time," she conceded, "when I read a lot about the war. It was when I was twenty or so, roughly the age my mother was when she was in Auschwitz. I did try to imagine what kind of experiences she had to go through. A friend of mine gave us the play, *The Deputy*, by Hochhuth, and somehow that made it more vivid. I knew the facts. I had always known the facts—gas chambers, the treatment, the dehumanizing atmosphere. I knew all about it. It was nothing new. But somehow in the form of a play it seemed much more real. It stopped being part of history and I related it to my mother.

"I also got myself *The Rise and Fall of the Third Reich*, but I couldn't read it all. My mind goes blank after a while when I read history. *Any* history. The play was different. I felt shock. It really dawned on me then what this experience meant and I felt very proud of her. She must be a remarkable person for having gone through it and not be scarred. I mean, you can't hide scars like that for more than thirty years without *anything* ever coming out. I don't think she ever felt any guilt about surviving and other people not. She does not dwell on these things."

Did she? I asked Aviva.

"I rarely do. It comes up in conversation with Germans, oddly enough, more than with anyone else. And it never happens because I want to talk about it but because *they* do. In Germany, people always try to explain to me exactly what they did and where they were during the war, and I haven't yet met anyone who admitted to doing anything at all other than try to survive. I arrived at an airport once and the man who came to meet me began talking about an American conductor who was not happy about performing in Germany. The man couldn't understand why. I mean, what had they done to *him?* I suppose I looked puzzled and he told me, 'You know, everything that's said about the war is much exaggerated. We suffered as much as everyone else. My boat capsized in the North Sea. Can you imagine how cold that water was?' To which, perhaps stupidly, I *exploded!* I told him I really didn't have too much sympathy considering what my mother had to go through in Auschwitz for an entire winter with no clothes. For the first minute, there was dead silence. Then he said, 'Of course, there were exceptions.'

"So what do you say? There is nothing to say!"

Throughout the interview, Aviva had waited, with a not-too-well-disguised restlessness, for my next question. This clearly was not worth our time, seemed to be her attitude. What was the point?

Sara, on the other hand, could not stop talking once she had decided to start. Our first interview had precipitated a succession of dreams and long bouts of crying. She came back the second time with notes and questions, along with a determination to sort things out in her mind.

"I was always trying to understand what had happened,

123

why my parents were the way they were, why I was always so angry at them," Sara said. "But in Israel, you don't talk about your feelings like in America. On the contrary, what's really being reinforced is *not* talking about them. At the agricultural school I attended, as in the youth movement, we talked about values. We argued ideology. We talked about Socialism and different leaders who played a role in the founding of the state. We were idealistic. Chauvinistic. But we didn't talk about personal feelings. We read about the heroes of the Palmach and went on trips to places they had fought. It was all very heroic, the stories of people going to fight and walking away in silence. No one ever said he was scared. No one ever cried. You could be a hero but you couldn't cry."

Aviva had cast herself in that mold, I thought. Sara could not.

"The most important thing about history as it was taught in Israel," Sara continued, "was fighting the British and the Arabs. There was something shameful about talking about the Holocaust. Something very degrading. Survivors were living witnesses to what had happened to the Chosen People. We were not taught about it at all in my school. I had to go find books.

"But the literature at that time was all about pioneers, beautiful stuff about the *yishuv,* the people who founded Petach Tikvah and Zichron Ya'akov. Building and planting. The period was so pure, so idealistic, so alive. Whatever literature there was about the Holocaust, it was always my feeling that it looked down on survivors. There was never a survivor with good qualities. He was always weak, helpless or crazy. On the kibbutz, for example, there's always a strange man who walks around alone and odd because he is a survivor. There were marriages that took place between Israelis and survivors that took place out of pity. I don't remember a survivor in the literature who came out all right. And you don't see them in Israeli politics. You don't see them in the arts. They talked differently, they weren't accepted, they lived together, like a minority group. The Israelis were so glorified that beside them the survivors were shameful. I still feel ashamed and sad and guilty about my parents."

Sara pulled at her hair.

"For a long time, long after I finished agricultural school, I wasn't able to trust anybody. The only thing I had heard from my parents was that the world was a jungle and there are no friends. There's nobody. It affected my relationships with people. I created walls. I did a lot of things: I was always busy; I seemed like the healthiest person in the world, always solving other people's problems. But I didn't touch other people and I didn't let them get close to me. In a way my husband is my first friend. The second day after I met him, I told him I had a secret, that my parents were in the war. It was not something I told just anyone."

She leaned forward on her plump arms.

"You see, it's something I live with, now, all the time. I'm afraid of my husband being taken away from me, even if he goes on a fishing trip. When I'm alone at home for a night by myself, I sleep in the living room, on the floor, with the lights on. Just in case. I feel guilty all the time for living. Today I walked around and the day's so beautiful and I felt so lucky to be alive. Normal people don't think things like that. They just accept it. The more I talk, the more I realize how preoccupied I was with all of this when I was younger. But I never talked about it. I kept it all inside. I'm very glad to begin. I want my son to be free of this. I see how it's being passed."

A few days after we had completed our last interview, Sara decided to see a psychiatrist who had worked extensively with survivor families. It would not be a long-term association, she felt. After all, she had a husband she loved, a job she enjoyed, a newborn son. She had a few close friends now and she had learned to cope with her parents.

125

But there was unfinished business she had been avoiding for too long, Sara said. She was thirty now; it was time to straighten out loose ends.

Nothing could have been further from Aviva's mind than psychotherapy. She had never considered it for any reason and she had no fondness for the profession as a whole. Certainly, she told me, she felt no ill effects of the Holocaust. "It has not influenced my choice of friends or my marriage or my choice of a place to live," she said. "The only way I can think that the Holocaust has influenced me is my identity as a Jew. I'm not religious in any sense of the word. I don't go to synagogue. I know the traditions because I grew up in Israel and you would have to be an idiot if you did not know what they were. But although I'm not religious, I have this strong feeling of identity. It's as much a part of me as being a musician. And I think *that* was affected by the war. It seems to me that the Holocaust was just another proof that you cannot run away from your identity.

"I don't particularly want to. The whole history of the Jewish people fascinates me. It took such a fantastic amount of determination to come out of all those miserable things that happened relatively unscarred. Somehow I have this faith that if it was possible for so long, it will go on forever. It's just not going to be possible to wipe this people off the face of the earth and that makes me feel good."

EIGHT

Not all the children of survivors I spoke with shared Aviva's pride.

Gabriela Korda* had grown up in South America pretending to be a Protestant. She was one of a number of people I spoke with whose parents had severed ties with Judaism. The racial laws of the Third Reich had persuaded them that there was no good to be had from being Jewish, and these survivors took advantage of emigrating to recast their identities.

Gabriela's mother, a tall, distinguished-looking blond woman, had her Auschwitz tattoo cut out of her forearm shortly after the war was over. She told Gabriela that her war experience had taught her to assimilate. Her concerns were now dominated by a need for security, and that need led her to raise her children in as un-Jewish a fashion as possible, so that what had happened to her would not happen to them. This attitude was typical of a certain kind of survivor and not difficult to carry out in the melting pot of the United States. It was much harder in Latin America, where Gabriela grew up. In Brazil, Argentina, Colombia, Ecuador, Peru, Venezuela and Chile, children of survivors lived in a cultural No-Man's Land. The Catholic church was predominant. Successive coups and shifts in government kept their parents primed to flee and sensitive to signs of anti-Semitism.

Their sensitivity was well founded. During the late forties and early fifties, South America had become a haven for ex-Nazis as well as for Holocaust survivors. It was perhaps the only continent where children of people with Auschwitz tattoos could find themselves in school beside the children of people who had manned the camps.

Gabriela had attended that kind of school for eight years, and by the time I met her she was practiced at camouflage: she had lived out an uneasy charade, a double identity, for a good part of her life.

We had met by chance at a cocktail party and I was struck, as were most people, by her quiet but staggering sophistication. Like many survivors, Gabriela's parents had done exceedingly well in business in South America and their daughter was proof of their success. She looked and dressed like a European model. She spoke five languages fluently. Years of travel abroad had made her as comfortable in the ski lodges of the Rockies as in the discotheques of Paris. She had completed graduate school in the U.S. after attending college at home, and now shuttled back and forth between North and South America, unable to commit herself to a future in either. "It's a question of where I can work," she would say, but in fact she had been offered jobs in both places. At thirty, she had worked at the United Nations, as well as for several American and South American concerns. "Nothing holds me anywhere; I have no roots," was another explanation for her travels, and that remark, unlike the first, was true.

128

People who met Gabriela rarely guessed her background. She had kept the Spanish surname of the South American she had married and divorced but her fine features and mysterious accent often led strangers to assume that she was Scandinavian. None had ever divined that her grandfather had been a rabbi in Hungary and this was not a fact that she volunteered. Not until she was eighteen had she begun to let people know she was Jewish and even now she preferred to leave the subject alone. She found Americans far too open about their private lives. She was more at ease discussing international affairs than personal problems.

When I told her that I was interested in interviewing her, Gabriela was intrigued but reluctant. She worried about repercussions: the Nazis in South America had a network of contacts that could cause trouble for her family. "You don't know the situation," she said quietly. "They're still powerful today. There was an understanding among people who went to my school not to discuss the backgrounds of our parents. I wasn't about to go to Wiesenthal in Vienna and say I know about this one and this one: they live under false names. I knew they changed their names. I never asked why. I *knew* why. We didn't have to talk about someone's parents being Nazis. It was obvious."

Gabriela said all this with some impatience, as if it was self-evident and part of everyone's daily life. "You don't know the situation," she repeated, but I suspected that there was more than that involved. Gabriela was not ready yet to "come out" as a Jew, let alone as a child of Holocaust survivors. Her tendency was to downplay the effect of the war on her parents to such a degree that, in her description, it became a minor interlude in the distant past. Her parents, like Aviva's, had not talked much about the war.

"Not because they had such bad experiences," Gabriela was quick to say, "but because nothing terrible actually happened to them. My father was in a labor camp and worked very hard, but he was in his early twenties, young and healthy, and he made good friends. My mother was taken straight to Auschwitz where she was for a year and a half. She worked in a section where they selected clothing for the prisoners who came in and they didn't have it that bad. The way she speaks about it—in a way it was a positive experience for her because nothing horrible happened *to* her although she saw terrible things happening around her. She was treated fairly well. The Germans were always asking her why she was there: they couldn't believe she was Jewish. One guy sort of took care of her and I don't think there was anything sexual there because she was very open about the way she talked about these things. He was an S.S. officer who brought her Ovaltine and kept telling her he wanted her to stay healthy and alive.

"That was her preoccupation too. During the winter she went out and washed herself in the snow because she saw people all around her who couldn't care less and who gave up hope. My mother still is a very disciplined person."

The Kordas, who had married before the war, were reunited in Budapest shortly after it ended. The war had radically changed Gabriela's father. Before, he had been an observant Jew who attended his father's *shul* daily. Now, he became areligious, and a committed Communist who worked for the Hungarian government through the Stalinist period and provided his family with a comfortable living. When, in 1956, the Hungarian Revolution broke out, Mr. Korda did not want to leave. "He was in South America on business," Gabriela told me, "and he wrote us that we should stay put. But my mother was frightened: there was a wave of anti-Semitism at the time. She took my brother and myself to Austria and presented my father with a *fait accompli*. There was no way back. We were in Vienna in a hotel. I was ten at the time."

The Kordas stayed in Austria for three weeks and then moved to Germany, where Gabriela's father had business contacts. The family stayed there for seven months. Gabriela attended school while her parents tried to decide where they would live. The best idea seemed to be to go to South America where Mr. Korda could work for a company run by a friend. The family moved there in 1957. Since most children of the European middle-class attended private schools and since Gabriela had just learned German, her parents decided to send her to a German school. It was a decision they made quickly and without deliberation. At the time it seemed logical.

"I hated South America," Gabriela told me. "It was strange. Shabby. People dressed differently and spoke a language I didn't understand. I wore slacks and people stared at me. Girls didn't wear slacks there. At first, I was quite happy to be in a German school. I knew the language and I was very well liked. Germans really appreciate three things: if you're good in sports—and I was excellent; if you're blond and blue-eyed—which I was; and if you're disciplined—which I was. I was very popular.

"In school, everything European was thought to be much better than anything native. The natives were considered lower class, a problem ... there was even a special name for them, the *hiesige*. Although the school had South Americans as well as Germans, it was far more pro-German. We learned German history from the beginning of the tribes. We read Goethe, Schiller, Kleist and authors who aren't even translated into other languages. I won prizes in history. I wrote a paper on the origins of the German language and got a letter of congratulation from the Dean. In school I was looked upon as an Aryan. One day, when they made up the catalogue, they took pictures of me and a native girl for the cover: me representing the German part, and her the local population."

Gabriela smiled, and it was impossible for me to gauge the depth or character of her feelings beneath that smile. Like many of the children of survivors I had talked with, Gabriela spoke dispassionately. Her manner was matter-of-fact; her voice flat and neutral. She could have been talking about a mildly interesting character in a novel.

"I was aware that I was Jewish," Gabriela continued. "But when people asked me what religion I was, I said I was Protestant. Somehow I didn't feel I should say I was Jewish. I didn't feel it would do me any good. I had heard remarks. Even when I was eight years old in Hungary, I remember remarks. *Jews, the moneylenders . . . the Jews who run the press . . . oh, don't be a Jew about it.* The school was very anti-Semitic. One of my teachers looked like the typical woman in all the Nazi pictures, with blond hair braided on top of her head. The third- and second-generation Germans were becoming nonchalant but those who were first generation in South America always walked very stiffly, their shoes polished, some of them even wore their hair combed in the Hitler manner. One girl I was friendly with had a house filled with pictures of Nazi parades."

Again Gabriela smiled. "I was very mature about all this. I didn't blame them for their attitudes. They were completely brainwashed. If I hadn't been exposed to both worlds, I would have been exactly like them. I did not discuss any of this with my parents. I was afraid they would take me out of this school and put me in another one. My best friends came from the school, even if they were the children of Nazis. I spent most of my time with them. Even on weekends we saw each other. I knew exactly how far I could go with them, how close I could be. I kept up the charade for the same reason I had started it. For self-defense. I didn't want to be excluded."

There were only a few times in Gabriela's life that her identity as a Christian was threatened. The first incident occurred when she was fifteen and an orthodox Jewish cousin from Brooklyn came to visit her family. "I took him to a party," she told me, "and for some reason one of my classmates asked him what religion he was. He said he was Jewish. He didn't speak Spanish and I don't know whether

132

they understood him. There was a lot of noise. But I got very upset. I kept on talking. The following morning I told my mother that my stupid cousin had said that and what would I tell my classmates now? Everyone would know I was Jewish. My mother told me that if my friends were truly my friends, it wouldn't matter but, for me, that was a very hard answer. I was quite desperate about it but when I went to school, nothing happened. I don't think anyone understood my cousin.

"Some time later, when I was going out with a boy from school, he asked, 'Why do your parents have Jewish friends? Are they Jewish? I don't mind if you're Jewish, you know.' I began to feel there was a rumor about me spreading through the school. But I was very well liked. I was chosen the most popular person in my class. I think that had the rumor been successful, my classmates would have considered me the victim of some Jewish conspiracy."

A small smile played around Gabriela's mouth at the memory of how well she had had the situation under control. "I did not confide in anyone about any of this," she said. "I think I was protective of my parents. My mother would have gotten upset about it and my father had his own problems about it. When I went out with boys from my school, my father would say, 'Maybe his father was a big Nazi' but he never told me not to go out. My father was involved with the German business community. In the beginning, in South America, he was working for a German company and it was in his interest to repress any anti-German feelings he had. He did not identify himself as a Jew—you know, people in business don't go around asking what religion you are. There was no reason to go out publicizing it."

Gabriela looked steadily at me, her hands still, her features perfectly composed.

"It was only when Eichmann was captured in Argentina that my father began to change," she said. "My mother

133

continued to want to assimilate but my father all of a sudden was reacting in a very strange way. I did not know who Eichmann was and what he had done. My father explained to me that this man had killed Jews, most of the Hungarian Jews in fact. Then he said he wished he could kill this man himself. My mother told him not to be ridiculous and say stupid things. I felt very uneasy. I thought: how can my father say this when he lets me go to a German school? I could have gone to school with Eichmann's children. I didn't but I might have.

"There was an outbreak of anti-Semitism at the time. We heard about incidents in the universities in Argentina, where the Nazi movement was active. There was one incident where they took a Jewish girl, branded her with a swastika and tortured her. There must have been many other unreported incidents like that. In my school, the teachers said it was all the fault of the Jews who were manipulating the press. We did not discuss the atrocities, and I was relieved. I certainly didn't want to hear about them. The teachers didn't want to talk about them. The other kids didn't care. I was very cynical about the whole thing. I thought: the Nazis did this but the Romans did that and why should I judge? I always tried to avoid talking about the war."

Gabriela lit a cigarette.

"When I finished high school," she said, "I went to England for a few months. When someone asked me whether I was Jewish, I said yes. I tried to make friends with Jews. I wanted to get myself involved in a Jewish atmosphere. I wanted people to accept me for what I was and not go on playing the game. I had come to that decision a long time before but I couldn't act on it. I couldn't just walk into school one day and say: *Listen everyone, I'm Jewish.* You can't do that. You can't."

For the first time, Gabriela's face showed some emotion.

"I started a new beginning in university. I wanted to be authentic. But even then it was difficult. So I try to get away from South America. It took me a long time to become indifferent to the whole thing. I still am not completely indifferent.

"My father has changed completely. Now he talks about Israel to people. He sends money there. Once my father achieved financial security, he returned to his Jewish feelings. That bothered my mother. She felt there was no need to disturb the way of life they were leading. Now, my father thinks that everything that went wrong with me, the fact that I was divorced, that I don't know what I want to do, that I am not settled, is the result of that school.

"If I had gone to a South American school," Gabriela said evenly, "my father thinks I would have assimilated better. He sees I have no roots and that it was a waste of time spending eight years trying to be part of the German community."

Her clear blue eyes rested on the table between us. "You know, if you go to a German school and you grow up reading German literature, you become very pro-German. I can very well understand those German Jews who stayed in Germany late into the thirties, even while they saw what was happening. I understand those Jews who returned to live in Germany today. I travel to Germany. For most of my life, I was very close to everything German ..."

Her voice tapered off and we sat together in silence. For a moment her manner, her expression of finality, her entire appearance made me think that Gabriela *was* German, that her whole story was some kind of elaborate coverup, an enormous and menacing joke. It made no sense to me and it frightened me. How could parents who had survived the Holocaust raise a German child? How could Gabriela embrace a culture that was responsible for killing off most of her family?

I turned off my tape recorder and tried to turn off my mind as well. Of course she wasn't German, I told myself.

Who would invent a story like this? It was no one's fault, I told myself. It was simply a matter of complications in circumstance, and misunderstood cues. I would try to make sense of it later; I could not sort out the reactions she had evoked in me now.

We talked about the other people I had interviewed, trying to reestablish the pleasant, professional atmosphere in which we had begun talking. We noted the extreme variety of upbringing that was characteristic of children of survivors. On the surface, it appeared that we were talking with detachment of things that were over and done with. But deep inside me, I felt a turmoil that I could not talk about to Gabriela. I recognized in her account of her family what psychiatrists had called "identification with the aggressor" and that recognition was not only unpleasant but painful to me. Gabriela had bought the Aryan myth along with much of the stereotype that the Nazis had propagated of the Jew. I could not cope with the confusion it created in me. I put her interview away in a folder and filed it in a bottom drawer, thinking that she could in no way be representative of others.

But in the following months, I came across and was told about others like Gabriela. Some were children of the 25,000 Jews who continued living in Germany after the war; others had never attended German schools but had experienced similar upbringings. Most disturbing of all these accounts was a news item that appeared in American newspapers in June of 1977. A Nazi coalition had planned a march to be held on the Fourth of July in Skokie, Illinois, and its leader, according to Chicago reporters and the Associated Press, was a child of survivors.

Frank Collin had been engaged in Nazi activities in the Chicago area since his early twenties. His father, Max Cohen, had been interned in the concentration camp of Dachau during the war. After liberation, he had emigrated to Chicago, changed his name to Max Collin, and had become a successful businessman. His son had first been arrested during a Nazi demonstration in 1969. A year later, the American Nazi party had discovered Frank's background and expelled him from their organization. Frank Collin responded by founding a new one. He had posed for the press alongside a portrait of Adolf Hitler and denied that his father was a Jew. "If the *Police Gazette* wrote something about me I wouldn't respond," he told reporters, "so why should I respond to gossip from people who lower themselves to using gutter sources for their stories."

Skokie became a symbol and Frank Collin was forgotten as lawyers and editorial writers across the United States argued the right of Nazis to stage a parade of provocation through a town whose inhabitants included several thousand Holocaust survivors. But the photograph of Frank Collin, a heavy-set, dull-eyed young man standing with his arms folded across his chest beside Hitler, stayed in my mind, far more vivid than any of the arguments for or against the Nazis' right to parade.

The truth was that it was far less difficult for me to understand Frank Collin or Gabriela than I cared to admit, and that their identification with Germans was comprehensible within the pattern of behavior I was beginning to see through my interviews. All the children of survivors I spoke with said they had absorbed their parents' attitudes toward Germany and the Holocaust experience through a kind of wordless osmosis. They had not been explicitly instructed to feel one way or another. Rather, they had picked up on cues, attitudes, desires that had never been expressed in words. Moreover, they had identified with their parents so closely that parental attitudes which had been forged during the war became their own.

The children of Jewish resistance fighters, for example, displayed a pride and strength in their identity as Jews that was strikingly different from children of Jews who had spent prolonged periods of time hidden or living as Christians.

Those children of survivors whose parents had sealed off their past responded by sealing off their own. Those whose parents had talked openly about their experience were most at ease with the subject while others, whose parents had tried to forget it, had little to say themselves.

Gabriela's parents had acted on deeply ambivalent feelings that were common to many survivors after the war, and it was that ambivalence which troubled me most of all. I heard things in her story that I had heard, in less stark a form, from others I had spoken to. Most of all, it touched off memories of my own family, things I had heard and seen as a child, which I had not put into any kind of order until now.

NINE

Every September until I was fifteen years old and my brother twelve, my parents enrolled us in Sunday school at the Stephen Wise Free Synagogue. By the end of November, after barely a dozen Sundays, we had already chalked up five or six absences.

It was not illness that kept us away, or even our own dislike of sitting in a classroom on a Sunday. My father was responsible for our truancy and he defended it with a clear conscience. In the fall, our Jewish education interfered with watching the countryside change colors; in winter, it interfered with our getting an early start to go skiing or skating; in the spring, how could one let children sit indoors poring over books when the ground was coming alive? What was more important: to breathe fresh air or to learn from books what every Jewish child should learn at home from the example of his parents?

"Sun's shining," my father would announce on Sundays

as he woke us up, huge and dripping wet from his cold shower. He whistled Reveille and made a clatter with doors and drawers. Sometimes he pulled himself up to his full height and beat his fists against his chest, chanting *"ooohlaah-meeh-neeh"* like Tarzan in the jungle.

In Prague when my father was young, there had been a swimmer who each New Year's Eve would plunge into the river which divides the city. Often a way had to be cut through the ice for him and when he reached the other side, blue and shaking with cold, he had pummeled himself, shouting *"Ulamene,"* or "Broken," at the top of his lungs. My father had always admired him.

"Wake up! It's eight o'clock!" he would say. "It looks like a beautiful day. A day for the country!"

My mother, my brother and I all tried to feign sleep, but then my father would drench a washcloth in cold water and hold it over our beds, threatening to shower us.

"It's Sunday, Daddy," I would complain from under the covers. "On Sundays people sleep late."

"Go ahead! Take a look!" My father would draw open the curtains of my room. "Look what a nice day! How could you want to waste it?"

Sunday school began at ten and let out at twelve-thirty, a great inconvenience as far as he was concerned. He worked all week in the dirty, congested streets of the garment center where the air was heavy with the exhaust of waiting trucks and all one could see of the sky was small swatches, as small as the swatches of cotton on the factory floor. Weekends were time to get out of the city, time to attend to his family's health. And good health was my father's overriding concern, far more important than any question of Jewish education.

"After the experience from the Nazism, see, I put three things down what were most important," he said, again and again. "First freedom. Then health. And in the third place contentment." The "country," which is what my father

140

called the collection of public beaches, reservations and parks located within an hour or two of New York City, was the place to pursue these three things. "Look here, your color is terrible. You need some fresh air," he would lecture us in the mornings until he had destroyed all possibility of sleep and succeeded in getting all three of us out of bed.

All through his childhood, his time in the army, and his time in concentration camps, my father had been made aware that Jews were considered physically inferior to Gentiles. The classic image of the Jewish scholar bent over scrolls in poorly lit rooms irritated him. What good was a brilliant mind in an unhealthy body? The chief thing he wanted to teach *his* children was a love of nature, a feeling for the pulse of life. The best way to do this, he felt, was by teaching them sports. By the time my brother and I were five, we knew how to row, swim, skate, and hit a ball with a tennis racquet. "If the American youth today would make some sport," he was fond of telling our teachers, our principals in school, and the rabbi of our synagogue, "there would be no smoking problems, no drinking problems, and no drug problem." The war had only confirmed his belief in the importance of athletics. In addition to building strength, sports encouraged discipline and established routine. They were an impetus to activity, and activity was a standard for measuring life. Illness, unhappiness and idleness were inextricably joined in my father's mind. They meant death, and every minute he spent with his children, my father seemed intent on infusing us with life.

Sunday school took us away from him, from air, from nature and, moreover, it was something of an alien concept to my father. He had grown up in Roudnice-nad-Laben, where there were three hundred Jewish families in a total population of 12,000 and where no special schooling was necessary to let him know he was a Jew. His grandfather had been the first Jew permitted to build a house outside the ghetto walls and his father, who owned a tannery and shoe factory, was a mainstay of the Jewish community. The Jews of Roudnice took care of their poor, observed the High Holidays and sent money to Palestine but their identity was cultural rather than religious. My father had studied Hebrew with the rabbi three times a week; he had had a *bar mitzvah;* and had attended synagogue out of deference to his parents. But the family had spoken Czech at home, they were citizens of the Czechoslovak Republic, and my father's primary allegiance, from the time he was small, was to the water.

His passion was swimming and, when he wasn't in school, my father could most frequently be found in the Elbe. "I would have to organize a group to go down to the river," he told us proudly, when he took my brother and me swimming. "You had to go in a group because the Gentiles would throw stones at us on the way. They thought Jews were too underdeveloped to become sportsmen. That was because of what they inherited from a life in the ghetto."

His parents, cautious burghers, were not enthusiastic about my father's activities. He was the only Jew in his classes and had already shocked the gossips in Roudnice by carrying the books of their Gentile neighbor's daughter Bosenka home from school when both of them were only ten. They wanted him to finish school and then help manage their shoe factory along with his older brother, Erich. But my father was not to be deterred. Business, school and his parents' view of his future all took second place to swimming. At seventeen, he helped found the Independent Swim Club of Roudnice and a few years later he began to compete internationally as a water polo player. In 1928, he had played in the Amsterdam Olympics and in 1936 he was one of only two Czechoslovak Jews who participated in the Nazi Olympics in Berlin.

"It was a big controversy," my father used to tell the friends my brother and I brought home from school. He would bring out a tattered album of sports photographs, men in old-style maillot bathing suits lined up beside a swimming pool. My girl friends and I giggled. We could see the bulges of the men's genitals against the suits, and their hair was shiny and slicked back like Count Dracula. My father paid no attention. He was absorbed in recalling the scores of the games played, places and dates. He wanted to impress upon us the importance of his participation. "The Zionist sports clubs made a boycott, see. The best water polo player in the country, who was a Jew, refused to go to Berlin. But I felt the Jews were obliged to take part, to refute the Nazi claim that they were inferior. You could in no way harm the Nazis by withdrawing from the competition. You had to prove that you were better, see."

My school friends and I listened gravely to his stories, then escaped to my room where we exploded with laughter. When I was eleven and twelve years old, my father's preoccupation with his sports album embarrassed me. No one I knew had ever even heard of water polo. No other father I knew took out old photographs and displayed them to us. My father seemed intent on showing his sports relics to people who came to our house, whether they wanted to see them or not. Sports were the core of his conversations with my friends. His life seemed to have stopped after the Olympic Games of 1936. He talked only intermittently about what happened after. There was a gap of about ten years in his recollections of his life. If, by chance, someone asked a question about this time, or if he began talking about it himself, his voice would taper off, his eyes would grow vague and he would lapse into silence, staring into space. Then he would return abruptly with a question like, "What's for dinner?" or "What's your brother doing?"

It was in bits and pieces, short, disconnected anecdotes that we heard what had taken place in those years. During the thirties, he said, as reports of Hitler's activities began to alarm Czech Jews, my grandfather had obtained a visa for Palestine. But my father's younger brother Bruno was brain-damaged; he did not receive a visa. My grandmother would not consider emigration without him and so the entire family stayed in Czechoslovakia. "Besides that," my father said, "I was with the opinion as a reserve officer in the Czechoslovak Army that I can't go and escape. I had the same rights as everyone else, so I felt I should have the same duties. In case of war, I should defend my country."

In September of 1938, the Czechoslovak Army mobilized and my father was called to his garrison in Terezin which would, ironically, become Hitler's model concentration camp. He stayed there for three weeks with his unit waiting, along with the rest of the country, for support from France and England against Germany's claim to the Sudetenland. When the Munich Pact was announced, surrendering the territory to Hitler, my father's garrison demobilized. "This I can remember was one of my saddest days," he told me. "When our commanding officer said good-bye to us, shaking every officer's hand and the tears ran down his face, I have seen the first and last time a high colonel cry like a baby."

My father returned to Prague, where his family was forced out of their apartment and where he was, as a Jew, suddenly barred from certain swimming pools and beaches. Three years later, in 1941, he again took the train to Terezin. This time he was not a lieutenant in the Czechoslovak Army but one of one thousand Jews pressed into forced labor to transform the Czech garrison into a camp and processing center for Jews.

"We arrived there, at the garrison we had used for 350 soldiers. The Germans put five thousand people there," he told me, with the careful attention to accuracy of detail that characterized all his descriptions of the past. "Of course, they used big rooms which were not built for inhabitants. They were used for stocks of goods and uniforms. When we came there the rooms were bare. There was not even one piece of straw on the concrete floors. At first I was working with the other boys to build up the rooms and to help with the incoming transports because every week there were com-

144

ing new ones. Later on, when they found out I had been a quartermaster in the army, I got the job to supply and take care of about 4,500 people three times a day. For breakfast, they got a very modest meal consisting of ersatz coffee and a piece of bread. Lunch consisted of thin soup. In the evening you got also coffee and some small piece of bread. The working people got a loaf for three days and the people who didn't work, maybe half that. Sometimes we got meat that was, of course, stamped 'Not for Human Beings.' It was delivered at four or five in the morning. So I was up very, very early. I supervised distribution to the different kitchens and I took care of one of them myself. And, of course, there were good people and bad people in Terezin and I had to make sure that the material for the meals would really come into them. For instance, margarine. Sometimes the cooks were stealing margarine for their own purposes, for eating and selling, instead of putting them into the soup. This I tried to prevent."

My father's voice took on a note of formality when he told me these things, as if he were giving testimony in front of a courtroom instead of talking to me. He did not look into my eyes as he usually did; instead, he fixed them on some invisible point in the distance. He was dignified. He was in control. He spoke like a soldier and I felt that he wanted me to listen the same way. I listened with my ears. I sent whatever hurt, whatever moved me, down to the iron box so my father would not see. I asked my father questions because I was afraid he would never tell us otherwise and there would always be a hole instead of a history behind me.

"I was in Terezin three years," my father said, "almost three years, and I was always with my parents whom I protected because of my position as quartermaster until May, 1944, when they were shipped to Auschwitz. It was the most difficult time in my life. I wanted to join them but the man in charge of the transport told me it made no sense; they had some intelligence that the older people went to one place, see, and the younger people were sent somewhere else.

145

We didn't know what was happening in Auschwitz but we had a feeling it was no good over there.

"In October, I was sent. Fortunately, we stayed only forty-eight hours. One factory owner requisitioned workers to replace Germans who were conscripted into the army so first we went to a quarry. Then to a propeller factory, to clean and polish propellers. My friend cut off two of his fingers and by a miracle survived. We worked twelve-hour shifts, one week during the day; one week during the night. We walked to the factory three miles in the winter cold and we got only seven hundred calories for our food. I lost about seventy pounds during the four months when we were in this camp, before we were liberated."

My father paused. I tried to imagine my father, who was more than six feet tall, weighing barely one hundred pounds. What had he looked like? It did not seem possible. The only signs on my father's body that I took for vestiges of the war were his toenails which were misshapen and discolored, and his teeth, which he said had never been the same since the war. But otherwise, my father had rebuilt his body. I did not want to imagine him as he must have been.

He hurried to end his story. "Already when I came to Auschwitz, I was told that my parents and both my brothers went to the gas chambers. So when I came home to Prague I was the only survivor of my family. Because I had lost so much weight, I had very low blood pressure and I didn't have too much strength to get up in the morning. I was very depressed. My foot was abscessed. But I had a good friend who was with me in the camp. When one of us was in a bad mood, the other one supported him. We were never both down. Then one day I met your mother on the street."

They had married as soon as they could acquire the necessary papers and set about reestablishing themselves in Prague. My father worked in his friend's business, coached water polo and was elected to the National Olympic Committee. My mother rebuilt the dress salon she had lost in the war. By late 1947, when I was born, they were comfortable again. Then, in 1948, there had been a Communist putsch in Czechoslovakia, and my father determined to leave, "in a bathing suit if necessary," he said. "I didn't want to make the same mistake like I did under the Nazis, see. To stay until it is too late. I wanted that my child should live in a free country without any experience of what I had to suffer."

We had arrived at Idlewild Airport in New York City in July, 1948, with fifty kilos of baggage and ten dollars apiece, the maximum amount allowed by the new Czech government. The Port Authority of New York took eight dollars from each arrival in tax, which left us with two dollars each. That was the point where the funny stories began, the stories about the Hotel Colonial where we lived across the street from the Hayden Planetarium and where my parents spent their first Thanksgiving eating hot dogs and wondering why the streets were so empty.

Like many survivors, my parents had been "vouched for" by rich relatives, people who had left Europe before the war began. They had provided us with $1,000, a refrigerator stocked with food, and a kitchen full of cooking utensils and silverware which my mother still uses. The first summer, when I was one and a half, they offered us the use of their home, a mansion in one of New York's poshest suburbs. They had locked all the bedrooms and brought cots down into the dining room, where my parents and I slept.

That summer was fraught with disaster. My father, while giving me a bath, had sat down on the Japanese wicker hamper in the guest bathroom and demolished it. The resident German shepherd had become frightened during a thunderstorm and had eaten his way into the house through the screen of the large porch. Worst of all, when friends from the city had driven up in a defective automobile, it had sprung an oil leak, turning the pale floor of the garage black and gray. After that summer, we were rarely invited back.

My father accepted that with philosophical resignation. He had resigned himself also to the fact that he would not be a water polo coach in New York, and when he had become a cutter, that he was unable to gain membership to the International Ladies' Garment Workers Union because unemployment among the members was high. When the ILGWU picketed the small factory in which he worked, and threatened his life if he refused to join, my father came home and made the event a humorous anecdote. "I have the good habit," he often told me, "of being able to adjust to many situations." When the monthly bills piled up on my father's desk in the living room and my mother grew pale and melancholy, my father remained the eternal optimist. "The U.S. government has a deficit of seven billion," he would say. "The Epsteins can have a deficit of a few thousand dollars."

His sense of humor seemed to disappear, however, when it came to questions of religion. Many survivors of the Holocaust had lost their faith after the war was over and my father's religious feelings, weak to begin with, had died entirely. He railed against American rabbis who tried to explain the Holocaust in their sermons as the "will of God" or as a necessary sacrifice to establish the state of Israel. Moreover, my father did not like the way rabbis ran their operations in America. He was offended by the practice of selling tickets to holiday services and by the membership fees that many congregations required. "In Roudnice," he told our rabbi, "a special meeting was held every year, see. The rich paid most of the cost of the synagogue; the middle-income people paid a part; the poor people didn't pay at all and everyone was happy." The rabbi had told him that such a policy was impracticable in New York City. The rich would not shoulder the burden. Who would then pay the bills?

The rabbi and my father communicated with studied cordiality on these and other matters. "He is a well-intentioned man," my father would defend him when we children came home complaining about a sermon. The rabbi had given us scholarships to nursery school; he was genuinely interested in our progress; one had to respect the rabbi, he was a learned man. Yet when my father himself went to synagogue, he too would often return home furious. "An idiot," he would mutter. "He talks about starvation! What does he know about the gas chambers? Americans! They think they know everything and they know nothing!"

It was this part of my father, the part which refused any interpretation of events he had lived, that made him even more reluctant to entrust us to Sunday school. He was not accustomed to hearing political allusions from the pulpit or to using synagogue as a social center. His life, his friends, were elsewhere. He did not attend study groups at the synagogue, did not join the Men's Organization and kept a polite but stubborn distance from the other members of the congregation. When on Sunday mornings we sat at the breakfast table, arguing whether to go to country or to Sunday school, it was my mother who argued for Sunday school. "You have to go so you know where you come from," she would say sternly, "so you know what it means to be a Jew."

She herself was unequipped to teach us. My mother had been raised in the heart of Prague, in a home that aspired to the heights of cosmopolitan chic. Her mother owned and ran her own salon for *haute couture*. Her father was an electrical engineer who owned a shipyard and a wholesale business in electrotechnical supplies. He was a member of the Deutsche Haus, the casino in Prague.

"Your grandfather would set foot only in the German opera house," my mother told me. "He never accepted the idea of Czech culture. He only opted for becoming a Czech citizen because he disliked the Monarchy. And he never identified himself as a Jew."

My grandfather had been denied admission to the University of Heidelberg, she said, because the quota for Jews had already been filled, and that instance of alleged discrimination had provided him with the last excuse he needed to break with his past. Just before the turn of the century he had himself baptized and vowed that should he ever have

149

children, they would not be exposed to similar humiliation. When my mother was born, in 1920, he had her baptized in the hospital over my grandmother's protests. Franciska Paulina Margaret Rabinek, my mother, would be a citizen of the world, without the impediment of being registered as a Jew.

He saw no need to change her surname, which means "Little Rabbi" in Czech, to anything less Jewish. "My father was very taken with the concept of the Czechoslovak Republic," my mother often said, with a curl to her voice. "In his opinion it was to be another Switzerland, where all the minorities would have equal rights and where religion was irrelevant."

My mother spoke German with her parents, learned Czech from the governess, the cook and the maid, and was sent to a French school.

It was a Catholic environment with two or three hours a week of religious instruction. The Catholics would study with a priest and the Jews with a rabbi. My mother studied with the Catholics, and one day the Catholic kids picked up a jingle they had heard in the street. It was an insulting jingle, the kind that children repeat endlessly in the yard at recess or in the halls between classes. My mother, as a Catholic, followed her Jewish friend Margit repeating it: *Jew, Jew, Jewish Jew, you have a poison tail.*

Finally Margit complained to her mother and the Rabineks received a phone call one evening. Emil Rabinek stalked into the nursery and demanded to know what my mother was saying to Margit. Then he told her never to say it again. But he did not tell her why. My mother thought that was the end of it until about a week later there were report cards and she got a three in behavior.

Her mother's brother, an observant Jew, was visiting from Bratislava at the time and the whole story came up at the dinner table. "See what happens when you bring up the child without telling her who she is and where she belongs!"

he shouted. Her mother defended her, saying that her report card had all "ones" except for that three in behavior. But no one told my mother that she herself was a Jew.

When it was time for her to be confirmed as a Catholic she told her father that she did not believe in the Virgin Mary and that she was not going to be a Catholic. He said, all right, that he would write to City Hall and have her papers changed to read that she was an agnostic.

My mother frequently told me that she had been a different sort of person before the war, and although I tried to find signs of it in her, I never succeeded. She said all she had really been interested in had been boys and parties and dancing. She had been frivolous, she said, and frivolous was the antonym for everything I sensed she was. "I quit school when I was fifteen to help run the business," she said, but I saw her constantly immersed in books. "I didn't read the newspapers," she said, but every day I saw her not only go through the entire section of the news in *The New York Times*, but also listen to the news on radio and television as well. Just before Hitler annexed the state of Austria, my mother had been skiing in the Tyrolean Alps, drinking hot milk with cognac and flirting with American movie stars, she said. It made no sense to me. My mother was somber. Her intensity was such that sometimes I thought she could make a piece of paper burn just by staring at it with her eyes. My mother was smart and skeptical: she was never taken in by anyone. Salesmen in stores would take one look at her, drop their sales pitch and get her what she wanted. Yet my mother had stayed in Prague while every day German newspapers lay about the house with detailed reports of Hitler's plans.

"I had just turned eighteen when Germany occupied Austria," my mother told me when I questioned her, for my mother was anxious that I get the story straight. Unlike many survivors, she told me in detail what had happened to her during the war. She talked in bits and pieces like my

151

father but her accounts were vivid and clear. "I remember that my father thought there was a certain logic to the Austrian annexation. It made sense, he thought, to make one big country out of two German-speaking countries. He disliked the Nazis of course but he did not feel threatened. We had our alliance with France. We had the best military equipment. Our armed forces were in good shape. The French wouldn't desert us. The British wouldn't let us down. Only a coward would leave Czechoslovakia, he said.

"On March 15, in 1939, at five in the morning, we were standing at the window watching them march through the streets. Even then my father was saying, 'I fought for Germany in the first war. They won't touch us. You're baptized. Technically, you're not a Jew.' I had seen Jewish refugees by then. There were three or four of them ringing the bell of the salon every day peddling pencils or ties or stationery from house to house. I didn't like them. They spoke a different kind of German than we spoke and my father was always making fun of them. He thought this endless stream of peddlers was a big nuisance. My mother gave them money behind his back. They talked to her. They told her what was going on in Germany and she began to worry. But my father didn't."

My mother would take another drag of her cigarette and then she would resume her narrative. Her face showed no emotion when she talked. The words poured out of her like blood but they no longer seemed connected to anything she had experienced. She did not show pain and I did not either. I imitated her. I took the words in as they came out. It was information. It was what happened, and there was no feeling attached.

"In the beginning, the occupation did not have any particular consequences for us. I got married shortly after the Germans came but my life did not change very much. Pepik moved in with us and I went to the salon in the morning as usual. There were rumors that the Germans had arrested dozens of political prisoners, Jews and Gentiles alike, Social-ists, Social Democrats, journalists. There was no special pro-gram directed against the Jews. As long as everyone was involved, my father said, there was nothing to be personally worried about. Besides, by this time, it was impossible to leave."

My grandfather did not acknowledge the reality of his Jewish identity until 1942, when he, my grandmother and my mother were forced into a train bound for Terezin. Only there, on the straw-strewn floor of a former stable where they waited to be "selected" for a deportation to the East did Emil Rabinek realize that his baptismal certificate, his fluency in German and all his political beliefs made no difference.

My mother, left alone in Terezin at the age of twenty-two, had had to accept an identity she had never known. For the first time in her life she watched Jews pray. For the first time she lived at close quarters with people who spoke Yid-dish. She talked with the Jews from the East whom her father had always derided. Added to the misery and shame of being herded into Terezin and the pain of losing her parents was an enormous confusion about who she was. She had made a vow then, just as her father had made a vow when he had been refused admission to the University of Heidelberg. She vowed that were she to survive the war and have children that those children *would* be raised as Jews.

In New York City, even by the time I was twelve, my mother had only rudimentary notions of what that meant. But she had been told by the parents of my friends in public school that in America, Jewish children were sent to Sunday school. I sensed, even though I had not been told the reasons in detail at the time, that my mother was acting out of duty rather than conviction. Her ambivalence was palpable. Even as my mother urged us to do our Hebrew homework and read our assignments in the Bible, she was reluctant to educate herself. That confused me for my mother devoured

153

books on far-flung subjects with passion. Usually too, my parents did not coerce my brother or me to do things we did not want to do. We were offered dance classes, art classes, music lessons and theater tickets, but if we made known our dislike of them, we did not go again. I knew without having to be told that my parents resented coercion of any kind. They were suspicious of anyone who tried to "organize" us or them. They resisted collectivity and stayed away from institutions and groups. Yet year after year, they insisted we go to Sunday school.

Sunday morning was, unless it was raining, a time when my parents engaged in an argument that was more formal than real. "The days are getting shorter," my father would say. "It's already dark at five. That leaves two hours for us in the country." My mother told us to get dressed and told my father not to exaggerate. "We were in the country yesterday all day," she would say. "They've missed too many Sundays already. What will we tell the teachers?"

My father drove us to synagogue and did not stay around to chat. Sometimes he took his ice skates with him and went skating in Central Park while we were in school. He let us off as if we were going to see the dentist, with a good-bye that implied, "It's too bad you need this and I hope it's over soon."

As I got out of the car, I would arrange my face in the artificially solemn, even grim, expression that seemed to me a requisite of admission to the gray stone building just off Central Park West. Going there was a formality I accepted just as I accepted giving up my seat on the bus to an elderly person or acting polite to strangers. It did not matter whether I liked it or not; it was convention and a mark of good upbringing that I would put on a white blouse and a skirt that was dressier than the ones I wore to public school and pretend to be part of something I felt no part of at all.

Inside the building, it was cool and always dim as a medieval castle. The halls and stairs were very wide, as if

154

built for processions. The classrooms were equipped with the latest in educational materials: there were arts and crafts workshops; folkdance rooms; a choir loft and a large social hall for carnivals and festive celebrations. The school enjoyed a reputation for young, progressive teachers. It was liberal, people said. But to me it was a lifeless world, dead as a museum. Although I sat there for nearly ten years, I cannot remember the name or face of a single teacher, nor the content of a single lesson.

I sat, surrounded by other girls and boys in starched white shirts and well polished shoes, tuning out the discussion, wondering listlessly why I was there. Some of the children came from my public school, others from elsewhere, but all of them seemed different from me. They were docile, soft and malleable children, content to sit and copy Hebrew letters into their copybooks while I grew restless and wanted to be outside. Most of them did their homework and seemed to be interested in the stories of biblical customs and heroes. When we attended children's services in the hushed Hall of Worship downstairs, they read the responses back to the rabbi in strong voices. They recited blessings in Hebrew. Most of all, they seemed to believe in God.

I did not. I could not remember ever having believed in God, any more than I had ever believed in Santa Claus. Everything about the religious services in our Hall of Worship enraged me. The thin cloying strains of organ music that seeped into the hall from behind the pulpit, the velvet and silver-sheathed Torahs which rested in a vault that looked like a Tiffany display case, the atmosphere of what I felt as affected sanctity, all seemed to me an outrageous hoax. I did not believe the rabbi in his long robe, raising his arms up to bless the congregation and all of Israel with everlasting peace, or the rosy-faced officers of the Men's Organization who stood beside him, resplendent in their well-cut suits. They asked me to revere and trust a God I could not see, of whom I had no evidence. The rituals were empty of meaning for me, their version of the Chosen People naive, like a fairy tale. It was an American movie version of history, full of hope and goodness and plenty. It was a Judaism that was unscarred, unburnt, fat and complacent.

When the children around me sang "There Is No God Like Our God," I kept silent. Some of the phrases in the hymn were pretty but none of them seemed true. How could there be a God who was all-knowing and all-merciful? Where was his mercy? Where was his power? Why had he let my grandparents die? Where was his justice? Where had he been? Why was my mother so sad and always in pain if God was so good? The rabbi was lying. The whole school was a lie. Behind the fancy words my teachers used to "prove" the existence of God, words I had to look up in the dictionary again and again to remember, there was nothing. "Teleological" or "ontological," I was sure that God was gone. He had brought his people out of Egypt three thousand years ago, and every year we commemorated it, as if we too had been slaves in the land of Pharaoh. But my parents had been slaves in Europe just fifteen years before. Where had he been?

Sometimes, in the hush that attended silent meditation in the Hall of Worship, I wanted to kick down the row of seats ahead of me, to fling mud at the pulpit or to stand up and dare God to make his presence known. I stared with contempt at the rows of children who prayed with bowed heads. "Idiots," I thought. "American kids. Babies. Goody-goodies." When in class our teachers referred to the "Six Million Martyrs," and the children around me dutifully wrote down what they said, I kept my pencil lying on my desk. For them, Six Million was a concept, a historical fact to be duly memorized and spit back on a quiz the next week. Once written down, it was forgotten. Silently, I determined not to learn anything at all in Sunday school. My parents had wanted me to know where I came from, that was why they had sent me there. But the effort was like trying to graft a foreign branch to a native tree. The graft did not take.

When the bell rang, I grabbed my books and tore down the stairs to where my father was waiting.

"Daddy, let's go!" I'd say as soon as I spotted him, erect, gray-haired and strange as a dinosaur among the young, smooth American parents in the lobby. He would be holding forth, he was always holding forth, to the other parents. When in the company of native Americans, he seemed to feel compelled to underscore his difference, as if his accent, his bearing, his manner weren't enough He was an American citizen now and thankful for the privilege, he told anyone who asked him and far more people who did not. "I wanted that my child will live in a free country, see," he was always telling people. "Without *any* experience that I had to suffer."

"Daddy, come on. Mommy's *waiting!*"

My father would be dressed for the country, in a thick sweater or jacket that made him stand out even more from the other men. I'd pull at his arm to get him away. There was something in the polite, bland, patient expressions on the faces of the American parents that I could not abide. I knew they did not really want to hear my father but suffered him, the way I suffered the discourse of the rabbi. I wanted to get away from them as fast as possible. I wanted to find my brother in the crowd of children, get into the car, and push off, leaving the gray stone building far behind.

My mother sat waiting in our old, black Chevrolet, reading *The New York Times*. She rarely looked up. She rarely left the car to greet another parent, and if she did there was something studied in the gesture, a social obligation that had to be met. "Nobody at temple ever made an effort to understand us," she told me later. "Nobody ever reached out to pull us in and make us feel a part of things. All they seemed to be interested in was how we survived and then when we got into the details, they would start talking about the weather because they couldn't take it. We were like an island."

My father started the car and pulled away from the

crowded street in front of the synagogue, the tangle of the children and parents who were going off to a brunch of bagels and lox, or to visit relatives, or home to watch television. My brother and I pulled on our blue jeans in the back seat. In a few minutes, we were speeding up the West Side Highway toward the George Washington Bridge and over the Hudson River where there was an open sky.

The space, the absence of enclosure, relaxed my parents like a drug. They began to sing Czech songs, my father first, in a strong, jovial voice, and then my mother. We sang rounds, Czech folksongs, about wild ducks who fell into brooks when they got confused on their flight South, and innkeepers, gardens and old times. My father would recite Czech poetry or intone homilies about the scenery and weather. *"Hory, jsou hory,"* he began to repeat as we left flat ground. "Mountains are mountains."

My brother and I did not have the slightest idea of what these sayings meant, but we warmed to the change in our parents. A sense of well-being pervaded the car; it was like a party, self-contained and happy, flying through the countryside unconstrained. My mother smiled, threw back her head and laughed, even though she often said that she had forgotten how to laugh since the war. We played guessing games and rummaged through the picnic lunch for Danish pastry, moving fast past the other cars on the road, watching out for policemen so that my father would not get a speeding ticket.

Our cars, which we kept until they broke down, were the only possessions my parents had which I felt they could not live without. The old black Chevrolet which my father cleaned and polished like old silverware, was no mark of status like the automobiles advertised on television, but a necessity, a vehicle for escape. The car was a ticket to the boundless space of America, where borders between states were casually noted by a welcoming sign at the side of the highway and one could travel unhindered until one reached

158

the sea. The vastness of America was a comfort to my father. He trusted its size and talked about its opportunity in a way I recognized from stories of the early American settlers that we studied in school. "Small countries are no good," he would tell me. "Look at Czechoslovakia, what happened. Look at Israel surrounded by enemies!" As far as my father was concerned, America had saved his life by entering and winning the Second World War. "The French actually betrayed us in the Munich Pact, see," he explained, "so I did not have much confidence in the French people. In England, there were very big restrictions on immigrants. The political system is a democracy but not the social system. Too many classes. I thought when I had to bring up children that America was the country of unlimited opportunities, that my children would be prepared the right way for the life."

In the fall and winter of the year, when the summer crowds had left the swimming pools of Tallman, Anthony Wayne and Bear Mountain State Park, leaving acres of empty forests, lakes and lawns behind, my father was satisfied that he had made the right choice. He parked our car in a near-empty parking field, got out and inhaled deeply a few times, expelling what he told us was stale city air from his lungs. He opened the trunk of the car and took out chairs, blankets, coals, a picnic hamper. Then the four of us set out for the woods to find a wooden table in the sunlight, shielded from the wind.

My mother was the expert in these matters; she could tell at a glance whether a fireplace was situated well or badly, and she knew how to use the wind. All her pain, the aches in her back, the migraines, the muscle spasms seemed to disappear as she set to work clearing out ashes and giving us orders. "Tommy, get some twigs. Little ones. Go on. Helen, bring the coals over here." My father set up the folding chairs and nibbled at the picnic lunch or found the sports section of the *Times* while my mother turned her concentration to the fire.

159

My mother knew how to make things work, I often thought as I watched her. Unlike other mothers, who always seemed to need repairmen or plumbers when something in their homes went wrong, my mother did things by herself. She knew how to change a tire when our car had a flat; she fixed old lamps and frayed wires: pipes, clogged sinks, leaking refrigerators did not intimidate her. She simply got down on her knees and began, methodically, to pull things apart until she had located the problem. Then she put them back together again. She had learned that in camp, she said.

"We were the first transport which actually *left* Auschwitz," she had told me. "Nobody believed it at first but there was a rumor going round that the Germans were going to pick out the young people, between fifteen and forty-five, who were capable of work, and were going to ship us out to Germany proper, to the Fatherland, because they were short on labor. We would actually leave Auschwitz alive.

"Sure enough, the order came that there was going to be a selection in the camp. The men and women in this age group were herded into one barrack. We had to undress. Completely naked. The clothes over the left arm. We had to walk up to Dr. Mengele who was the top S.S. medical officer in Auschwitz and we stood there for hours and hours in line. I was watching what happened in front of me and I noticed that the weak ones and the ones with glasses and the ones who looked old were turned to one side; the other ones were sent to a table where the numbers on their arms were written down. That obviously was the better side. By the time I got to him I was a little worried because I had a scar from an appendectomy and Dr. Mengele didn't like people with scars.

"You had to announce to him your name, your age and your profession," my mother had told me. "I had been listening to what went on before me and it turned out that out of those thousands of women, every other one was a dressmaker all of a sudden. Now I was *really* a dressmaker but suddenly I thought: that's not original enough, and I have a scar from my appendectomy on top of it! So by the time I got to him I had made up my mind that when he asked my profession I would say *electrician.*

"That stopped him dead in his tracks. He said: you must be kidding. I said no, *Hauptschar Führer,* I am an electrician. He said, 'You mean you can install wires and things like that?' I said, 'Yes sir!' So he said, 'Over there!' That was the side where they took the numbers. I didn't worry too much about the electric business. I figured God knows where they would send us. Nobody would ever find out that I got through the selection by claiming to be an electrician. My father was an electrical engineer. Why shouldn't I know something about electricity?"

Each time I heard that story, a flush of pride would rise up inside me, making me want to smile and cry at the same time. I wanted to hug my mother then, touch her, tell her how smart and brave she was. But somehow, at those times, my body would go numb, the lid of my iron box would bulge and then flatten out again. The moment would pass.

"I need some more twigs," my mother would say, without moving her eyes from the fire that was beginning to flicker. "Get me some thicker ones. Make sure they're dry."

My brother and I foraged for twigs, leaving them in a small pile beside my mother. "All right," she said then, satisfied that the fire was burning properly. "Bring me the coals."

When the coals were laid out over the wood, she rose to her feet. Then my mother set about unpacking the meat that was to be barbecued. She worked efficiently, without wasting motion. My father would look up from his sports pages, sniffing the smoke in the air. He beamed at us in the sunlight and made another big show of inhaling the air.

"Daddy," my brother or I would say with the disgust particular to pre-teenagers, and my mother would laugh. Her deep, troubled eyes sparkled; she looked pretty.

"Who will we meet in the country today?" my father began to speculate. "Who knows? Maybe someone from Roudnice?"

My brother and I looked at each other in the way that meant, "Here he goes again." Then we ran off into the woods to play until the meat was cooked, leaving my father musing out loud about which other refugee family might have chosen to go for an outing to the same state park that day.

Dimly, I sensed that my father came to the country looking for company as well as fresh air. The people we met there and sat with at picnic tables made up a society completely different from the one which congregated outside the steps of the synagogue. It was an informal gathering of exiles, Czech, German, Hungarian and Austrian refugees who found in the great green expanse of public land the contours and colors of Central Europe. These were grownups who were like my parents, vastly different from the American parents of my friends at school. They owned no country homes, they dressed for comfort rather than style, and when they spoke, their English was laced with phrases in French, German and other languages.

Unlike other adults, all seemed to have double identities: the person they had been in Europe and the person they had become in the United States. Money seemed to have lost its power to exalt among them. They had all lost so much of it, along with property, profession and place in community, that the lines which normally position people in a given class had been broken and blurred. Emigration had cut them loose from the social hierarchy of their home countries and created a new community. There were Christians and Jews, and all of them had suffered in the war. The women worked for a living as well as the men, and their lives had been adventures, each one of them. I had my favorites and, early on, I had adopted those people I liked to replace the grandparents, aunts and uncles I did not have.

I chose Liza as my aunt. Small, thin, with long, elegant fingers and jet black hair, she was so sharp-elbowed and sharp-tongued that the very air seemed to quicken around her. She had been high society in Czechoslovakia, the daughter of the general director of the largest steelworks in the country. The German general who took charge of the company during the war fell in love with her and, to escape marriage without provoking retaliation, Aunt Liza had married someone else and run away to Portugal.

Although she was a Catholic, Aunt Liza had been raised in Prague among Jews. She returned there after the war was over and the Czechs were restored to power. But, on paper, Liza was a Sudetenland German. There was a shortage of apartments in Prague after the war and the Czech janitor of the house in which she lived had wanted hers. He reported Liza to the city police as a collaborator, a quisling, and she was slapped into Pankrac, Prague's central prison. "Your Mama was put there when the Nazis came to Prague; I was there because of the Czechs," Aunt Liza would say in her amused, pointed way. "I want you to remember that. The Jews weren't the only ones who suffered. I was in prison too."

Aunt Liza's eyes would glitter as she talked. Her pointed fingers would wave a cigarette in the air. "Life was a roller coaster for every one of us and don't you forget it!" she seemed to be telling me sternly, and then she would flash a white smile and zero in on some other target. Later on, when I was much older, I remember Liza sitting in a French restaurant ordering Camembert. When the waiter brought it the cheese was hard and cold. She impaled it with her fork and, swinging it around her head like a lasso, wailed loudly, *"Ce n'est pas la France, ce n'est pas la France."* Her outrageousness had become tinged with bitterness. Every day, she mourned a lost world. But earlier, at the picnic table, in the green woods, there was a vivacity in her that brought out the life in everyone. Her sarcasm was a goad to enjoy the

163

moment, to wrest from it all one could. She was impatient with pretension: she pricked balloons before they were even fully blown up, and accorded respect to no one until they had felt and survived her barbs.

Her husband, Uncle Willi, was Jewish. His sister had been my father's brother's wife before the war, and so he was a real relation, by law if not by blood. He had been a law student in Prague before the war, had escaped from Czechoslovakia and made his way to Palestine where he joined the Czech brigade of the Royal Air Force. He had served as a captain; he had been at Tobruk; he had picked up the accent and manners of the British. He had rescued Liza from a Displaced Persons camp in Germany, to which she had been deported by the Czech authorities. When they came to New York, he worked as a night clerk in a hotel in Harlem; Liza was a bilingual secretary. Then he began to sell religious goods. His pockets were full of rosary beads and crosses which he called "goods" the same way my father called the sample aprons and pedal pushers he brought home "goods." Willi talked about the army in a different way than people did on television or in books. He said there were no heroes, only men who were afraid. He had earned decorations but disparaged them. He talked with my father endlessly about the events of 1938 and 1939, whether Czechoslovakia should have fought, whether the British waited too long. The names Yalta and Chamberlain, Roosevelt and Churchill recurred in their conversations, along with Czech names, dates of battles, movements of armies across national boundaries that no longer existed on the maps we were taught to draw in school.

My brother and I would listen for a while. Then we got lost in names. The intensity bewildered us. There would be shouting arguments over people who had died and events that had been forgotten before we were born, references to what Churchill had written in his memoirs, or Truman, or some European writer whose book had not yet been published in the United States but whose views had been passed along the refugee grapevine to New York. My brother Tommy would pick at his piece of broiled chicken or frankfurter and then go off to the nearest stream to search for tadpoles and salamanders. He did not like noise and did not make an effort to follow conversation that was not in English. He found other things to do when people talked about the war. "I didn't want to hear about any of it a second time," he told me when we were much older. "It's not the most pleasant thing to talk about and if you know the information already, that your parents were locked up like animals, there's no reason to hear it again. Mommy and Daddy definitely went back over it again and again, and I didn't want to hear it."

Sometimes, I didn't want to hear it either and I ran off to play with my brother. But more often I stayed at the picnic table listening. The stories told there were like treasure. They proved my parents came from someplace, where people knew who they were. They were my folklore: they taught me lessons and truths. They also bound me to the grandparents I had adopted: Milena and Ivan Herben. I knew that they were not real grandparents, that we bore no physical resemblance to each other, that our names were different, and that they were Christians, not Jews. But that did not seem to matter. They were the right age, they had no grandchildren of their own and, most of all, they understood my parents; they had come from the same place. They were the people we met most frequently in the country, a gray-haired, sedentary couple who spoke almost no English and seemed to be the kind of people my grandparents would have been were they to have come out of their sepia-toned photographs and joined us in the country.

Ivan Herben had been editor-in-chief of *Ceské Slovo*, the largest newspaper in Prague, before he came to the United States. He had been against the Nazis from the very start, my mother said, and it was an honor to us that his wife

165

consented to be my nurse. Ivan had been among the first Czechs to be arrested by the Gestapo in 1939. He had spent six years in concentration camp and had been badly beaten in Dachau. Milena had remained alone in Prague during the war and although she had been closely watched and harassed by the Germans, had managed to hide a Jewish baby. After peace came, there had been less than three years of relative quiet for them. Then the Communists had taken over Czechoslovakia and the Herbens had fled, on skis, into Germany. Like Aunt Liza, they had waited in a Displaced Persons camp until they received visas for America. In New York, Ivan had found a job broadcasting for Radio Free Europe and Milena had worked taking care of me.

The Herbens, Willi and Liza and dozens of other displaced lawyers, diplomats, businessmen, writers and artists strolled through the state parks around New York City in the fifties and early sixties, a hermetic society, a secret one, set entirely apart from the world I was taught about in either public or Sunday school. There my father became eloquent in his own language and my mother seemed to blossom, throwing off the wariness that marked her relations with people in the city. There, our family seemed normal and connected to other people. There was community, an interweaving of lives that went back in time, that formed frail bridges over the great gap that was the war.

That gap was always there, a great dark pit into which, sooner or later, the conversation would inevitably fall. All of the people my parents knew had been part of it and it had become the ultimate standard by which they judged and were judged. "It was like a finishing school, a very strange finishing school," my mother told me once. "I think it made me more socially conscious. I was quite a frivolous, superficial young girl when the war broke out. But after three years in camp, I learned an enormous amount about human nature, about loyalty, about treachery. It was a very condensed education in coping, in living, and in sorting out a sense of values. You had to decide what was important in life: was it money or possessions, or people, or love, or friendship? I think that is, in a nutshell, what it was: a humanitarian finishing school."

That moved me very deeply. What my mother and father had lived through was more compelling to me than anything I had ever read or learned in school, inexhaustibly rich, a mine of stories and choices between good and evil, life and death. The Germans themselves, the people who had been responsible for the camps, the deaths, the losses, seemed not to enter into the picture on those Sunday afternoons. The subject was life and how to live it and it was listening at the picnic table that I received the Jewish education which my mother had hoped I would receive in the morning, at Sunday school. The Jewish heroes we learned about there, biblical figures, Zionist figures, American labor leaders, all lost their stature when put beside my parents and their friends. My mother and father were real heroes, living ones, whom I could see and touch. My father had a reputation among the society of former concentration camp inmates as one of the incorruptible men in Terezin, a prisoner who never stole from or denounced a fellow inmate although, as one of eight quartermasters, he could have easily done both. My mother had outsmarted death. She was clever, more adroit than the Greek heroes whose exploits we called myth in English class.

Often during those afternoons, I would wander off into the woods by myself, moody, filled with thoughts and yet unable to articulate a single one. I felt as if I carried unwritten plays inside of me, whole casts of characters who were invisible and voiceless, who could only speak through me. The people at the picnic table were voiceless in America. There, in the woods, they spun stories and told jokes and formulated theories, but once back in the world of the city, their voices were stilted and halting. They could not find the right words. The wide, bright, sprawling fan of their experience snapped shut among people who spoke English. They were forced into a groping that changed the nature of what they had to say, that made them appear helpless, that distorted what they were. They became outsiders.

I had access to both worlds. I could move back and forth, serve as courier, interpreter and spy. It was I who asked for instructions when we got lost on the back roads in the country: it was I who corrected my father's spelling and syntax when he wrote letters to the mayor of New York. I taught my parents American history and politics as I learned them at school. I explained the structure of the judicial system, and the principle of separation of powers, making large diagrams on pieces of white paper. I felt confident then, seeing America in outline form, the way my teacher showed it on the blackboard in school. What had happened to my parents could never happen in this country, I thought. There were too many checks and balances. I planned on making my career in government, in the foreign service where I could best represent America. Then I would have a platform from which to vindicate my parents.

Great speeches formed on my lips in their behalf. In the woods of Bear Mountain State Park, I addressed Hitler, Roosevelt and Chamberlain, the General Assembly of the United Nations and the President of the United States. I did not have to gather my thoughts: the words came into my mouth fully formed, as though I were a medium and other people were speaking through me. My body swayed with waves of feeling. My arms gestured to fallen leaves, bare branches. I spoke about injustice, an injustice so deep and deadly that the names people gave it seemed like Band-Aids on a gaping wound. I stumbled through the woods, not watching where I was going, mumbling phrases, buffeted by visions of saving, of reclaiming, of healing.

The landscape of my parents' past was so vast and empty, like the world of the Greek tragedies we read in school. The small details of life, the interlinked episodes of waking, eating breakfast, catching cold, buying a candy bar, hanging out, loving a teacher or forming a crush on a friend, were all missing in their accounts. Every story they told was a matter of life and death, of loyalty or betrayal. Nothing that upset me—the fact that my boyfriend had asked another girl to a dance, or that something I had counted on didn't turn out right, or that I could not fathom some homework assignment from school—was important compared to the upsets my parents had known. "Worse things have happened, you know," they said, and I saw the war rise like a great tidal wave in the air, dwarfing my trouble, making it trivial.

I wondered what I could do in my life that would even register on the grand, heroic plain of the past. My mother's sighs and sarcasms, my father's push toward health and air, as well as his lapses and faraway stares, the aggregate of stories told at the picnic table all kindled inside me. My iron box became a furnace then, generating energy, burning rage. Sometimes, when I felt it burning inside me and there was no activity to channel it, I picked a fight. In kindergarten, my mother told me, I had been sent home from school for fighting another child and until my brother and I were well into our late teens we, too, fought, passionately, with fists and nails and whatever came to hand. Once I hit him on the head with the telephone receiver in our kitchen in a gesture so deliberate and unequivocal that I remembered it in amazement for years afterward. I wanted to kill.

There were, of course, sanctions applied. I was told it was unacceptable to hit anyone, especially my little brother whom I should love since he was my closest relative besides my parents. Relatives were irreplaceable. Any anger I showed at home was quickly quashed. My mother could not bear any anger directed toward her. She would withdraw into tears or else order us into our rooms where we could address it to the four walls. Ordinary bickering, the kind almost all siblings indulge in, unnerved both my mother and father. They could not tolerate it. When we scrapped over

169

little things, things that were of no great importance to either of us, our parents often intervened with anger themselves. It was as if a lid had to be put on our energy: otherwise, it might get out of control.

I felt it coiled up inside of me, so bottled up that sometimes it caused aches and pains in my legs. I let it out in running and talking, in pounding on the piano, in making things, in school. But there was so much of it. At times, my life seemed to be not my own. Hundreds of people lived through me, lives that had been cut short in the war. My two grandmothers, whose names were mine, lived through me. My parents, too, were living through me. They saw in my life the years they had lost in the war and the years they had lost in emigrating to America. My life was not just another life, I thought often when I was a child, it was an assignation. "Every one of you is a miracle," my mother would say about children of the people she had known in camp. "None of you was supposed to have been born."

I did not like it when she said things like that, or when other refugees in the country eyed my brother and me as if looking for some defect in the manufacture. At those times I felt like a vindication of their collective lives, a great golden egg to be ohhed and ahhed over, not just an ordinary child like the others at school. I wanted to be ordinary, free of history, no miracle but just a matter of course. Sometimes when my parents recalled the past, puzzling for the thousandth time about why they had come out of the camps when so many of their friends had not, they concluded that the reason was to have us children. When my mother told me that, I shut the words out. I did not argue. But I did not want to hear her say anything more. What she said frightened me. It implied expectations I could never meet. It made me special, important and precious but it deprived me of carelessness, the carelessness of childhood. I rambled through the woods on Sunday afternoons with a serious face. Even at twelve, I was purposeful. I thought about the reasons for things.

"Give me a smile," my father would cajole when he spotted me and automatically I would smile for my father. He could not bear to see my brother or me unhappy: he took it as a personal affront. "What can you be thinking about that makes you look so serious?" my father always asked me. He was suspicious of too much thinking. Too much thinking led nowhere good; it weakened one, it interfered with living.

"Time to go. It's getting cold," my father said.

My brother was called back from his station at the stream: the folding chairs, hamper, newspapers and coals stood ready to be taken to the car. My parents' friends gathered up their belongings, and we all walked back to the parking lot, a small group, chatting in German and Czech. It was the end of the weekend, the start of a new week. During the week, all of them worked in different neighborhoods of the city. Sometimes, if one fell ill, or someone died, or there was an extraordinary political development somewhere in the world, they would telephone, and I would overhear my parents engaged in long conversation. But most of the time, my parents' friends met and talked on weekends over picnic tables, apart from the world of everyday.

We said our good-byes and got into our cars. Slowly, we drove past the unmanned parking lot booth, one by one. Then we were on the highway, among dozens and hundreds of vehicles. The small group of automobiles first loosened, then disappeared.

TEN

On Sundays Joseph and Deborah Schwartz's family would often pile into the family car and, on an impulse that recurred whenever a few weeks had gone by, drive for two hours through the Blue Ridge mountains.

"My father's friend Moishe lived there," Joseph recalls, "and later his brother Yankele moved there too. They were from my father's town in Hungary, and they were like family. They went through the war. They had Jewish books in the house. They talked politics. They talked about *The New York Times*. And my father was comfortable there.

"It was a refreshment to drive down on Sundays. We'd be all together in the car, everyone would be in a happy mood, there'd be some fighting but in a good spirit, and it was like a cool bath on a hot day. I saw my parents in a different atmosphere. I saw them with old friends, and I saw that that was good for them. They relaxed. My father was calmer. Everyone would talk and eat and we'd stay so late that when we drove back, all the stars would be out. We used to get back at midnight, or one in the morning. Or even two in the morning, sometimes. I'd fall asleep in the car and everything was quiet except for the sound of the road and the driving and maybe my mother and father talking in the front seat. Gently. Everything was relaxed and refreshing, those Sundays. Because it was like going home in a way. It was going somewhere where there was someone like us."

There was no other family like the Schwartzes in the rural town in which Joseph lived. It was a small place, set high in the mountains, above horse farms, trailer parks, Baptist churches, and neon-lit motels, which serviced the tourists who came there for their health. Fashions came there five years after they appeared elsewhere; school integration came only in 1970. The community was sharply divided by race, class and religion. Labor was, for the most part, not unionized, wages were low and opportunities were elsewhere. Mountain people, city people, suburbanites, blacks and whites, and about three hundred Jewish families lived separate lives in this town which was really not one community at all but a mosaic of several.

Joseph, who had lived there for most of his life, had always felt different from all of them. "I always felt different," he told me, "I always felt alone. Every school I went to, I felt apart from the other kids. My parents always wanted me to have the best education, so after going to two public schools, I went to private school in grade four. It was beautiful. Tudor-style buildings set in the hills, a Catholic school run by nuns and old retired army types. Very English. Everyone had to wear a jacket and tie. The jacket had a little emblem. Everyone was issued a complete football uniform and had to participate in the athletic program. I was very self-conscious. I wasn't athletic. I made one good play the whole time I was in that school. I ran into someone carrying the football by accident; I think I was trying to get out of the way. I broke my arm there the day before field

173

day, jumping a hurdle, and that made me happy. I didn't have to compete. I was always looking to be a little bit happy in that school.

"I never felt like one of them and I don't think I was treated as one of them. I didn't make a cross over my heart in the mornings and I used to only mouth the prayers. In the morning, in home room, the cross was up on the wall as it was in every room in the school. We'd have to stand up, cross our hearts and say *Our father who art in heaven, hallowed be thy name, thy Kingdom come, thy will be done on earth as it is in heaven.* Sometimes I used to say the *Sh'ma*, as they were reciting Our Father. I used to say *Sh'ma Yisrael* in my mind in order to block it out. I had to say: What's going on here?

"I knew I was in that school because my parents had a notion that what was private was better than what was public, and my parents always thought that if you could afford it, you sent your children to the best schools. My parents hadn't been educated themselves. Education was something of an alien thing to them. My older sister, Deborah, went to private school and I went too. I trusted everything my parents did implicitly. With no question. I never wondered what I was doing there. When I asked my parents about saying Our Father in school, they said I should try to do what I felt was right and yet preserve my identity, that I should remember who I was. I believed that was what I should do. My parents appeared so strong. I never saw them in a reflective moment. They couldn't be mistaken. So I tried to preserve an identity I was just beginning to learn about."

Joseph's parents were both living in small rural towns when the Second World War blew apart their lives in Hungary. His mother had been deported to a ghetto and at sixteen was in Auschwitz. His father had been ordered to a labor camp from which he later escaped to join the underground. The two had made their separate ways to the United States and met in 1950 on a blind date in the Williamsburg section of Brooklyn.

A very short time later they were married, and in 1951 their first child, Deborah, was born. At this time Joseph's father worked in a garment factory as the operator of a pleating machine and then a sewing machine. By 1953 he and another survivor had pooled their savings and started a tucking business. They worked doggedly at it, driven by the need to rebuild. In 1954, Joseph was born and in 1956 the family moved out of Brooklyn to a house near the ocean, where the children could grow up "in a better atmosphere."

By 1958 the tucking business was a success and the family could afford to take a vacation. They drove down South to visit other survivors from Hungary. Joseph's father had lost his entire family—six brothers and sisters, two parents, one grandfather—in the war, and now viewed his childhood friends as relatives. They stayed several days in the South and liked what they saw. They looked at a manufacturing plant that was for sale and decided to buy it. "There was less competition there than in New York. I thought we'd have a better chance," Joseph's mother, a small, sharp, no-nonsense businesswoman told me. "I thought it would be better for the kids to grow up in the mountains and I just made up my mind. Life is short and I'm impulsive. I make a change very fast."

Joseph's father also liked the mountains, the small-town atmosphere and the simplicity of Southerners he met, the people who would be buying the cotton and polyester pants, suits and skirts he manufactures. "These are the roofers, the mechanics, the people who build bridges and maintain equipment in America," he told me with satisfaction, as we watched a group of cloggers dance to the music of a blue-grass band one night. "These people work hard. They never think of moving. They've been here for generations. Even the Jews have been here for two or three generations. It reminds me of home. That's why I like it."

Less than twenty years after they had arrived in the South, Joseph's parents had built up a thriving business in the ladies' sportswear industry. Their factory employed sixty

175

people. Their four children always had the best money could buy. A Cadillac was parked behind the patio and a housekeeper came in daily to cook and clean. But their lifestyle, like that of many survivors who had done well, was relatively modest.

"Most people here furnish their homes lavishly," their black housekeeper, Mary, told me. "They play golf, belong to clubs, have a lot of cocktail parties. Entertain. Most women let their husbands do the work and their husbands don't work so hard neither. The two of them, they work so hard! They don't have time for parties. They're working."

Joseph's parents often worked seven days a week. "Sometimes I'm here eighteen hours a day," his father told me in his factory, "and I don't sleep here. I *work* here." He worried that the United States seemed to have stopped producing young workers and instead young people wound up either in universities or on welfare. Work was the center of his life as it was for many survivors: it was his duty to his family, it was his passion, it was a discipline and a source of real pleasure. Talk was cheap. It accomplished nothing. "My parents don't want leisure time," Joseph's younger sister told me. "They want to keep busy. One of the reasons they work so hard is that it gives them no time to think."

"I don't think she meant thinking rationally," Joseph said, when I told him this. "I think my father loves his work and works hard because he reaps rewards from it, but he also works so hard because he doesn't want to think about his brothers and sisters and mother and father; maybe there's this incredible guilt he has. But I don't know. He doesn't talk about it. He's silent. He just doesn't talk."

Joseph liked to talk. He could talk until five or six in the morning when he got involved in a subject. He was a graduate student in sociology, tall, slow and heavy-set, with the fair-skinned pink complexion of a redhead. He was in his early twenties but his wide, freckled face could change to make him look like a wondering adolescent or like an astute,

176

demanding professor. Part of him wanted deeply to become an academic. He enjoyed a reputation in his department for being a serious student and good teacher, able to clarify issues, patiently take them apart and then put them back together again. Yet another part of him saw entering university life as an abandonment of his parents. "If I were a Jewish boy in Hungary," he said, "there would be no question about it. I'd go into my father's business and get married and that would be the end of it. I wouldn't even have an opportunity to go do a master's degree and feel guilty about it." The prospect of examining his background and tracing the origins of his attitudes threw Joseph into confusion and a great deal of ambivalence.

"The reason I'm talking to you at all about this is that I'm showing good faith," he told me the first time we met. "I'm talking about it because I'd give up anything for community, for sharing it. This whole field for me—every time I reach out to make it intelligible, all I find is chaos. It's tumultuous. Someone must ask questions or else it won't come out. It doesn't come out by itself. And at the same time, I don't want to be part of something that may hurt my parents. They've been hurt enough. Of all the things I know, I know the love I have for my parents. It's the model, the reference point, the point of departure for all other things.

"I always wanted to share with my parents; I wanted to feel what they felt. And my problem is that I can't feel what it was like to have a parent murdered. As a child I was overprotected from knowing that my uncle died. I was always protected from death. I wanted to feel it, to be a part of suffering. I could *never* feel it, and that made me helpless and guilty. Whenever there's an opportunity for me to be helpful, I'm always helpful. I couldn't be helpful here. There was nothing I could do. I couldn't even convince myself that listening was helpful."

Joseph stopped abruptly, as if he felt he had already said

more than he intended. His light brown eyes turned opaque and he shook his head at conversation. For a long time, our discussion of the way the Holocaust had affected his life was bumpy. It happened in bits and pieces. He was guarded in what he said, and worried about appearing disloyal to his parents. Like all the children of survivors I spoke with, he did not believe that any pain he had felt as a child could compare with what his parents lived through. His problems had been inconsequential compared to theirs; he did not wish people to think that he thought himself of the same stature as his parents. "I'm of no comparable stature," he repeated. "I didn't suffer."

His loyalty to family appeared extreme to Joseph's friends. He lived in a neighborhood his parents had chosen for him. His mother had chosen his furniture. He was readily available to his older sister's family as driver, confidant or babysitter. Several times a month he would have long fatherly discussions on the telephone with his younger brother and sister. He had broken off at least one relationship with a woman because he felt his parents would not approve, and often spoke of finding a daughter of Hungarian Jewish survivors to marry.

"I was always painfully aware that my parents had survived the concentration camps," Joseph told me. "The fact that it wasn't talked about made me know it more. All I had to do was look at my mother's face and I knew I'd better not ask questions. The effects of the war on my mother are obvious. Her strength seems to last only as long as my father's strength is behind her. She cries easily and I didn't want to make her cry. Even my older sister didn't ask my mother questions. My father's stronger. She asked him.

"My father was like God to me. Unquestionable. He was strong. He was good. So giving, so generous. I felt my father had been appointed to survive. I felt he had been given something that had been taken away from everybody else. Everyone else was an image to me, not a reality. And I couldn't deal in images. I could only deal with what I saw. It looked like my father had survived and sustained a good life. It looked like it hadn't changed him. I always wanted to know more about him. I always wanted to ask my father questions as a son. I never could. He would lapse into thoughtfulness and for me the lapse was an answer."

Joseph's features sharpened as he concentrated.

"The way my father covered up his pain was so complete! My father seldom if ever talks about his brothers and sisters. And it was so hard for me to hear. I don't remember him describing their qualities. I don't remember him speaking about his mother or father. I don't remember him talking about any of them. He's silent.

"I used to tell my friends about him when I was a kid. I used to tell them what a hero my father was, how he had not killed a man when he could have, when he was in the partisans. I don't know how or where or when I heard stories from the war. It's as if they came through thin air to my ear. I only picked up on the heroic parts, on the human parts. I could never remember the details. I always had to ask dates over and over again. I could never retain it."

Joseph stopped abruptly. "It's incredible. Just one month ago, when I was home, I heard the story chronologically and I've forgotten it again. I was sitting there listening and I said to myself, *This time I'm not going to forget.* But I've forgotten. I only remember chunks of it ... those same chunks that came up inside me as a kid ... the same feelings. ..."

"Tell me what you remember," I asked him.

Joseph threw up his hands. "I don't like telling it because I'm sure I'm going to make mistakes. I should have it recorded. But I couldn't bring myself to do such a thing."

He paused and lit a cigarette.

"As far as I can remember, they came on a Passover and my father received orders to go to a labor camp. He took care of horses there. When the Germans sent for the Jews, the man running the labor camp let them know and my

179

father and his friends escaped. He ended up in the underground. He was in the Swiss Embassy in Budapest for a while. There were Jews hiding in the basement there. In a space where there was room for five hundred people, they put two thousand. My father was responsible there. There was another story too. He was in a building and a bomb came down. The bomb went through three floors of a building and didn't explode. My father was standing right there."

"No wonder you thought he was like God," I said. "Those stories made him seem invulnerable."

"Those stories made him invulnerable," Joseph repeated. "Whatever suffering my father did, he did alone. I always resisted it when my older sister asked questions. To talk about it minimized the impact. She would take on a peculiar voice. She had to make a transformation in herself to ask the questions. There was a contrived neutrality in her voice. I heard it and I would condemn her for asking. I never needed to hear words. It was the looks, the vibrations which gave me the feeling I have.

"You know, the fact of the matter is I know almost nothing. As a historian, I mean. I can never bring myself to recount. Even though I've heard it and know it inside out. I want you to know it's a big thing for me to submit myself to these questions. I don't do this kind of thing."

Joseph glanced at me half angrily and then went to the kitchen for a glass of water. His apartment, which was situated over a kosher grocery store, was quiet. He lived alone, and unlike most other students, he did not have to worry about money. He owned a car, stereo system, expensive clothing, shelves of books, and when he saw a record or artifact he wanted, Joseph bought it. Like most survivors who had done well, his parents had always been generous with their son and Joseph was well aware of this. People in school reminded him of it; so did his friends; so did his family. He did not like the idea of being a "rich kid," yet living in Canada as an American without a work permit made getting a job impossible he said, and working illegally was a risk he was not willing to take. It seemed clear to me, though, that nothing in Joseph's upbringing had encouraged financial independence.

"Other kids didn't have all I had," he told me. "They used to tell me that their parents couldn't afford it. They told me that they only got toys at Christmas while I got them all year round. They were disciplined kids. When their mothers called, they went. Whenever I was mischievous or did something wrong, I was never really scolded. My parents always protected me. I always thought I should be punished more."

Like many children of survivors whose parents were preoccupied with financial security, Joseph spent a great deal of time at home alone. When school was out and the bus dropped him off near the road to his house, he would walk through the woods and then up the steep asphalt driveway, making zigzags up the incline, the way his father did. He would sit down in front of the television to watch "Star Trek" or "Mr. Ed." and when they were over and no one had yet come home, he built models or took them apart.

Unlike his older sister who was always busy with lessons and activities, Joseph always felt himself to be "in a different gear than anyone else. I was questioning morality when I was eight years old. When a kid was ill treated by the group, I would go to that kid and try to comfort him. I was always interested in justice. I thought about it. I saw that my parents were just people. Even in Hebrew school, I felt different from the Jews. They were nice boys. I liked them. But I felt their Jewishness was a matter of rituals and traditions. I had those too but more than that I felt that I was a Jew with suffering attached to my name. And for some reason, suffering made being Jewish sweet. I didn't think anyone else in my class studying with the Rabbi had that feeling."

Joseph broke off again. He was uncomfortable recalling

181

feelings, he said. He wasn't good at it. He would be of much better use analyzing my findings than contributing to them. He did not like to lose control.

"Your sister told me that when you were younger you thought your parents were angels," I said. "Do you remember thinking that?"

"I thought they were more than human," Joseph said. "I thought they were more than great. They were different from the other people in the street and different from the other people in the *shul*. Because they had known the taste of inhumanity that others didn't know and because of that they were better judges of humanity than other people. I don't know whether they told me that, or other people told me that, or I thought that. I don't know where I got the idea. But I believed it then. And to some degree I believe it now.

"Family is the first loyalty: it always was in our house. You always forgo your friends for family. Let's say I wanted to go out at night, which I did all through high school. They didn't want me out with my friends until one o'clock in the morning. I'd say we were talking till late and my parents said: You don't talk. You come home. They would always say: Who's your loyalty to? They don't support you. They'd always say: Why don't you run to your friends? See if they're going to take this from you!"

Joseph's voice had risen and his face had lost the calm, reasoning expression it habitually wore.

"I was a disobedient, raucous, rowdy kid by the time I was in high school. I was angered easily. I cheated in school. I got kicked out for smoking. I had temper tantrums. I wanted my voice to be heard and I thought my parents never responded. They didn't listen to me the way they listened to a business partner. They never said to me: How's your friend? So I assumed that my parents were not interested very much in what I did. They were interested in what they did, which was work. And they wanted me to be inter-

182

ested in what they did. I was always wondering why they worked so much but after a while I took it for granted.

"At any rate," Joseph continued, "they were always working, and I resented it terribly. I resented that I was never taken out the way other kids were taken out. I was not doing what I saw other kids do with their parents. Like fishing! I got angry about fishing one day. I said, 'Daddy, I want you to take me fishing for the weekend.' We had a wonderful time together but on the way back we had to stop at the store. We couldn't go straight back to the house. We had to stop at the store first.

"The explanation was: We have to work to support you. We have to work to make you *something*. My parents wanted me to be a success, a doctor or a lawyer, someone big. If they worked it was implied I would have a chance at being *something*. It was implicit that if they didn't work I would become nothing. So what incentive did *I* have to work? Why should I even take it seriously? I was always changing schools. I had a hard time making friends and when I finally made friends, I thought I couldn't keep them because that was a betrayal of things that were to be shared in the family even though they *weren't* being shared in the family!"

Joseph looked at me to make sure I appreciated the absurdity of what he was saying. He was talking easily now. The words were coming out at full steam.

"My parents taught me not to expect much from the world. My parents always said: Even the best friends we had in Europe came and robbed us and threw us in the gutter. Why should it be any different today? *Why* should it be any different? We had the same feeling you have for your friends. And that's a very strong argument. I didn't believe them but whether I believed it or not was irrelevant. It was my parents speaking and what my parents said always had the most impact on my life."

Their philosophy was buttressed by events at the various schools Joseph attended. "The other boys knew I was Jewish. They seemed to make a point out of the fact that I was Jewish," he recalls. "I had to go to summer school when I was fourteen and I had to live on campus. It was like going to boarding school in the middle of my own town: I couldn't leave and go home. I had had my bar mitzvah the year before and kept all my Jewish paraphernalia—my tefillin, and a little Torah and prayer books—in my room.

"I came into my room one day and they were all over the floor. I was forced to be Jewish. And I was forced to feel it more when I told the headmaster, who listened but didn't do anything. There was an instant there when I felt unified with my parents. I felt that what had happened was a teaching. I called my father and he complained to the headmaster. It turned out that the school didn't want me to come back in the fall anyway."

That fall, Joseph entered the sixth and last school he would attend before college. He was fifteen years old. He was tired of readjusting to new environments. Although this last move again put him in an exclusive school, filled with students from a neighborhood where, it was rumored, no blacks or Jews were allowed to live, Joseph began to apply himself. "I got involved. I started making friends. I started to value myself a little bit," he says. "Some of the people there seemed anti-Semitic but I used to dismiss their comments. . . ."

A year later, however, he found himself in a situation he could not disregard. He had been playing chess with a friend after lunch, during a break between classes, when a fellow student began to annoy him. "This boy had bothered me a couple of times about being a Jew," Joseph recalled. "He looked over at me and he said, 'Hey, Hitler missed one.' I was shocked. I thought: What do I do? I didn't even know what I felt. I just knew he had hit something very sensitive. He said it again and I got up and walked out of the room. I began to cry and my body began to shake. I did a lot of crying as a kid. I went halfway down the hall and then I turned. I went back, tapped him on the shoulder and struck him so hard in the mouth that he fell down on the floor. I felt like an angel had pushed my arm."

Joseph stared at me. "I'm feeling this as if it were yesterday. Things are crystallizing as I talk and I don't know what to do with them."

"What happened after you hit him?" I asked.

"I walked out," he said. "I walked out of the room and he came after me. He grabbed my coat and I slipped out of it. In the middle of the hall I pushed him up against the lockers and then the fight was broken up. I had to go to a private place. To be by myself. I felt terrific and terribly guilty. I was shaking. I never felt so polarized in my life. It forced me to think about everything I never thought about. All the things that were so unapproachable. I not only felt in a sense that I had avenged my father but all the images of my uncles and grandparents. I felt I could look at the pictures my father kept in his shoe box. I had that feeling that my sister always had to put into words."

His parents knew very little of this at the time. All they knew was that their son persistently had troubles in school and shrank away from hearing anything that had to do with the past. Joseph's mother and sisters were afraid of him. He would bang on the car when he had one of his tantrums. He had slashed his father's favorite chair and run after his older sister with a kitchen knife. They would compare him to their friends' children, to his cousins in Phoenix, to his older sister and demand: What's with you? Why do you have so many troubles?

"I also wondered why I had so many troubles." Joseph smiled at me ruefully. "I was terribly angry. I was angry they were in the war. I was angry that they worked all the time. I was angry at my older sister. That she achieved things. That she was a beauty queen. My mother wanted very much to have peace at home. She always used to throw up her hands and ask: Why can't there be peace? She was

185

terribly upset by me. When she got to the end of her rope she used to say, 'Did I leave Auschwitz for you?'

"I would be rendered speechless by that. Everything was taken out of me in that one phrase. My whole life. I felt as if someone took a hypodermic needle and sucked all the life from me. I was nothing. I was weak. I'm weak right now even remembering it. I'm just empty. She said that a few times. When things got crucial and she came to the end of her rope, that's what she said. And she used to break down and cry."

Joseph stopped talking and I realized that I was feeling as tense as he was. The scene he described had been a staple in our household too. I had watched my mother and younger brother do battle. I had watched Tommy come home from school with bad report cards, lock himself up in his room and stay there for hours building models. My mother too had been frightened of my brother, unable to discipline him. She too had invoked Auschwitz and death and suffering, and I had seen my brother's face close off in much the same way as Joseph's was doing now.

"My mother decided to send me to a psychologist," Joseph continued, with a note of sarcasm in his voice. She said, 'We'll try anything,' as if the world was coming to an end because of me."

I smiled in recognition. My mother had used the same words, done the same thing.

"I resented being sent to a psychologist. I resented it because I felt my mother was trying to solve her own problems. She couldn't handle me. She didn't know me. She portrayed me as being out of her control and yet she didn't have time to talk to me. My life revolves around talking things out. And my parents would always say: Enough talk! You have to *do!* I could never distinguish between what a problem was and what a problem wasn't because when I thought I had problems my father put them into perspective too quickly. He decided on a solution and—*boom!*—that was it. So going to the psychologist wasn't all bad for me. I went for about four months and I felt I was communicating with someone who gave me an ear. Just the fact that he brought my parents in to talk about *me* made me feel good. Because at least there was a beginning of a conversation and I could say what was bothering me. He'd tell my parents: You have to give Joseph a chance."

Joseph's voice had gained so much in volume that he was nearly shouting at me.

"I went to the University of Miami my first year, and I got into every vice I could possibly get into. I smoked dope in Miami. I drank in Miami. I got beaten up and I beat up in Miami. I was not socially accepted. I didn't give a fuck about school in Miami.

"I *sent myself to the psychologist.* Because I *believed* there was something wrong with me. Maybe I just can't do it, I kept thinking. Maybe I just can't do all that's expected of me. Maybe I had no intelligence. Maybe I *was* really nothing."

Joseph stopped to light another cigarette.

"The psychologist gave me all these tests. Three or four days of intensive testing. Then he sat down with five pages of typed notes about me and there was a *paragraph* on each of my features. How I was with honor, and how I was with dignity, and how I was in vocational tests. And I said: My God, I have to write this down! I wrote down everything the psychologist said. That I would make a good doctor, a good psychologist. That I wasn't too gifted in mathematics. That I'd make a good social worker. That I'd make a good sociologist. I folded up this piece of paper and I put it in a safe deposit box in the bank.

"I failed miserably that first year in Miami. I went home and I sat my mother and father down on the patio and told them I wanted to talk to them. I took out the piece of paper I had put in the bank and I said: *Look,* this is what the world thinks of me! I was at a loss for what to do. I was thinking of quitting school and going into my father's business. Then my sister and her husband convinced me I should study in Toronto."

Joseph paused. He slowed down.

"I came up here and enrolled at University. I got interested in school. People liked me and I liked them. And I liked the school. And I got good grades."

He said this deliberately, as if he still had to reassure himself that it was true. In fact, he had received a teaching assistantship for the coming year. Other students sought out his help. His teachers took a special interest in him.

"I became settled here in Toronto," Joseph said. "I was on my own, away from home. I began to mature a little bit.

"And I guess I'm still doing it."

ELEVEN

On Sunday afternoons in the late fifties, in Rochester, New York, Ruth Alexander remembers sitting on the public beach at Lake Ontario with the rest of the *greeners*. They ate sandwiches, kept an eye on their children, and spoke Yiddish, the language they used at home and often at work. Almost all of them were Polish Jews. Many had met before, during the long decade that began with the Nazi invasion of Poland in 1939, and saw them move from ghettos to labor and concentration camps to post-War Displaced Persons camps, and finally to the United States. Most of their eldest children had been born in 1946, in Germany, like Ruth's older brother Eugene. The Alexander family had been brought to the United States by the Hebrew Immigrant Aid Society (HIAS), three of nearly 150,000 Jewish DPs relocated between 1947 and 1951.

HIAS had sent the Alexanders first to Cairo, Illinois, and then to St. Louis, Missouri. Neither place felt comfortable and when one of Ruth's two surviving uncles moved to Rochester, the Alexanders followed. They lived in the very center of the city, the then Jewish section, which boasted five synagogues and the densest concentration of *greeners* in upper New York State. They worked in the factories of Rochester, where English was not a requisite for work. Jake Alexander, Ruth's father, had been a tailor before the war and he found work with a uniform manufacturer. Her mother, like many of the *greener* women in Rochester, stayed home with the children.

By the early sixties, most of the survivors had scattered into the suburbs. They worked six days a week and kept long hours. Many would leave their homes at eight in the morning and work with only a lunch break until eight or nine at night, much as they had done while they were incarcerated by the Nazis. Eventually, some bought businesses of their own. Ruth's uncle, one of the more successful *greeners,* owned a fish market; Ruth's father had opened his own tailor shop. Both still worked six days a week although they were now financially secure.

The survivors who had sat together on the public beach on Lake Ontario now could sunbathe in their own back yards. They drove large cars and some had built ostentatious houses. Although they no longer congregated at *"the kloob,"* a branch of the New Americans Club where Ruth and her brother remembered having birthday parties as children, they kept tabs on each other. Their community was hermetic and small. Their children were closely watched and it was for this reason that whenever Ruth returned to Rochester for holidays, she kept a low profile.

"I really hated the *greeners* when I was a kid," she told me as we walked down the clean, leafy street where her parents now lived, a street that felt like typical middle-class America. Children rode their tricycles; men were hosing down their cars. Although it was Saturday, Ruth's father was at his tailor shop. Her mother was at home, cooking.

190

"I always felt suffocated by the *greeners*. I hated the way they talked. I hated the heavy, look-what-I've-been-through atmosphere they carried around with them. They scrutinized me always. I was Hella's child. They looked me over from head to toe. I was always too skinny or too pale. I didn't feel like a regular child. I felt like a novelty. I felt like I had to do a song and dance for them. They'd always ask me: Do you speak Yiddish? Some of them had numbers; others didn't. I remember looking at them and feeling very self-conscious about it. Almost ashamed for them. I was very glad my parents didn't have numbers. It embarrassed me."

An uncertain smile passed over Ruth's face. At twenty-seven, she was one of the second ring of survivors' children in Rochester and one of the few who had not yet settled down either to a marriage or a steady job. Ruth had finished her Bachelor's Degree at New York University and then worked as a secretary. She was a slim, small person; pale, with black curly hair tumbling over an old-fashioned face that looked as if it belonged in one of the pre-war photographs in her mother's bedroom. She had a small, flat voice which did not vary much in volume, tone or quality. When she laughed, even the laughter was subdued. She seemed to embody the notion of quiet.

When Ruth Alexander was four and a half years old, she had been hospitalized in order to have a tumor in her foot removed. The thing she still remembers most vividly is that she had hardly any visitors. "Basically, only my mother came to visit," she told me, "and sometimes, late, after visiting hours, my father came. Before that he was working. I shared my room with this other little girl who had a mother and father, aunts and uncles and grandparents coming in. I remember envying her, thinking: I wish I could have that kind of family. My father had had seven brothers and sisters and only one sister survived. My mother also had seven brothers and sisters. I guess seven was standard. Two of the brothers survived but one lived in Israel. I got very

191

confused when people talked about family. I remember once my father saying something about brothers and sisters killed in the war. I didn't understand. What was an uncle? What was that to me? When he talked about brothers and sisters, I thought they were mine.

"In kindergarten I remember celebrating Easter and how you were supposed to go put flowers on people's graves. I came home and asked why I couldn't put flowers on my grandma's and grandpa's graves. My parents told me why and when I went back to school I told my teacher that all my grandparents were murdered. That got her very uptight, I remember. She told me that they weren't murdered, that they were killed, that I didn't understand the difference between murdered and killed. I knew she was wrong. I remember wishing they had been killed instead of murdered. It was not as personal a thing.

"My whole childhood I wanted a grandmother. I'd tell my mother that my best friend had two grandmothers and I didn't have even one. I always felt a lot of big spaces, a lot of empty spaces at home. I felt a lot of emptiness. I went through a period when I was ten when I used to cry every night. I always felt that I loved my parents and that they loved me, but there was a sense of despair in the house. I know that I got the idea while I was quite young that people weren't all that wonderful. *'Nazis did this. Some Jews collaborated or sold out. Other people didn't want to know.'* There was always a sense that life was tenuous. Things weren't that secure."

The Alexanders, like a certain number of survivors in Rochester and elsewhere, talked very little to their children about the lives they had led before or during the war. Ruth knew that her mother had been born in 1915 in Warsaw, into a family of religious Jews. Her grandfather, she thought, had owned a factory. Her father had been born in the same year, into an extremely religious and very poor family in Lodz.

192

"His father was one of those guys with long beards who didn't work because he studied and prayed all day. My father started working when he was very young. About eleven. He was apprenticed to a tailor in order to help support the family. I don't know too much else. I know he was sent to Auschwitz and Dachau, where he was liberated. I know he experienced and saw a lot worse things than my mother did. I don't know exactly what they were. My father was very quiet. He never told me any specific stories. I feel that my father's family was obliterated. Erased. I felt very nervous asking him about his family; I do even now. I knew it was horrible, very upsetting to them. It was also upsetting to me. It was my responsibility *not to ask*. I knew that they didn't want me to know but I did know. So I pretended not to."

Ruth's face, which had remained almost expressionless while she talked, now showed faint signs of annoyance. "I got this double message. My parents didn't explain things to me but they did a lousy job of hiding the evidence. My father has a couple of remnants from Auschwitz: a Nazi armband, actual photographs of bodies. He used to bring them out sometimes when other survivors were over. I knew where he kept them. They were up on the top shelf. If they had wanted to really hide them, they would have found a place I couldn't see or get to. If I really wanted to, I could take them down and look. But I knew I wasn't supposed to know so I pretended I didn't. Over the years, I heard and saw bits and pieces. I felt like I got them through osmosis; I always tried to block them out. I was sorry I knew. I resented it. I really hated to have to see pictures of bodies and stuff. I felt: *I'm not supposed to know this. I'm a child.* I felt very wise when I was a child. I always wanted to be more of a child and I wasn't—because of that awful knowledge.

"I hated the bits and pieces I heard. If it was snowing, my mother would say, 'I used to have to walk miles and miles in the snow without shoes. Can you imagine that?' I'd look outside and I couldn't imagine it. I remember walking home from school and making things a test for survival. Each block, I used to pretend, was a mile. I remember fantasizing what I would do to Hitler. I would torture him.

"I was very stubborn, very angry as a child. It seemed I was very angry at everyone. I had tantrums. I'd yell. Dinners were always the worst thing. I guess my parents didn't understand how it was possible to have food and not want to eat it. I was always being forced to eat. My mother sighed, my father would get crazy. There's this famous story in my family. I was only three years old and my mother told me to drink my milk. I said, 'No. I'm not going to do you any favors.' My mother told me that a lot. I think she was proud of me for that. She'd say: 'You were such a smart kid, even then.' My parents were pretty permissive. After my foot operation, they were very afraid of losing me. I never pushed it but I knew I could get from my parents whatever I wanted.

"The only thing my parents could not tolerate was when my older brother and I fought. We fought a lot as we were growing up and this would drive them crazy. My father rarely got angry, but he had these outrages whenever anything went wrong in the house, when it was not calm. He never hit me but I thought he'd get angry enough to throw something at me. He wanted everything at home to be peaceful. I began to bottle up my anger as I got older. By the time I was in high school, I was very withdrawn. I felt very ... clutched. I felt I was living just to keep the bad things from getting me. I don't think I felt the whole spectrum of feelings that people feel. I tried to keep myself on a monotone. I lived a very monotone existence."

At high school, Ruth kept to herself. "I had no school spirit and I felt extremely alienated. Even though there were a good number of Jews in the school I always felt there were less than there actually were. I wasn't attracted to the jock and cheerleader clique: I didn't go to football games al-

194

though that was a big thing at school. The smart kids had another clique but I didn't feel part of that. I pledged for a week to a Jewish sorority but that turned me off too. I don't like organizations. They make no sense to me. I was a loner. I couldn't plunge into a group. I felt different from all of them and I *was* different. My parents were older than everyone else's parents. They were European. They didn't play bridge and do all the suburban things that parents in Rochester did. I felt different from the kids who weren't Jewish and I had this hate for American Jews. I didn't understand them and they didn't understand me. To be Jewish in high school meant joining the Jewish social group and going to synagogue. I felt the strongest Jewish experience I had was the Holocaust. *That's* where I identified being Jewish, and not with anything else. I felt very alone."

We walked back into the Alexanders' house and sat down to have coffee. Mrs. Alexander sat down with us. She was, like her daughter, a small, pale woman. Both she and her husband had the pallor and the soft round contours of people who spend most of their time indoors. There was a heaviness to her movements alongside a purposefulness that reminded me of my own mother. She poured us coffee and gave us cake, listening with interest to our conversation. She and her husband were proud that their children were taking an interest in their history, she told me. Of course children of survivors were going to have special problems, she said. It had never occurred to her that they wouldn't. "We all came out a little bit crazy, all of us," she said. Then she shrugged, a movement that seemed to eliminate the need for any doctor's or specialist's opinion. "Of course it affected the children."

Ruth listened to her mother impassively. Then we went into another room and continued our conversation.

"I always felt that my parents had expectations of me that I could never fill," she said. "It's not that they wanted me to *do* something specific. It was more a way they wanted me to be. They expected me to be really happy. They kept saying that they had done everything for me: Why wasn't I happy? In high school I would just sit and be quiet for hours and hours. I felt numb most of the time. My mother used to say, 'When I was your age, I went dancing. I was happy. I didn't mope like you.' I was happy when she said that because it meant there had been something good about her life. I imagined her growing up a very tanned, tall young girl who had a lot of boyfriends. I had no boyfriends. I had a few friends. But basically I was waiting for the time I could leave Rochester. I had this fantasy that I'd find new friends once I left town."

Leaving for college was, for Ruth and most of the other children of survivors I spoke with, the only acceptable way of leaving home. Family separation was more than separation for survivor households. It carried implications of impotence and loss, sometimes death.

"I had gotten a Regents scholarship," Ruth told me, "so when I decided to go to New York University it looked like I was doing the right thing. It was a very legitimate form of running away."

Ruth laughed a short, dry laugh. "When I got to New York, I was really confused. Everything was fast. Everyone was into drugs and sex. I had never been exposed to either. I felt that I was very wise, that I was very aware, but in terms of experience I was less than zero. I felt very lost. My first year I really fucked up at school. I felt like an outsider. I used to go down to the Lower East Side, down to Essex Street, just to look at Chassidic Jews. Just to see their faces. It made me feel that I could have been living among them. That they were who I would have seen had I stayed in Europe. I would look at them as if they had the answer or, at least, as if they had a secret. I was sure they had some kind of secret.

"The people in my dorm and at school seemed very complacent. The dorm was filled with Jewish princesses from

Long Island. They were very well off. They had all this abundance, this superficial life. Nothing really bothered them much. There was a lack of concern. I wanted to find people who had suffered in some way, who had some identifiable pain. I wanted friends who were dissatisfied with the way things were, or who were gutsy, or driven. Maybe it was all that anger in me I was trying to link up with. Anyway the first person I met like that was black. First we were friends. Then we had a very long involvement."

Ruth looked up at me with a faint smile.

"It was, of course, the supreme rebellion against my parents, the greatest rebellion I could have staged, but the fact that he was part of a minority group, that he had a sense of being the underdog, made me feel close to him. I felt more connected to him than I felt to most Jewish people in New York. He was a pretty charismatic character who hung out at the dorm. From Mt. Vernon, tall, a beard, glasses. He seemed aware of things. He seemed to know life pretty well. I wasn't into talking about my background then, but I could relate to pain and to oppression. I could feel something in common with someone who suffered. He seemed to be someone who had a lot of pain inside and, like me, someone who was alone. The relationship was very stormy, on and off a long time before it ended.

"It was during this time that I learned that my mother had been married for two years before the war and that she had had twins."

Ruth stopped here. This part was harder for her to talk about than the rest.

"All my life, she had made remarks to me that someday I might have twins, that twins run in the family. There were no twins I had ever heard of in the family, but I never said that to her. I never said: Well you don't have twins now, Mom. I knew not to say that. I don't know how I knew, but I *knew*. My parents had come to New York to visit me. They didn't approve of my boyfriend and they tried to talk me

197

out of the whole thing. We had an argument, and in the middle of it, my mother said, 'I know you don't think you can fall in love with anyone else but you can. I know. Because I love your father but before him, I loved someone else.' I knew she had been engaged to someone but I didn't know she had actually been married. 'I never told you this,' she said then, 'but I was married to someone else before I married your father and I had twins.'

"That was the first time, that was the *only* time ever with them that I started crying. That upset me more than anything. I was crying really hard and then my mother got upset too. She said she had no idea that it would upset me so much. It stayed on my mind long after they left. I always wondered if somehow they had managed to stay alive. The twins were born in the ghetto. They were taken away right after they were born. My mother told me how her mother told her it would be better this way, that they wouldn't suffer. I always wondered if somehow someone might have rescued them and they were growing up in Poland somewhere not knowing they were Jewish."

Ruth looked down at her small hands, and I thought of Rochelle Rubinstein Kaplan looking at photographs of children at an exhibition in Israel, wondering if one of them might be her half-brother.

"All this, everything about my parents' background, I kept secret up to now. I couldn't talk about it. I thought no one would understand it. Or that someone sensitive enough to understand would be freaked out by it. In college, I might mention it to people I was close to, but it would be in the form of an announcement. They wouldn't pursue it. Maybe it was implicit in the way I told them: you can imagine what went on; you can imagine what my parents are like; you can imagine what I'm like. Case is closed. And even that kind of communication was very personal for me.

"When I was a sophomore everyone was going to a shrink. It was the peak of the fad. A lot of my friends were even going to the same shrink, which really turned me off. I didn't want any part of it. But I was having problems with everything. I had always been an above average student but suddenly I couldn't study. One semester I was put on probation and the school made me see a counselor.

"She talked to me and asked a little bit about my parents. She was the one who convinced me to go to therapy. They gave me tests. How many times have you had sex? Zero to thirty? That's how they would talk, exactly like that. I was twenty-two when I was doing this. I was even quieter than I am now. Very frightened and withdrawn. I was sent to the New York University Clinic and had an appointment with a therapist there.

"It was clear the shrink thought I was yet another stereotypical student: middle-class, female, having typical female college student problems like not knowing what I wanted to do, boyfriend problems, loneliness problems. I was homesick but I didn't want to go home. I didn't want to be in school. I didn't like my roommate. It was very boring. He was just as bored as I was. Then he asked me about my parents. I said they weren't born in this country, that they came to the United States in 1948. That surprised him, as it does most people, because most Jewish refugees came to the United States before the war, in the thirties at the latest. He asked where my parents were during the war and I told him they were in concentration camp."

Here Ruth grinned, and a giggle sneaked out of her throat.

"The psychologist *sat up.* His eyes lit up. I could tell he thought I was really interesting. After all these years of middle-class college girls, finally, a real Case! It made me feel very weird. I wanted to get out of there. I wasn't at all in touch with my parents' experience at that time and I felt he had a lot of nerve getting in there between us. There was such an obvious change in the way he treated me, in the way he even *looked* at me. He rolled out a set of questions that I thought were just insane.

" *'Do they socialize a lot?'* he asked.

199

"And I said, 'No.'

" *'They stay home a lot, don't they? I know they do.'*

"And I said, 'Yes, they do.'

" *'They don't have a lot of friends, do they?'*

"And I said, 'No. They really stick together.' I really didn't know what he was getting at.

" *'They have a lot of intestinal problems, don't they?'* he asked.

"And I said, 'Yes, my father has back problems and intestinal problems.'

"I started to feel very strange. Very uncomfortable. I felt that he didn't know about me and he thought he did. I didn't like the way he started pulling out all those questions. I thought: Who the hell does he think he is? I felt really resentful. I was very angry at my parents at that point and I felt I had to protect these people I was angry at.

"The interview ended then. I was sent to other therapists who gave me a whole battery of tests. I read the results of one where the examiner, who knew nothing of my history, concluded that I was 'pervasively saddened.' I thought that was a good description of me at the time. I thought I came to therapy out of depression or unhappiness. But it wasn't really unhappiness because if you're unhappy you at least have feelings. I was very, very numb. I had no feeling at all.

"I was not the best patient. I was sent to the Yeshiva University Graduate Clinic and for the first year I never, ever talked about my parents. The next year, I was assigned to another therapist, a young Jewish therapist who had been in Vietnam and had worked with the Vietnam War Veterans Rap Groups. He was very curious about the effect of war experiences on people, especially on someone who hadn't been there. I connected more to him because he had been in Vietnam, but I was still very withdrawn. I don't think I started talking for about six months.

"He told me to read *The Survivor* by Terence Des Pres. Reading it brought up a lot of stuff. I carried it around with me. It took me forever to read. I couldn't digest a lot at a time. I could read three, four pages, a chapter at the most. Then I had to do something else right away. I cried a lot reading it. I identified; I put myself there. I couldn't believe my parents had to see this and do that. Things began to make sense to me: why I always expected the worst, why I was always getting myself into painful situations. I always had the attitude: I can take anything—as if I knew I would have to."

Ruth took a breath.

"It wasn't until two years ago, when I was twenty-five, that I connected any difficulty I was having, any part of it at all, to the fact that my parents had been in the war."

TWELVE

I began looking into the professional literature on children of survivors with mixed feelings. Like most of the people I interviewed, many of whom had studied psychology or psychiatry themselves, I disliked the way the psychiatric profession had portrayed our parents. Hundreds of articles and books focused solely on describing Dr. Niederland's "Survivor Syndrome" which had, over the years, become a label stuck to survivors as a group. While it collected demonstrable characteristics many had in common, it also made their condition appear to be an insidious disease contracted in equal measure by every Jew who had survived the Holocaust. "Survivor Syndrome" ignored the strengths that I and other children of survivors had observed in our parents. What was most disturbing to me was that the term set Holocaust survivors apart from other, "normal" people, including the psychiatrists themselves, some of whom had barely escaped concentration camps and shared the prob-

lems of displacement, discontinuity and unresolved mourning. "Survivor Syndrome," it seemed to me, was an
extremely narrow and negative term which did not take into
account historical, cultural and social considerations.

As the Wayne State Conference on Massive Psychic
Trauma and other sources made clear, survivors were part of
a far greater group of people—other, non-Jewish prisoners
who had survived concentration camps under Hitler, under
the Japanese government, in the Soviet Union; prisoners-of-
war who had returned home after being interned in Europe,
Korea or Vietnam; the survivors of Hiroshima and
Nagasaki; and the vast numbers of survivors in every part of
the world, the gypsies, the Armenians, the Asians and Africans who had escaped wholesale slaughter, had been forced
to emigrate, and who had rebuilt their lives elsewhere. All
these people had developed extraordinary survival skills as
well as suffering trauma. The term "Survival Syndrome" did
not address itself to these beneficent changes in personality.
It seemed to imply that a defective human mutant had been
created, intrinsically different from you and me. Novels and
films had elaborated on this characterization, portraying survivors either as saints and martyrs, people who had survived
the worst and could do no wrong; or, alternatively, as little
more than shells of their former selves, near-criminals who
had stooped to inhuman measures in order to prolong their
lives.

Children of survivors knew that the truth was far more
complex. We had all grown up in situations of great com-
plexity, acutely aware of how our parents were driven by an
impetus toward life as well as death. But while many professionals also knew this and personally expressed admiration
and respect for survivors they knew socially or had treated,
the image of the survivor in their writings was overwhelmingly negative.

It was with this knowledge that I began to look into the
psychiatric literature on children of survivors. There was

very little to look at. As late as 1978, when the first crop of my peers was turning thirty-two, there were fewer than two dozen studies which had been published anywhere in the world. Several described less than a handful of cases. Only two could be termed substantive.

This was a surprising find because, by even the most conservative estimates, there are half a million children of survivors alive today. Moreover, they are clearly part of the demographic pool which seeks out psychotherapy: middle-class, college-educated people who live in large metropolitan centers, who have access to health insurance and for whom psychiatrists are more a part of contemporary life than a milkman. Many of the people I interviewed had, in fact, seen some sort of therapist during high school or college. Some had been in psychotherapy for as long as three or four years. But most of them told me they had never talked about the effect their parents' wartime experiences might have had on them. "The shrink never asked," was a common explanation. "It never came up," was another. "I just didn't trust him with that kind of stuff." One young man, now a social worker, found that, "Whenever I talked about it, my therapist said, 'You're an American now,' and I let it drop."

The earliest published writing on children of survivors appeared in 1966, in a small Jewish-Canadian journal called *Viewpoints*. Its author, Dr. Vivian Rakoff, was then Assistant Director of Research at the Jewish General Hospital in Montreal, a city in which several thousand Holocaust survivors had settled. He had deliberately chosen to publish his work in a general rather than professional journal because he was not sure how representative his findings were. His approach was cautious. "Within the last year or two," he wrote, "it has been my experience—similar to that of other psychiatrists—that I am seeing more adolescents than one would expect whose parents are survivors of the Holocaust. In most cases, they are only children ... The parents, the actual victims in these cases, are not conspicuously broken people. Without probing for difficulties and without knowing that they had been in concentration camps, there would not be evoked an easy reflex of pity for their suffering. Yet their children, all of whom were born after the Holocaust, display severe psychiatric symptomatology. It would almost be easier to believe that they, rather than their parents, had suffered the corrupting, searing hell.

"I am aware that not all children of survivors display such symptomatology but ... how many have suffered with the same quality but less quantity?"

Rakoff went on to describe three case studies. His first patient had been a sixteen-year-old girl, the best student in her class according to her teachers, who at exam time became convinced that she knew nothing and would "at last be exposed." She had been examined by a neurologist because she fainted frequently, had intense migraine headaches, and had suffered paralysis of her legs for six months. The neurologist found nothing organically wrong with the girl.

In subsequent interviews with her family Rakoff pieced together a story similar to many I had reconstructed in my own interviews. Both parents were sole survivors of their families. They met after the war, the girl was born in a Displaced Persons camp and they arrived almost penniless in Canada. They lived in a working class neighborhood and both parents worked sixteen hours a day in an effort to establish themselves. By the mid-sixties they owned their own house, enjoyed music and skiing, but continued to work hard. This was what the father had done in concentration camps. "I kept myself very busy," he told Rakoff. "I kept myself very busy." His wife claimed to have survived by becoming a shadow. "I gave them my name when I had to," she told Rakoff, "and the rest of the time I tried to disappear." Their daughter, with a smile on her face, listened to them explain. She had heard these explanations many times before. "Although both [parents] had told the story of their survival many times and apparently believed their individual reasons for having escaped," Rakoff noted, "it did not take much probing for them to admit that they had no real idea of the reason for their survival. They had used these explanations for years to give a semblance of rationality to their lives and therefore some rationality to their total existence in the post-war world."

The two other children of survivors Rakoff described had both attempted suicide before they were nineteen.

The first was the eighteen-year-old son of parents who had married after the war, "with the explicit understanding that they were marrying for companionship, in an attempt to fill the vast loneliness of their lives after the concentration camps were liberated."

The mother had been married before the war and her only child had been murdered. The father was a passive figure, absorbed in his work and depressive. Their son told Rakoff that his repeated suicide attempts, like his threats to kill his parents, were ultimate expressions of anger at them. "I have been existing for the past some odd seventeen years," he wrote in one of his suicide notes, "and as of tonight I hope I shall *cease to exist.*"

The third patient, a girl, also displayed a terrible anger against her parents, who retained the ambitions of pre-war German Jewry for their daughter. Their arguments centered around religion and politics, with the parents taking the stance of Canadian patriots and their daughter emphasizing only the flaws in Canadian culture.

The three cases, Rakoff conceded, could have been three case histories selected at random from almost any psychiatric clinic dealing with adolescents. However, he noted, they shared striking features that were different from the bulk of adolescents he had treated. All three had been born in Europe, were intimately aware of their parents' concentration camp experience, and had been relatively good and obedient children, protected from a world their parents perceived as hostile. Their difficulties had surfaced during adolescence when the first girl had become "phobic," the boy had become "an untameable, pleasure-seeking, hysterical, histrionic teenager whose only concern was to get kicks out of life," and the last had become "argumentative, sullen and so depressed that when she finally could not stand the tension between herself and her parents she tried to kill herself."

Rakoff noted that the three bore a heavier load of parental expectation than most children. "These parents," he wrote, "by virtue of their concentration camp experiences, have become almost sacred figures. The children were ceaselessly exposed to the story of the parents' sufferings and more than normal children they felt guilty when they disobeyed or misbehaved. They could not express toward their parents the aggression that is part of the usual process of growing up. When the growth of their bodies and emotional maturation in adolescence necessitated some expression of independence and of dammed-up anger against the parents, it could only emerge in a distorted form.

"A life that is not simply a 'given' but an almost unexpected gift, may seem to be not a life to be lived, but a mission," Rakoff concluded. "It is almost as if the parents, in an attempt to justify their survival, demanded qualities of the children which were the accumulation of their expectations of all the dead who were murdered. The love and ambitions of whole families were resurrected in memory and imposed as hopes on the children, who were expected to supply the gratifications normally coming from mothers, fathers, brothers, sisters, cousins, uncles and aunts, and to live out in their lifetimes those truncated lives."

Over the next few years, Rakoff and his colleague, psychologist John Sigal, continued to examine the case histories of children of survivors who turned up at the Jewish General Hospital in Montreal. By 1972 they had seen 144 survivor families, enough to justify mounting a formal study. They applied to various funding agencies: Canadian, American, Jewish, scientific, but despite their success at obtaining grants in other areas they could get no funding for this research. "I think people thought we were 'making research,'" Rakoff told me later. The case studies, however, continued to accumulate, regardless. In 1973, Rakoff and Sigal, joined by two more colleagues, published "Some Second-Generation Effects of the Survival of the Nazi Persecution," the first systematic study of children of survivors. Their premise was that a homogeneity of parental experiences may lead to a particular homogeneity of behavior in their children. They found that a clinical sample of mid-teenage children of survivors did, in fact, have more behavioral and other disturbances and less adequate coping behavior than a clinical control group.

The researchers emphasized that they had studied only those survivor families that had sought help, and had no data at all on those who did not. But the problems and tendencies they discovered were consistent with earlier clinical observations.

Children of survivors tended to report greater feelings of alienation than the children in the control group. Survivors perceived their children as being more disturbed than parents of the control group perceived their children. Children of survivors appeared to be more dependent on their parents than the control, and also had more difficulty coping.

John Sigal explained these differences chiefly as a result of parental preoccupation. Survivor parents, he found, "are an extremely preoccupied group, preoccupied with the unending mourning of the loss of their parents, siblings, etc., and with the various psychological and physical illnesses that have beset them since the war. Because they are so preoccupied, they respond to their children's normal robust activity and need for control as an interference with this mourning process or as an extra burden imposed on their already taxed resources. As a result, the children become anxious and more disruptive."

In Detroit, Dr. Henry Krystal extrapolated another reason for the children's disruptive behavior. Survivor parents, he postulated, might unconsciously encourage aggressive behavior in their children, aggression they themselves could not permit themselves to express toward their own dead families. None of the researchers took this point farther, but it seemed to me that survivor parents also took a secret delight in their children's aggressiveness because during the war, whether the parents were in concentration camps or in hiding, they could not allow themselves to express the aggression they felt toward their oppressors. To do so would be to invite death.

The great degree of dependence the researchers observed in survivor children might be related, they thought, to the children's fear of their own bottled-up aggression, and to their fear of the outside world. "In adolescence," they wrote, "the difficulties become compounded by the usual identity crises typical of that age. Identifying with their parents would lead to anomie and depression, and the guilt over not doing so could have the same consequences."

The studies conducted at the Jewish General Hospital in Montreal were buttressed by the work of Dr. Bernard Trossman, who in the late sixties began to see children of survivors appearing at the Student Mental Health Clinic at McGill University, also in Montreal. Their problems ranged from academic difficulties to stuttering. They all shared the same family history as Rakoff's first three patients. Trossman found several common features among his group.

"The first and perhaps most innocuous," he wrote, "is that these parents are excessively overprotective, constantly warning their children of impending danger.... Consequently, many of the children have become moderately phobic, others locked in combat with their parents as they try to throw off the smothering yoke.

209

"Another feature consists of the child being used as the audience in the relentless recounting of their terrifying memories. It is hard to assess the effect of this since the student often treats it with bored disdain. It is likely to contribute to pathology of a depressive nature—the student feeling guilty about his better fortune.

"A third frequently-met family outlook consists in two bitter, hardened Jewish parents presenting a suspiciously hostile attitude to the Gentile world around them and expecting their children to follow suit. We see the children in the phase of active rebellion, where they may insist on dating non-Jewish partners to their parents' mounting rage or as in one humorous yet pathetic situation, an angry young girl failed all her subjects but one—German!

"Perhaps the most deleterious parental attitude is the spoken or unspoken communication that this child must provide meaning for the parents' empty lives ... Thus the expectations on the child are enormous. He is treated not as an individual but as a heavily invested symbol of the New World ... High parental expectations are difficult for any college student but the redemption of unhappy lives is well nigh an impossibility, and so many even good students either give up in despair or seethingly rebel."

Trossman found that in several survivor families, one of the parents had ceded parental responsibility entirely, continuing the "shadow identity" adopted during the war years. "I haven't got a father," one of his patients told him. "The war killed him. He is a weak and frightened man." In such families, the children experienced great difficulty in identity formation, especially when "the emotionally absent parent" was of the same sex.

At about the same time Rakoff, Sigal and Trossman were working in Montreal, children of Holocaust survivors began turning up in the office of Henry Shaw, Director of the Hillel Foundation at Monash University in Melbourne, Australia. Shaw was not working in a clinic, but as director of the Hillel Foundation he did a certain amount of student counseling, and was well acquainted with the Jewish population in the State of Victoria, Australia. That community, which lived almost entirely in Melbourne, numbered 35,000 Jews, and a high proportion of them were post-war immigrants. By the late sixties, Shaw had noticed that many of the students he counseled were children of survivors and, unaware that anyone elsewhere in the world was studying them, began to keep his own records.

"There is a particular Melbourne pattern of these survivor problems," he wrote to me in 1975. "A man who lost his wife and kids in Auschwitz meets a woman who lost her husband and kids in Buchenwald. They get together in a DP camp and there is just enough 'time' for the woman to have a baby. They get away from Europe—as far away as possible, some of them say—and settle in Australia in the 1950s. There is a great economic expansion, they become rich in a few years. Property deals, textiles, the usual business. The kids I meet have parents who are old enough to be their grandparents. They can't speak English too well, are terribly protective, and grudge their children nothing. The kids treat them with contempt. The parents have one fear—their children must not mix with Gentiles.

"An overwhelmingly large proportion of the Jewish students in Melbourne are the sons and daughters of 'New Australians.' With parental memories of Europe during the Holocaust years and the sudden transition from imminent death to affluence, an unusual tension develops between the parents and children, a 'chasm' rather than a 'generation gap.' All Jewish welfare agencies speak of this difficult relationship.

"A typical outburst (by no means an isolated instance) made to me by a brilliant honours student was, 'I hear about Europe, the Nazis and anti-Semitism every day of my life. I'm fed up with it. If I have to meet anti-Jewish agitation, I want to do it my way. I'm responsible for my own future.' If I dare to suggest to members of 'The Association of Victims of Nazi Persecutions' that they should stop talking about Auschwitz to their children so frequently, they look upon me as if I were completely unsympathetic. Many of them have no Jewish association or affiliation other than the memory of their wartime experience. Most of them expect a kind of 'privileged' position and expect their children (in some cases their second families) to relive their lives with them. Additionally, the university-trained young men and women have little in common intellectually with their parents and the clash of intellectual attitudes as well as their totally different experience tends to create severe problems.

"This is likely to be a problem," Shaw concluded, "for a good many years."

In Israel, despite its large survivor population, there is an amazing dearth of information about children of survivors. "None of the many medical congresses held in this country after the war concerned itself with these [survivor] problems," wrote R. Z. Winnik in the *Israel Annals of Psychiatry* in 1969. "Only as late as July, 1967, the Psychoanalytical Society held its first symposium dealing with the psychotherapeutic experience of its members in the treatment of Nazi victims."

The only systematic study of children of survivors living in Israel published to date is by Hillel Klein, who between 1967 and 1970 interviewed twenty-five survivor families living in three *kibbutzim*, the collective settlements. The group he studied was significantly different from the ones observed in Canada and Australia. It was unusual in Israel as well. Most survivors who emigrated to Israel did not settle in *kibbutzim*, in part because the communal way of life reminded them too much of the camp experiences they wanted to put behind them. There is, however, one kibbutz in Israel, *Lohamei Ha'Ghetta'ot*, in which the majority of members are survivors, and other *kibbutzim* where they constitute a distinct minority.

Klein's group had rather specific characteristics which distinguished it from the more heterogeneous communities of survivors elsewhere. All the families originally came from Poland; most had been adolescents during the war; most came from the lower-middle class and had belonged to Zionist youth organizations before 1939; and at least one partner in each marriage had joined with the partisans in Nazi-controlled Europe or else had escaped to the Soviet zone. Perhaps because they were a younger group, most had not married directly after the war was over. Some had waited up to seven years to marry. The oldest child in each family had been born four to eight years after liberation and was raised entirely in the kibbutz.

All of the survivors, Klein found, had gone through an acute emotional crisis within three years after liberation but none sought psychiatric help. Almost all fifty had been left without close family and while their death was provable, the survivors tended to deny it. They continued to fantasize that someone had survived, had emigrated to another part of the world, and would eventually be found. The survivors also fantasized, Klein found, of being rewarded for their suffering through special treatment by their fellow kibbutz members or special considerations for vacations or work arrangements. Many had expected Israel to be a mother, who would make up to them for their pain. Here they were disappointed, for the country first became engaged in its War of Independence and then began a harsh period of severe economic recession.

Survivor parents in kibbutz, like those elsewhere, saw in their children a source of security and gratification. They tended to spend more time together than non-survivor families in kibbutz and "the dominant motif in the family seems to be the restoration of the lost family and the undoing of destruction." Their children, like almost all children of sur-

213

vivors, were named after relations who had been murdered in Europe, and the parents seemed to experience them as magical replacements. That the children were healthy and all in one piece seemed a continual blessing to them. During pregnancy, some of the mothers had been sure that they would give birth to monsters. Even after the children were born, the parents worried that they themselves had been damaged and that their children had inherited that damage. "We have such good children in spite of all the persecutions we have suffered," was a remark often expressed to Klein.

None of the children he studied showed any conspicuous disturbance in behavior, although ten of the twenty-five children bit their nails or sucked their thumbs. At school, their performance was above average. They showed very high intelligence and verbal ability. Moreover, Klein noticed several tendencies which seemed to characterize them as a group.

"The youngsters show an unconscious denial of conflict situations with the world of surrounding adults—parents, teachers, and homeroom teachers—and avoidance of overt expressions of anger or aggression toward parents," he wrote. "There is a marked tendency [on psychological tests] to change frightening situations into pleasant ones, and to invent happy and positive endings. Denial is prominent where aggression-provoking situations are represented, especially when they are confronted with separation and death.

"When confronted with open aggression (from children and adults as well) or with the danger of war, the children's tendency is to react passively, to escape, to hide, to cry, to stick to the group of children and not to respond by active aggression. When they observe children fighting, they try to persuade them to stop or ask for adult help."

Klein found that all the children tended to stay as much as possible with their parents which, in the setting of kibbutz, is fairly unusual. Because parents and children do not live together, and because parenting is shared with other kibbutz members, many kibbutz children are extremely casual about spending time with their mothers and fathers. Children of survivors, Klein found, disliked any kind of separation, even for a short trip. "There is a wish to protect the parent who survived the Holocaust—to take special care of him and to avoid asking any questions that might hurt him. There is severe anxiety aroused by separation from family members, educators, or friends, and a great deal of emotional energy is mobilized in the avoidance of separation or denial of it."

During his interviews, Klein reported, the children showed a very low tolerance toward traumatic memories of the past. "The children tend to emphasize the heroism of the parents," he wrote. "They are proud of the active part their parents took during the persecutions and even today as defenders, saviors, or representatives of the persecuted. There is no reference to suffering or any traumatic situation which occurred to the parents. It seems there is a common denial by the children and the parents who never tell about the suffering and the torture they went through in the ghetto or the concentration camp. They handle this memory like a common secret: they negate and deny."

Children of survivors in the kibbutz, Klein noted, did not identify fully with the victimization of their parents. "They view the past somehow as a lost battle," he wrote, "compensated for by more recent victorious ones leading to the rebirth of Israel." The kibbutz setting in which they lived provided them with a super-family in place of the relatives who were lost. All lived, studied and worked within the framework of a peer group. They and their parents belonged to a community in which they bore some responsibility for decision-making. Also, Klein found that survivor parents worried less about justifying their own survival in kibbutz than elsewhere in the world. "As the years passed, survival has been seen by them to be part of a total situation in the service of national survival ... aggression could be turned against an external enemy (the Arabs) and the feelings of humiliation, degradation, and helplessness which had to be endured during the Nazi persecution could be corrected through victory. In addition, the futility of the suffering is denied with the idea that it was a necessary historical development which led to the rebirth of Israel. In some fantasies expressed by the survivors, there is a kind of resurrection of their own communities and families as well as of their own fathers and mothers."

In general, Klein found survivor families in the kibbutz setting far more integrated into their society than survivors elsewhere. The survivors he spoke with were satisfied with their positions in life and thought that their war experiences had not diminished their capacities. "On the other hand," he wrote, "their fear of the possibility that their families might be destroyed is conscious and manifest, and sometimes very realistic as during the Six-Day War or in other dangerous situations. Still, the survivors and their children have a profound fear of being sadists or aggressors. During the war with the Arabs they had the need to repetitively stress its defensive character. The war and its danger were identified with their own experience ... The first realization of victory gave rise in the survivors to an uneasiness with the new role of victors. They had the need to deny identification with the aggressor and to justify aggression as defensive and temporary."

In the kibbutz, Klein concluded, the past did not manifest itself openly in the everyday activities and concerns of survivors. Their children knew no more specific historical facts about the war than children from other families.

The Child Guidance Clinic of Shalvata Hospital in Tel Aviv also saw survivor families but there, according to L. Rosenberger, survivor parents fell into two categories. The first type appeared to disregard their children's emotional needs and, instead, to shower them with material possessions. This reaction was interpreted as a response to the

216

material deprivation survivors had suffered during the war. The second type of parents were those who attempted to relive their childhoods through their children and often used them for gratification they could not find elsewhere. Both groups were apt to interfere with their children's therapy when the process began to threaten their children's dependence on them.

The few professionals writing in the United States corroborated most of the Canadian and Israeli findings. "Among these children one sees apathy, the inability to formulate professional goals, a preoccupation with reliving traumatic experiences," wrote Dr. Henry Krystal, who worked with survivor families in Detroit. Other researchers reported that children of survivors tended to be "anxious, depressed and somewhat estranged from society," and passively accepted their parents' wishes, particularly in ethnic or religious matters. Some pointed out that the survivor's child learns depression as a primary response to stress of any kind. Others pointed out reactions of extreme guilt and hostility, and confusion about Jewish identity. All cited patterns of ambivalence in the feelings of survivors' children. "Guilt seems to be quickly infused into any hostile thoughts directed toward the parents," wrote Stephen Karr in 1973, after studying a non-clinical group in the San Francisco Bay area. Another ambivalence concerned success. While most children of survivors complained of the high expectations their parents had for them, some also felt that they had received an implicit message not to succeed, not to exceed the levels of achievement that their parents had set.

In 1969, New York psychoanalyst Judith Kestenberg began examining the question of second generation effects of the Holocaust. A few years before, she had analyzed a young adolescent, "who behaved in a bizarre way, starving himself, hiding in woods," and treating her as a "hostile persecutor." She soon made the connection between her patient's behavior and the experiences of his family in Europe during the war. "Haunted by the image of this patient, who came to me emaciated and hollow-eyed like a Musulman in a concentration camp," she wrote later, "I looked at children of survivors in Israel and thought that I could recognize in some faces a faraway look, reminiscent of the stare of survivors from persecution."

Kestenberg subsequently devised and sent off 320 questionnaires to psychoanalysts in six countries, asking them if they had analyzed any children of survivors and, if so, whether their analyses were characterized by any special features. She found that only twenty children of survivors had been analyzed, and that she was able to draw more certain conclusions about the analysts than the patients she had originally sought information about.

"On the basis of rather uniform experiences in America, Europe and Israel," she wrote, "we may fairly generalize that psychoanalysts themselves resist the unearthing of the frightening impact of Nazi persecution on children of survivors. Attitudes of psychoanalysts revealed themselves directly and indirectly, ranging from great interest in the topic to forgetting they had seen the questionnaire. A vast majority of those questioned revealed an amazing indifference to the problem. Some regretted that parent-survivors who consulted them did not follow through on their recommendation for analyses of their children. Some were startled by the questions because it never occurred to them to link their patients' dynamics to the history of their parents' persecution."

Nevertheless, by the mid-seventies, the notion that certain characteristics of Holocaust survivors were apt to appear in their children who had never been inside a bunker or concentration camp was widely accepted. In 1977, when an Israeli psychiatrist who had been treating survivor families in the Shalvata Psychiatric Clinic in Tel Aviv, took a sabbatical at Stanford University in California, he found colleagues there who had been conducting their own research. Stanford University Medical School had an excellent press service, and when Shamai Davidson, the visiting scholar from Israel, began to lecture on his findings, the service sent press releases of the data to several American publications. *Time* magazine published a paragraph on Davidson's research. Suddenly the question of "Second Generation Effects of the Nazi Holocaust" became a hot topic. Conferences of various professional groups were planned around it; doctoral students in sociology and psychology began to write their theses about it: the field which had once been the province of a few scattered researchers now became a prime target of investigation.

At first, it appeared that children of survivors and their concerns would be defined entirely by the professional community, as had largely been the case with our parents. But there were important differences between the two generations. Our parents had moved into their new countries late in life. They were not, for the most part, engaged in academic or professional pursuits. Many did not have the language facility necessary to speak publicly about themselves. Although many were angered by the way they as a group were represented to the world at large, they lacked the contacts and the emotional energy required to correct that image.

Children of survivors, on the other hand, were an extremely well-educated group in each of the countries to which their parents had emigrated. Those who had been raised in the United States, particularly, were sophisticated in areas of which our parents were ignorant. While our parents had come from an extremely wide social spectrum that included poverty, illiteracy and the parochialism of *shtetl* life on one extreme, as well as highly assimilated, cosmopolitan European intellectualism on the other, we were, by and large, middle-class. We had grown up during the sixties at a time of great psychological awareness, when

219

group after group became involved in examining concerns that were more than individual problems. We watched women, blacks, homosexuals, ethnics, even *block associations,* organize, brainstorm and air vital issues. Some of us joined other groups but we did not, at first, form our own. Most of the people I interviewed expressed a distaste for large rallies or demonstrations of the kind that were popular among students in the sixties. They spoke of an uneasiness in crowds, regardless of whether people had come together to protest the American military involvement in Vietnam or to express solidarity with the women's movement. Moreover, most children of survivors I spoke with had never been active members of any organization. Almost all described themselves in one way or another as "loners" or people who did not like groups. "I never thought of myself as a child of survivors," several people told me, with some dismay at the fact that they constituted part of a larger entity.

As I talked to more and more of my contemporaries, I began to feel that they were all carrying around a version of my iron box, the contents of which they had left unexamined and untouched, for fear it might explode. It also became clear to me that our parents' wartime experiences had not given rise to a handful of clinically categorized symptoms but to a particular world view. Our parents' past had been, whether we admitted it or not, a dominant influence on the basic choices we had made in our lives. In some cases, as Judith Kestenberg and other professionals had remarked, children of survivors seemed to be actually living out either the actual experience some of their relatives had undergone during the war or, more dramatically, the lives they might have lived out had they been free to act.

THIRTEEN

When Albert Singerman first walked into my apartment in the spring of 1977, he frightened me. A short, well-built man with a sandy mustache, receding dark brown hair, and muscular arms, he looked ready to knock someone flat. He was wearing a wool sweater, blue jeans and a stained olive-green army jacket, an indication to me and the world at large of his identity as a Vietnam war veteran. "All my friends are Vietnam war veterans," he said shortly after he came in and that announcement served to draw a distinct boundary between us.

Al Singerman had actually been in a war, living out what the rest of us had only imagined. He had been a soldier. Killing people had been his job. That thought triggered in me a variety of reactions ranging from awe and fear to the same kinds of suspicions I had heard expressed about survivors. What had he done? Had he killed many people? Was he liable to do anything weird?

The realization that I was thinking these things embarrassed me. *Don't be idiotic,* I told myself. *If you didn't know he was a veteran, you couldn't pick him out of an office full of young accountants wearing glasses.* Still, I felt uneasy. So did Al. He had been interviewed before, during the time he was an anti-war activist, and he didn't much like journalists. Reporters had a way, he said, of asking stupid, stereotyped questions to which there was no way of replying. He hoped I'd be different, he said. And so we sat down. Nervously.

Al talked in short, throwaway phrases, like a sportscaster tracking the progress of a hockey game. He had begun his anti-war activities, he said, by helping to put out and distribute an anti-war newspaper while still stationed at an army base. He had married early, completed a master's degree in accounting and become a member of the Vietnam war veterans' Rap Groups. Had I seen the book about them? Yes, I said, I had. He was thirty now. He worked for a large American bank. He lived on Staten Island with his wife Miriam and five-year-old daughter and was very proud of being a father. "I'm the best on the block, I want you to know," he said. "When I come home from work, it's not only my daughter, all the kids come running."

Miriam's parents were the Mr. and Mrs. Fiszman whose arrival in the United States on the S.S. *Marine Flasher* was noted by the *Boston Herald-Traveler.* Both the Singerman and Fiszman families were from Poland. Miriam was twenty-nine and taught children with learning disabilities. They had been married nine years and although Al said he had been impossible to live with during a good part of that time, the marriage had somehow survived. Their common background probably had something to do with that, Al said, although he and Miriam had never once discussed the Holocaust. "I'm not sure we can," he told me.

Both Al and Miriam had been born in Displaced Persons camps in Germany and came to the United States as small children. Miriam's parents first settled in the South Bronx

222

but when a neighbor's child was mugged shortly after their arrival, they repacked their metal suitcases, sold the furniture they had just bought, and moved to Brooklyn. By the time Al was twelve, his family had moved to Brooklyn too. Both remembered their fathers working long hours—Al's as a tailor; Miriam's as a capmaker—to establish a foothold in America. Their mothers were strikingly different. Miriam remembers her mother walking the half-mile to elementary school with her every morning until she was in the sixth grade to make sure that she arrived safely; Al claimed to have never felt any solicitude from his mother at all. "She once said, 'People like me shouldn't raise children,' and I think that was true," he told me. "Neither of my parents are really capable of showing love or affection. My mother especially. The camps had just screwed up her mind. She never could go to work. She was just too nervous a person to tolerate anything."

The two met when Al was eighteen. Miriam's family had moved into the house his parents owned, and Al's mother had sent him downstairs to paint the kitchen cabinets for the new tenants.

Now they lived in a row of semi-attached duplexes on Staten Island in a neighborhood that had the shorn, raw look of a new development. The homeowners on their block were policemen, firemen, and white-collar workers, many of Italian descent, and their yards were strewn with tricycles, red wagons, and picnic equipment. The Singermans liked living there. They took their five-year-old daughter Jennifer for walks along the beach that fronted New York Harbor. They had barbecues in their backyard. Their home was open to the neighborhood children who came over to play. Neither the uninspired, prefab architecture of the houses that impinged on theirs, nor the fact that they were at least forty minutes from Manhattan disturbed them. Their lives were centered around their home and their daughter. They were planning a second baby.

223

When Al grew restless, which he sometimes did, he got behind the wheel of his low-slung Datsun 280 Z, his one extravagance, and sped off across the Verrazzano Narrows bridge to the expressways. It was his way of relaxing, and of figuring out what was on his mind. He often remembered things when he was driving that were inaccessible to him at other times. When he arrived at my apartment to continue our interviews, the drive would have often dredged up bits of dreams or half-remembered scenes from his childhood. Like several children of survivors I had talked to, Al Singerman found it very difficult to remember much of what he was like before he was a teen-ager.

"I've repressed a tremendous amount. I must've blocked it all out," he said, and his face gave way to an unexpectedly engaging grin. "I think the reason I can't remember must have something to do with my parents and that they were in the camps, but I don't know for sure. That subject is very important to me. I'd say since the age of about nine or ten I can't remember a time when it wasn't on my mind. At times, it's completely engrossed me. I've always had a rage about it and nowhere to go with it. I've never talked about it with anyone before. It's damn hard to talk about."

I asked Al what he knew about his family's activities before the war but he could recall very little. He knew his parents had come from Lodz, Poland, and that his father had been married before and had children in his first marriage. He knew nothing about his mother. "I'm not one hundred percent sure where they were during the war," Al said. "I think my father was in Auschwitz. Both of them were in the camps and they went in early. My father was a tailor and they used him to make uniforms. I don't really know where my mother was. I've always been afraid to ask. I don't know the names of the brothers and sisters who died. I don't know how many there were. Both my parents came from very large families and I must have been told. Of course I was told. But I don't remember."

Al's earliest memory was of moving to a new apartment when he was seven years old. The new place had three rooms: a kitchen and two tiny bedrooms. "There was no living room, there were mice, and this was moving up so you can imagine what kind of place we lived in before," Al said emphatically. "When we went to look at it, I remember my mother getting me to promise to behave myself if we moved, that we wouldn't move unless I promised to be good. I was constantly getting into trouble. Really *bad* trouble. Once I threw a rock at a kid that nearly took his eye out. I always beat up other kids. People on the block wanted to send me to reform school and my mother would tear up and down the street telling people she wouldn't stand for my being taken away. I wished they *would* take me away. I always wanted to get away from her."

Al leaned back in his chair and shook his head.

"I always think in terms of my mother. I never say 'my parents' or even mention my father because it's as if he was never there. I cannot remember him. Until my teen-age years, I barely remember my father being alive. The only reason I remember him at all was that I used to have to beg him to play ball with me. Just to toss a *ball* back and forth!

"He used to just sit there and fall out. He'd sit there like a fixture, staring at nothing. He read the paper—he read *The Forward,* in Yiddish—and then he'd go to sleep. I used to yell at him, '*You're not my father!* You never act like a father to me!' Then he used to tell me that when I was two, he carried me on his back, that he went to work so that we had a place to live and brought home food. What else did I need?"

Al looked at me, as if to ask how I would have felt if my father had said that to me. Then he shrugged.

"That was it for him. I saw my friends' fathers do things with their sons. They'd go fishing with them. They'd play ball with them. They'd *talk* to them. I felt as if I never had a father at all. I was ashamed of him. He was like a nebbish.

He was completely out of it and I felt myself becoming the same way. I didn't know how to act as a man. It was almost impossible for me to make friends with boys and, later on, with men. I had no concept of how men behaved together.

"My mother was always an extremely nervous person. Very highstrung. She always had a closetful of pills because every ailment in the world, she had. She used to faint at the drop of a hat. Anything that involved stress, she just couldn't take. During the Eichmann trial, she did a real swan dive. She had a nervous breakdown and a relative from Nebraska came to stay with us for a while. My mother was more of an active person than my father. She liked to go to the movies. To read books. To go places. But my father never wanted to go anywhere. He just wanted to sit home and rot."

The bitterness in his voice made me want to find something in his home that he had been proud of. Hadn't he had any good times alone with his mother? Hadn't they gone places together? If he was such a good father, wasn't it likely that he had learned some of it at home? Nothing?

Al insisted that he could not remember any moments of levity or gladness at home. "You don't understand something," he kept telling me. "In my house, people didn't talk to each other. My father stared into space. My mother screamed at my brother and me. When we disobeyed her, she would yell at us: *Enemy of Israel! Enemy of the Jews!* She yelled in Yiddish. That I was not a Jew because I didn't obey her. Boy did I hate that. Because I knew what she was talking about. I knew she meant it in the same way as she talked about the Germans.

"I knew about the war," Al said, raising his voice as if I were trying to start an argument with him. "It seemed they never talked to me *except* to tell me what the Germans had done to them. I was told that my mother was struck in the head. My father told me they did things to his hands, his nails, his back. They pulled out his fingernails and they beat

226

him. You can see that something was done to his finger-nails—they grow all bent—and he's had trouble with his back as long as I can remember.

"There's probably a lot more that they talked about but the only thing I remember is the torture. I was able to sit and listen to it for maybe ten minutes. At most, fifteen. They would want to go on and talk and talk and talk. I'd have to yell to stop them. I'd have to block my ears and yell *'I don't want to hear!'* or leave the room to make them stop. They felt I had to know. They never explained to me *why* I had to know but I had to know. I don't know what made my mother the way she is. I think she was an unhappy person before, and the war only made things worse. I've always been afraid to ask what actually happened to her, where she was. I think I don't want to know."

I asked what Al was afraid to hear.

He smiled, his cheeks dimpling like a small boy's. "God-awful things."

"What specifically?"

"The worst."

"Like what?"

"That she had been raped."

Both of us were silent. I had often thought about that possibility in regard to my own mother. In wars, women were always raped. In *The Pawnbroker,* a film both Al and I had seen as teen-agers, female concentration camp inmates were shown working as prostitutes, waiting naked in small rooms until the next S.S. officer entered. That image too had been forced down into my iron box and now it hung in the air between us. I had never had the courage to ask my mother whether it had happened to her.

"I guess that's been in the back of my mind for a long time," Al said softly. "I've never even said it out loud before. It's hard to even say ... but I don't really think she was raped. Because she was with her family, I think, throughout the whole thing. The whole family went in very early, in

227

1939, and they managed to stay together during the war. My mother's father died at the very end of it, a few days before they were liberated. He died on a forced march. My mother also had a younger brother who was sixteen at the end of the war. They went back to Poland together after the war was over, and he was killed by the Poles. I was devastated when I found that out. I found that out recently, this past year.

"When I was a kid, I couldn't stand them talking about anything that had to do with the war. They would show me pictures of the family and I didn't want to see them. I would get enraged. I would get furious. I couldn't look at them."

"Why?" I asked him.

"Why? I don't know why," he said. "Look, when they talk to you about the camps and the torture and they show you pictures of the dead relatives, they don't have to tell you they're angry. You *feel* it. It's in the air. But at the age of ten, what are you going to do with that? When they talked about the family I got enraged that they were all *dead*. That stands out in my mind. The fact that they were all dead, and I couldn't do *anything* about it."

His response was twofold. He picked fights with almost every other boy in the neighborhood and with his younger brother, who also was developing a reputation as a tough, disruptive kid. And he withdrew. From the time he was a small child, Al had liked school. He remembers doing his homework as a way of tuning out what was going on in his household. Also as a child, he was very religious while his parents were not. That gave him an excuse to spend Friday nights and all day Saturdays with his religiously observant relatives whose household he preferred vastly to his own.

By the time he was fourteen, Al says, he had made his break with his parents. "They didn't know how to cope with my brother and me. My mother would complain to my father and he'd come roaring into the room and start beating us up. He was never around when I needed him, but always there to beat us up. When I was fourteen, I hit him over the shoulders with a chair and threatened to kill him if he ever came near us again."

Al Singerman straightened his back and held up his head. "I took a job in a grocery store and from that time on, I supported myself. I made my own money. I bought my own clothes. I came and went as I pleased. That's the way it was. I started working out with weights at that time too. I was enraged by the idea that in the war, Jews didn't fight, that they were passive. At least, that's all I knew at the time. I wasn't going to be that kind of a Jew. I was going to fight."

At the same time Al was concerned with building up his body and running his life by himself, he felt an ever-stronger undercurrent pulling him away from activity of any kind. "Starting at fourteen," he told me, "I remember wanting to be dead. If my parents hadn't survived the war, I wouldn't have been born, I thought. Death was something good. I hated my parents. I felt afraid to talk to another person. I didn't know how to befriend a person. I didn't trust anyone. It got so bad that in school I wouldn't answer when my teachers called on me. You can imagine how whacked out I was. I was in another world. And yet I continued to do well in school. I read a lot. Science fiction and Russian novels. Nothing about the Holocaust. I just couldn't take it. Not even the *Diary of Anne Frank.* I read science fiction because I liked anything unreal. The Russian novels I read because I saw the people in them destroying themselves, and that was what I saw myself doing."

When he was sixteen, Al Singerman decided to see a psychiatrist. He went to two appointments, but found himself unable to trust the man. And his parents were against it. It cost too much money, they said. "By this time, things were so bad," Al recalled, "that I just lay in bed and stared at the ceiling for hours at a time. I went to City College, to major in engineering. I had a girl friend then, a steady girl friend who lasted about two years. We never got close. She never knew the first thing about me. We had sex but sex for me was another weapon, a way of hurting people. I was off in my own world. Nothing touched me.

"At eighteen, my second year of college, it was almost impossible for me to concentrate. I decided to go to therapy, quit college and take a job. I didn't know one shrink from the next and so I wound up with an analyst. I lay on this guy's couch for five months talking about my dreams and why I thought there were no grown-up people in them. He'd be taking notes and all I ever got out of him were grunts and nods. Great profession! I felt like I was getting worse instead of better and I didn't even know what was bothering me. I never told the therapist my parents were in the camps. He never asked me. I don't think that, at the time, I had the slightest idea that any of my problems had to do with that."

Al Singerman sighed. "Well, the army seemed the perfect place to go into. I wanted to get lost. I wanted to go someplace where nobody would see or care that I was around. Like in a big sea. Everyone else I knew was trying to get *out* of the army. I volunteered. By that time I was nineteen, a walking vacuum. I was so numb you could have banged *nails* into me and I wouldn't have felt it. Going into the army seemed the natural thing to do. I'd been watching war movies on television all my life. I had an obsession with them when I was a kid. I loved to watch the Germans get killed.

"At the time I joined the army, I knew I'd be going to Vietnam. There were a couple of times—two, three times— when I realized what I was getting into and I felt a sort of panic. But it went away. I felt good about going. I had the sense that finally, in Vietnam, I could prove that I, too, could be a survivor.

"I didn't realize till a long time after I came back that growing up I had felt my parents' rage and that I had felt a lot of guilt. But maybe the strongest thing they passed on to me was this 'showing me,' this *'We survived the camps.'* It

230

became something I had to prove to myself. And my survival was going to be Vietnam."

The theme of survival and of testing himself did not begin for Al Singerman at age nineteen. Like Ruth Alexander, who had tried to imagine that every block she walked to school was a mile; like myself, riding in the subway as a schoolgirl, Al had always had survival fantasies. Often, as a child, he would visualize himself entering a large room filled with shower heads and forced himself to hold his breath, to see how long he might have lasted in a gas chamber before dying. The showers were a staple of the imagery that recurred among many of the people I interviewed. Another common experience had been testing our endurance and tolerance of pain.

"I broke several fingers when I was a kid playing football," Al suddenly rememberd. "I didn't go to a doctor. I enjoyed the fact that I could endure whatever happened to me. When I was nine, I was climbing a fence and got a huge splinter in my hand. Any kid would have been screaming. I went home, boiled some water, soaked my hand and pulled the skin away with a needle. At the dentist's, I never had novocaine. Like I was preparing myself for something. All the years I've been preparing myself in case ... I never finish the thought. In case of what? In case they come to get me."

In November of 1966, Al left the United States for Southeast Asia. "I was seasick. Sick as hell. But happy. We stopped at Okinawa and *everybody* on the boat got off. A last chance to let loose. I stayed on the ship almost entirely by myself. When the guys came back, they gave it to me. 'How could you not come? You don't know what the hell's going to happen to you in Vietnam. You might get killed. And you missed this.' I looked at them as if they were crazy. I said: 'What are you *talking* about? I'm coming back *alive.*' I mean, there was no doubt in my mind about that. That was why I was there. Sure, everyone thought they'd come back alive. But for me it was a little different. I was there for the specific reason to prove I could get through it alive."

At this point I began to shift around in my chair. Until now, I could identify with everything Al had been talking about although the tensions and problems in Al's home were perhaps the most extreme of any I had heard about. My parents had never told me torture stories. They had never even admitted to me that they had been beaten. But I did not need to be told these things as a child and I could easily put myself in Al's place. I, too, had felt the numbness Al described and I had now begun to tap the anger that had driven him most of his life. It was comprehensible to me. Nothing he told me was new.

The war in Vietnam was different. All the young men I knew had done their best to stay out of it. My friends and I had been among those who sang protest songs, attended anti-war rallies, and worked for politicians who took a stand against intervention in Southeast Asia. More to the point, I often reduced situations I observed into a conflict between two parties: aggressor and victim; the Nazi and the Jew. To be an oppressor in any way, I had always thought, was to betray who I was, and to hear Al Singerman talk about *volunteering* to be part of the oppression threw me into confusion.

What I saw of the war in Vietnam on television reminded me of many scenes I imagined from the Second World War. The American strategy of clearing out and burning village after village reminded me of Nazis clearing out Eastern Europe *shtetls*. In the photographs of long, straggling lines of Vietnamese civilians, abandoning their homes, unaware of their eventual destination, I saw the faces of displaced Jews. Soldiers in uniform wielding guns and manning tanks frightened me. It made no difference what flag they fought under, what color their uniforms were. It was difficult for me to accept that the young man in my living room, with whom I shared so much, had been one of them. I was afraid to ask him questions. My manner changed.

Al felt it. Until now, he had been speaking to me almost as if I were a sister he had never had, who knew implicitly what he was talking about. Now suddenly I was another outsider, and his manner changed too. Before, he had been caught up in memories, letting them slip out of him without censure. Now he became more careful, slowly choosing his words. I felt a tremendous loneliness in him. His sentences were more deliberate. I had difficulty listening but it was nothing compared to the trouble he was having explaining.

"Vietnam was a very strange war," he began, looking straight out into the middle of my living room. "You didn't see who you were shooting at. You could kill people without getting emotionally involved. It was a faceless war. Being in the infantry was a day-to-day thing. You got through it thinking you were going to make it to the next day. The thing that really kept you from going crazy was that you knew you were going to be there 365 days, so you counted those days. That's what really kept you going."

But did you make a connection? I kept thinking. *Didn't you feel like a German?*

"I mean, fighting the Viet Cong wasn't the worst of my problems there by far. It was constantly having the leeches on you. The bugs. And the malaria. The dysentery. Most of all, the mud. Constantly up to your neck in mud. We were in the Mekong Delta and that's the way it was. But as much as I complained about it, I was like a pig wallowing in it. I got a perverse pleasure out of it. It gave me a good feeling to know I was *there,* that I was able to endure all that."

Al paused, then continued in a very low voice.

"As I said, most of the time you never saw who you shot at, except for this one incident that occurred. We were walking through a pineapple plantation. There were a bunch of old foxholes surrounding it and we were given orders to throw grenades into all of them and to blow them up. We were all laughing about it. We didn't think it was possible that they were still being used. And one foxhole I threw a grenade into, a body blew up in front of me. I don't know if it was a VC or a farmer. And the clothes were blown off and landed right in front of me. At the time it happened I thought it was funny as hell. I started laughing. And I think by the next day I'd forgotten it. Just blocked it out. Must have blocked it out for about five years. But after that incident, there were a lot of times when if I thought there were civilians around, I didn't fire.

"There's a particular incident I remember, as if it happened yesterday. And it happened ten years ago. We were in a very heavy VC area and I was on guard. We had set up an ambush next to a house and that upset me because I knew something could happen to those people living in the house. During the night, I heard movement next to that house. The first thing that occurred to me, since this area was heavily VC, was that there were people trying to hide something or possibly trying to get guns out of hiding. But I couldn't be sure. And I had my hand on the trigger mechanism for the Claymore mine. The Claymore was set up to cover every inch of territory around us. I had three triggers in front of me and one of them would have killed the person out there on the spot. No one would have said a thing about it. Probably would've gotten a Bronze Star for it.

"I couldn't press it. I could not press the trigger. There were other incidents like that where I couldn't shoot. The thing that really upset me most was going into villages. . . ."

Al's voice tapered off. *Didn't you make the connection then?* I asked silently. *Didn't you see?*

"When we went into the villages," he continued slowly, "most of the time it was in the Mekong Delta. There was a strategy employed in my unit that the artillery would shell a village we were going into. Then, by the time we got there, of course, a number of the people were usually dead. The rest would have escaped. Usually. Sometimes, though, there would be people left behind. We would search the village and then we would burn it down to the ground. The thing I remember upsetting me so much is that we would leave

234

these people behind. Just lying there. We wouldn't *do* anything to them. But we would leave them sitting there. Just sitting there in the middle of this burned-down village."

"Did you ever," I said after a pause, "make any connections in your head between the Second World War and what you were doing in Vietnam?"

Al shook his head, unsurprised by the question. "Not at first. No. I don't think I could have taken it. I think I would have gone off the deep end if I had made that kind of connection. Just trying to survive in Vietnam was enough of a stress. I didn't have enough room in my head to make those kinds of connections.

"Once. Once I made the connection between the camps and Vietnam. Very much so. I befriended several Catholics in Vietnam. I talked about religion with two of these guys because it was on my mind. I told you I was quite a religious little kid. Then I pulled back from it but I always believed in God. In Vietnam I was becoming more and more of an atheist. I hadn't thought much about these things before then. But there I started thinking. I thought: if there was a God, he would never have let the Holocaust happen and he sure as hell wouldn't have let Vietnam happen. *I felt that it had happened twice to me.* I had heard stories when I was a kid that the Holocaust happened because God was punishing the Jews. That was hard to believe. That God would destroy six million human beings just to prove that they were sinful. And in Vietnam, it finally became clear to me. I thought: There can't be a God. Somebody's pulling the wool over everybody's eyes. If there was a God, there's no way he would allow such atrocities to happen."

I began to understand that Al saw himself as a victim of the war. While he may have wanted to go into it as the aggressor, the Jew who would fight back, he had returned from Vietnam a survivor who identified himself among the victims.

"You know, when I first came back, I actually supported

235

the war. I couldn't believe that. Then I realized I wasn't supporting the war because of the war. I was supporting the war because I had survived it. It became my personal war. I was elated that I had survived it.

"I found it even harder to get close to people after I got back. The problems I had were fairly common to other guys who were out on the line. Feelings of extreme hostility mainly toward the American public. A rage toward everything connected with Vietnam. I had no friends. I found it very hard to make friends. Miriam and I had trouble. I didn't talk to my parents. I even had trouble opening up in the Rap Groups and that was four and a half years after I came back.

"One night in the Rap Group, I remembered the incident with the hand grenade. I recounted what had happened, how I had laughed when the body flew into the air and the clothes landed on the ground in front of me. People told me later I was white as a sheet. I was soaking with perspiration. That was the first time I really *felt*. The first time I was capable of feeling anything. The whole time I was in Vietnam, I didn't seem to care whether people lived or died. I didn't feel anything. The numbness about the war started breaking down a little bit.

"But even in the Rap Groups, I didn't say anything about the camps. I wouldn't let myself feel about the camps the way I had let myself feel about Vietnam. That numbness that had been there all my life was still there—only worse. I talked about it in the groups. I described it. But I couldn't place it. I would talk for hours about this wall I had felt around me since I was a little kid but I could never *place* it."

Al stared at me for a while in silence. I felt drained. I wanted the interview to be over. Al's face, which I had seen as such a tough guy's face when I first met him, had softened. He was tired too. He had opened a door that had been stuck shut for years and was dumbstruck at what he saw when it opened. He rubbed his eyes, then shook his head.

236

"You know," he said, "it came out once in the Rap Groups. We were all in a cab one night going to radio station WBAI for a talk show about veterans. We were all in a pretty happy mood and all of a sudden one guy started singing a German song. I became very upset and told him to shut up. He wanted to know why. 'What do you mean *why?*' I told him. 'You know my parents were in the camps.' And he was incredulous. He said he didn't know. And I said, 'What do you mean you don't know? I've *talked* about it.' And he said no. Never. And several of the other guys in the cab confirmed it. I was amazed. These were the only people in the entire world that I trusted.

"I was shocked. They were shocked. But by the time the group met again, I had put it out of my mind. I didn't know how to talk about it. How to bring it up. In the group I'd talk about my dreams. Bits and pieces of what I'm telling you now come up, but I could never put them together. Now all of a sudden all the pieces seem to fit."

Al shook his head. "I guess all my life I wanted to be able to tell *somebody.* I mean, even if this wasn't some thing that was going to be printed, I wouldn't give a damn. This is the first time I've talked about it, the first time I've been able to do it. It's just that the power of it is so great. You have to *want* to do it. You have to know what to ask. You have to have the courage to ask.

"You know, I don't know my parents. I'm thirty years old and I don't know my parents."

His face showed a mixture of sadness, anger and utter bewilderment. "I'm thirty years old and I don't know my parents. They're like strangers to me."

FOURTEEN

Yehudah Cohen *, a slim, dark, bearded research scientist was born within months of Al Singerman into the same community of Displaced Persons in Germany which in 1947 numbered nearly one quarter of a million stateless Jews. His father, like Al's father, had been a tailor first in Lodz, then in Auschwitz, then in the United States. His mother, like Al's mother, had stayed home to raise the children in the working class section of the small Midwestern city in which the family had settled. But unlike Al, who recalled being overpowered by his parents' wartime experience, Yehudah remembered being sheltered from it. At sixteen, when Al had withdrawn into his own world, Yehudah had joined Habonim, a Zionist youth group. While Al barely spoke to the people around him, Yehudah was an extrovert, known among his friends for a sharpness of mind and a penchant for making incisive, mirthless jokes.

238

Even today when guests arrive at the Cohen home, the thirty-one-year-old scientist often greets them with gallows humor. "I introduce visitors to my wife, my daughter, and Uncle George," he told me, pausing like a stand-up comedian for me to grasp the setup for his punchline. "Then I point to the nearest lampshade.

"Some people turn green. They find it in terrible taste. Okay, I suppose it's really sick. It's really disgusting humor. But I don't consider humor as being degrading in any way. It's something I picked up from my father. He never told me horror stories about the war. If my father told any stories at all, they were humorous ones. They were jokes. I think the way my father can look at something and verbalize only the humorous aspects helped him—not physically, but emotionally—through the camps. I don't know whether it's an acquired or inherited characteristic, but it's something that I'm proud of."

I took a deep breath. Gallows humor has never appealed to me. I tend to see the gallows and miss the humor. Lenny Bruce and the line of "sick" comedians who had followed him had always put me off, and I had often wondered at their popularity. Yehudah Cohen, however, did not exhibit any of their self-deprecating quality. His life in Israel had influenced his bearing, manner and dress. He held himself very straight, wore his shirt open at the collar, sleeves rolled to mid-arm, and spoke in brusque, unequivocal terms, as if doubt were a luxury.

When I told him I didn't think his joke was funny, he shrugged. "Look," he said, "I wouldn't call my father's sense of humor normal but I always felt proud of it. He has the right to make sick jokes. It's in no way an insult to anyone's memory. I'm told to bow my head and shed a tear? No, thank you. I'll shed my tears in private. There's something in my father's vast understatement that expresses horror much more than saying, 'They shot. They killed. They raped.' I think you can tell a lot more through humor. I feel

239

proud that my father can tell me humorous anecdotes about the war and feel sure that I can understand the rest.

"One of his classic stories went like this: Me and the boys one day were starving, so I figured we have to do something. They got a broom—this was in one of the subcamps in Auschwitz—and my father began sweeping the sidewalk in front of the Kommandant's quarters. He stood there and out of the corner of his eye he saw the curtain of a window move and then close. Then one of the Gestapo men came out and said: *Du, du bist ein fleissiger Jude.* You're an industrious Jew. My father said: *Jawohl mein Kommandant.* The Gestapo man asked his profession and my father told him that he was a tailor.

" 'You have your equipment?' asked the man.

" 'Oh, of course, *mein Kommandant.'*

" 'Fine. Come back tomorrow at seven. I have work for you.'

"My father ran back to his barracks, spent the whole night unraveling clothes to get thread, found a needle, and next day bright and early ran back to do some sewing. Repair work."

Yehudah paused again. A practiced story-teller.

"Okay, nothing happens. They're still starving. A few weeks later, two armed guards come and ask for my father. He figures, well, this is it. Shook hands with everybody. See you up there wherever we meet again. He figured he was all finished. So, they take him over to the officers' canteen. They gave him several cans of condensed milk and a few foods in payment for the work he had done. He had to sign for it, he said. Typical German bureaucracy. So he went back to his barracks and said he was not sure what amazed him more. That he had come back. Or that he had come back with food.

"So they each had a sip of milk, my father said, and a little bit of food, and that's the way they got through the winter. I thought it was a tremendous story. I thought it was tremendous that he could *tell* this story."

Yehudah thought he had been at least sixteen or seventeen before he had heard that story. Before that time, he said, his parents rarely volunteered facts about the past. Like many children of survivors I had interviewed he described his parents as private people, people who did not talk much about themselves. Also, Yehudah was not sure of his memory regarding what he had heard about the war as a child. He felt that his parents had sheltered him from it and yet he could not remember a time when he had not known about the war. "I couldn't tell you when I found out about it any more than I could tell you when I first realized I was breathing air," he said. "I certainly never thought of myself as different from anybody else. All of my peers were born in Germany and all of their parents spoke Yiddish. None of them had grandparents, and I don't remember ever asking where grandma and grandpa were. When I was a kid, I used to think that all the Jews had come to America in 1946. I didn't know about any other kind. Some of my parents' friends had numbers on their arms, but I took it as a fact of life. I don't remember questioning it."

Although Yehudah's parents were among those survivors who lost a good deal of their orthodoxy during the war, his family maintained the Jewish traditions. On holidays and Friday nights, his mother lit candles and served traditional foods; his father said *kiddush* over the wine. They hung *mazzuzot* in the doorways of their house and sent Yehudah to Hebrew school over his objections. Theirs was a consciously Jewish household, very much like the other homes Yehudah visited as a child. It was not until his father began to earn more money and the family moved into a better neighborhood that Yehudah became close friends with children who were not Jewish.

"There were three of us," he said. "One kid was from a

241

typical WASP family and the other kid was Polish. We played together every day without any problem. I don't remember ever being hurt or insulted because I was a Jew. The only time things ever bothered me was when I had to go to Hebrew school and they didn't have to go. I asked why, and my parents said: 'Because you're Jewish.' That was an irritation," he conceded.

Yehudah flashed a grin through his beard, and I had the sensation that he was trying to sell me something. There was a glibness to the way he summarized things that did not ring true to me. I felt that he was sliding over events that either he did not wish to remember or else that he did not wish to go into. He spoke so quickly that it was difficult to interrupt him, and his tone was tinged with a sarcasm that discouraged intrusion. Both his younger sister and his mother had told me that Yehudah had been beaten up as a child; I asked him if he had any memory of that.

"Oh yes," he said, "when I was in first or second grade, there were real anti-Semites in the neighborhood. Ukrainians, mostly. Several times I was beaten up and called a dirty Jew. Once I was kicked around, literally kicked around, by two older girls. I would come home crying and, a couple of times, my mother called the police. They were tremendously upset that this was happening in America. She told the policeman, 'Haven't we suffered enough?' The cops' reaction was that they couldn't arrest a fourth-grader. If there's no breaking in, what can they do? But my understanding was that they went to the families and talked to them."

Yehudah did not think I should infer much from those incidents. They happened all the time, he said, to Jews who lived outside of New York City. "I should also make it clear," he said, "that some of these things I invited by myself. When I was ten, I ballooned from a skinny kid into a ball of putty that must have weighed 190 pounds. I was a perfect target. On Jewish holidays, I didn't go to school, which caused a certain amount of resentment."

He had never, Yehudah said, consciously thought about how his parents' experience had affected him. It was painful, private and, besides, his parents did not want to dwell on it. "They didn't go to the extreme of denying it had happened," Yehudah explained. "I mean, a friend of mine from Sweden—his parents left Poland and moved up someplace near the reindeer, away from all Jews, in order to forget. My friend grew up celebrating Easter instead of Passover. But when people came over to our house and talked about the war, my parents always said '*Shah!* The children will hear us!' It's very difficult for me to remember what I thought about it then. I remember that in the morning, one of my parents might say to the other: I had that dream again last night. It was clear what the dream was. It didn't have to be talked about. When I watched war movies on television, I never associated them with the Holocaust. Whatever it was that had happened to my parents was not a movie. What had happened to them happened because they were Jews. Not because they had done anything wrong. I assume my feeling then was: that's not right. Somewhere, also, I had the very strong feeling that it should never happen again. But I never verbalized those feelings. The only time I ever remember having verbalized them was just before the 1967 war in Israel."

Like most of the first-born children of survivors in his community, Yehudah did extraordinarily well in school. In high school, he was at the top of his class, had close friends and does not remember any serious quarrels with his parents. However, he disliked the social cliques at school and remembers not wanting to be part of any of them. "In high school, you had to conform," he told me. "You had to carry a briefcase—that was one of the fashions then. You had to wear your hair a certain way. I never joined anything in

243

high school, until I was a Junior and a friend of mine said to come with him to a meeting."

"What kind of meeting?" Yehudah wanted to know.

"What do you care?" the friend answered. "You have nothing better to do."

The meeting turned out to be a group of Jewish high school students interested in Israel and the social movements that had preceded the establishment of the state. It was part of the Habonim movement, which had chapters throughout North America and aimed to eventually bring young Americans over to kibbutzim in Israel.

"The people there were friendly, so I started going," Yehudah told me. "There wasn't a feeling of being in an organization. There was no doctrine, no dogma, no structure. It didn't feel like a youth group but like a very friendly get-together. In Habonim, you were accepted for what you were. It didn't matter how much money your parents made, or what you looked like, or how you spoke, or whether you smoked cigarettes or not. You were accepted as an individual and I felt comfortable there. I could be myself. We happened to come together because we had common interests, although we all came from different backgrounds. Instead of reading a whole book by yourself, in Habonim we each read one chapter of a book and then talked about it. I began to do a lot of reading about Jewish nationalism and Socialism. I also read a book called *Like Sheep to the Slaughter,* through which I found out for the first time that there had been Jewish resistance in the war. Here was a whole area of history that had been neglected. I found out that Jews did fight. I wanted to know why people didn't talk about it. Why didn't they know about it?"

Here, for the first time since we began talking, Yehudah seemed to drop his guard a bit. The edge of sarcasm that had made his voice sound tight became softer. He spoke more slowly.

"I suppose the seed of going to Israel was already there, even before I joined Habonim," he said now. "We had family in Israel. My mother had a brother, Menahem, who left Poland in 1933, before the war, and I was always told that the people who got out of Europe with him were all okay. They were smart. They were all alive. They got out at a time when the whole family should have gotten out. They were never persecuted.

"But I didn't then and I still don't consider Israel as a place to run to," Yehudah said quickly. "In high school, there was a lot of fun involved in being part of Habonim. There were parties, games, hikes, weekends. I met people I liked. I met my wife. It also gave me something I didn't get in either public school or Hebrew school, and that was a sense of Jewish history. That was something I wanted.

"There was no pressure from my parents to stay in Habonim. On the contrary. We met on the other side of town and my parents were annoyed that it took me one hour to get there and another hour to come back. They weren't crazy about the whole idea of Israel. As soon as I started talking about spending a year working in a kibbutz, they got really turned off. I wanted to go right after high school and they refused. It took me another year to convince them and they were sure that once I left, I would never come back. They thought I'd become a farmer someplace in the Negev. I had to assure them that I was just going to see what it was like and that I would be back. That was the truth. I wanted to see what it was like. 'So I'll finish college a year later,' I told them. 'So what?' "

Yehudah finished his freshman year at Columbia in New York, then flew off to Israel. The way he described it was markedly different from the often sentimental, everything-is-rosy attitude of many American Jews, and strikingly similar to the attitudes of other children of survivors who had been there. "What got to me the very first day I was in Israel,"

245

Yehudah said, "was this sense of normalcy. I saw Jewish cops, Jewish pickpockets, Jewish pimps, as well as the kind of Jews I was accustomed to at home. There was a positive shock: we are a normal nation. It was a Jewish state, a place where a Jew could be the master of his own destiny. I didn't think it was an island where everything was good and green. Israel is a place where anyone can be a Jew the way he wants to be a Jew, but he has to fight for it—whether it means fighting the bureaucracy, or fighting the orthodox Jews, or fighting the Arabs. But he can fight. He does not have to depend on the good graces of a government that is not his.

"My feeling is obviously influenced by my parents' experiences. I consider myself very Jewish. Not very religious. But very Jewish. There are certain things on which I agree with the Russian authorities. They classify Jews as a nationality and I accept that. I believe it. Sometimes, I feel that the religion is almost secondary. That's my basis: everything else I believe is built on that."

Yehudah spent the school year of 1965-1966 working half-days on his kibbutz and studying Hebrew and history the other half. At about the same time that Al Singerman had begun his basic training, Yehudah was adjusting to communal life on what was essentially a large farm. He was finding that the country he had come to "check out" had a special claim on him, that he felt better there than he had felt anywhere else. Yet, at the end of the year, he returned to the United States and resumed his studies at Columbia. "I left with the depressing feeling," he said, "that it would be years and years before I got back."

Ten months later, the Six-Day War broke out. In May of 1967, newspapers were carrying daily front-page accounts of growing tension in the Middle East. President Nasser of Egypt closed the Straits of Tiran to Israeli ships; United Nations peace-keeping forces were asked to leave their posts in the Gaza Strip. Yehudah was preparing for finals at the time. They were scheduled for the end of May. Word began to filter down through the youth movement that volunteers might be needed to replace Israeli workers who would be called into the army and Yehudah began to grow extremely excited.

"I didn't want to shoot," he told me. "I don't like guns. But I felt this compulsion to go there. The connection for me was clear; it shouldn't happen again. If all I could do was to pick fruit, I was going to pick fruit. I was not going to sit in the United States and watch. I would have gone crazy sitting in New York listening to news reports. The connection to the Holocaust was obvious. It was typical. Here we go again. The world sits by, people send complaints to the United Nations and no one does a damn thing.

"All these feelings had been seething and growing for a long time, I guess," Yehudah said, "but this was the first time I had verbalized them. I was convinced that nothing had changed. I kept thinking: they're going to surround Israel; they're going to attack Israel; and if Israel is destroyed, they're going to send flowers. To hell with them. I can't do that."

Yehudah finished his exams and then flew home to his parents with a release form. He needed his parents' signatures in order to leave under the aegis of the youth movement. "My parents were hysterical," he remembers. "Literally hysterical. It was the only time in my life that my mother pulled rank on me. It was clear that war was coming. The question was only when. Nobody then knew that it would last less than a week. My mother just broke down. 'Haven't we suffered enough?' she said. 'After we lost so much, we have to lose you too?'

"I told her two things. One was that of all the people in the world, how could I not go? We could not allow it to happen again. Two, I told her that if she didn't give me her permission I would go anyway.

"Neither of my parents could argue with my position.

247

They signed the release. They just asked that I spend the Sabbath with them. I was on the last plane that left the United States. We didn't leave until June 4, a Sunday night. It took us forty-eight hours to get to Israel and by the time we landed, it was the second night of the war. There was a blackout at the airport. We landed with a Mirage escort. Almost before they sorted out and settled us, the war was over."

Israel was flooded with volunteers that summer of 1967. Thousands of young Jews from Europe, North and South America and Australia had had the same feelings as Yehudah and poured into the country in the days before and after the Six-Day War. The Israeli Army demobilized shortly after the cease-fire and the men returned to their jobs. There was a sudden glut of manpower. Yehudah, like many other volunteers, went from kibbutz to kibbutz to volunteer his services but found that none were in need of help. He stayed the summer, nevertheless. By that time, he knew he would be coming back for good.

He finished college and decided to do graduate work at the Weizmann Institute in Rehovot. He married the young woman from New Jersey whom he had met in Habonim and, in 1969, they moved to Israel, where they became citizens. "I served in the army," Yehudah told me, "I had the pleasure of being in the 1973 war. And lived happily ever after," he finished quickly, just as his mother walked into the room.

She was a small, cautious woman, careful not to intrude upon her son.

"What are you looking for, Mom?" he asked.

She said nothing, looked about the living room, and then went out as quietly as she had come in. Yehudah said nothing more until he heard the door to the kitchen click shut.

"I don't want to feel as if I'm performing for her," he explained to me. "Maybe also I don't want to hurt her. I

248

don't want her to hear me discussing these things seriously. She might take it the wrong way. She might worry. Maybe I just don't want to verbalize feelings in front of her."

I told Yehudah that his mother had told me she worried about having burdened her children with stories of the war, and Yehudah looked surprised. "Not at all," he said. "I told you. My father is an extremely private man. You have to read between the lines with him. My mother verbalizes more, but she didn't say much either. Certainly she never told me where they were."

Now that I had asked all my questions, Yehudah seemed more relaxed, even reluctant to end our conversation. "I don't know whether the feeling I have for Israel comes from the Holocaust, or from tradition, or from religion," he mused. "As I said, I never really examined the whole subject closely before. Obviously, the Holocaust was a crucial aspect of my parents' lives and everything that happened to me— the way I was brought up—had to do with that. I feel the Holocaust in a different way from someone who watches a documentary about it or studies it from books. I feel I understand it better than they do or ever will.

"I don't trust the world. I always have the fear, and I guess it's because of the Holocaust, of sitting by and watching. I'd say that my background made me aware that being Jewish carries certain responsibilities. You have to make sure no one's civil rights are trod upon. And you have to make sure that you yourself won't be trampled. There are still Nazis in America. I think people are afraid to see them. It's the old attitude: if you pretend you don't see them, if you keep quiet, they'll maybe go away.

"It's just not true," Yehudah said forcefully. "I don't agree with everything Israel does either. But if I don't like the government, I vote against it. If I don't like the politics, I try to do something to change them. I feel the same way about Soviet Jewry. I think they're being destroyed and that people aren't doing enough to try to save them. Same old story: most of the world doesn't care. We *went* to Russia. We saw what's happening there. We write to people and they tell us it's like a lifeline. I don't like working with organizations, but here's something you can do by yourself. Just write a letter. I'm just appalled that more people aren't doing something, when the whole world knows what's going on."

The door to the kitchen opened again, and Yehudah again fell silent. This time it was his three-year-old daughter who wanted him to stop talking.

Yehudah's dark eyes turned to her.

"Go play in some traffic," he said jokingly.

His daughter did not budge. She looked up at her father without blinking.

"All right," Yehudah said. "Enough of the Holocaust," and got down on the floor to play.

FIFTEEN

How could I not go? Me of all people?

I had thought the same thoughts in May of 1967. I too
had picked myself up and flown to Israel filled with ideas of
putting my life on the line. I had visions of trees being
burned to stumps. *I couldn't allow myself to sit back and watch,*
Yehudah had said. *Israel wasn't a refuge for me. It was a place
where Jews could be masters of their own destiny.*

Like Yehudah's parents, my parents had strong objections
to my going to Israel. The last thing they wanted me to do
was to put myself deliberately in danger. Like Yehudah, I
found myself at odds with my parents for the first time in
my life. I had always been extremely protective of them, like
almost every other child of survivors I had spoken to but I
had not previously found it difficult to do what they wished.
They had wanted me to grow up free, healthy, happy and
close by. So did I. Their wishes were not hard to fulfill. We
had never had a major disagreement on the choices I had

251

thus far made, and my insistence on Israel gave them pause.

People in Israel, my parents felt, were not free. They could not travel beyond tightly controlled borders and were dependent on the good will of the West. The country was patently unsafe, very hot, and six thousand miles away. My father thought that Palestine, like Czechoslovakia, had always been a way station for invading armies, geographically vulnerable, ultimately indefensible. My mother, the cosmopolitan, did not like the idea of so many Jews segregated in one place. It reminded her of concentration camp, she said. It would be narrowing my horizons.

I had to be ingenious in finding reasons to go there, so I told them that the Hebrew University was a fine institution based on British university models and that it boasted an excellent English Department. Besides, it had an international faculty and student body. Just as Ruth Alexander had left Rochester to study in New York City, I left home ostensibly to broaden my education in Jerusalem.

My parents did not buy this explanation entirely. Why, they asked, could I not go to Paris or London, someplace where there was no war? Because I didn't have the money, I told them. I had obtained a scholarship earlier that year from the American Friends of the Hebrew University. I had worked part-time throughout high school and college. I was not asking for financial support. My parents took a certain pleasure in my stubbornness, although my father alluded to my abandoning the family and my mother made vast sarcasms about the ironies of history.

"Your grandfather would turn over in his grave if he had one," she said tartly. "To think that his granddaughter, the granddaughter of a baptized Jew, would become a Zionist! He wouldn't understand it."

I did not understand it very well either at the time, but my mother's penchant for reducing things to black-and-white seemed to me misguided. I was certainly not a Zionist, although this is what my New York friends also seemed to think I had become. I knew virtually nothing about Zionism and, if anything, I was put off by what I knew. I had never dreamed about going to Israel. I had never been intrigued by stories of pioneers turning marshy swamplands and deserts into gardens. I did not like the few export items I had seen from Israel: the religious artifacts and the turquoise and imitation-gold plates sold in Barton's candy stores in my neighborhood. I did not like the American philanthropists who seemed to make a lifestyle of attending banquets for the good of the Jews; the Israeli politicians who exhorted Jewish youth in the Diaspora to make *aliyah* to the Homeland; or the good kids in Sunday school who took their bar mitzvahs seriously and planned to visit Israel on organized youth tours.

I felt nothing in common with any of them and yet, although I could not explain it to the satisfaction of anyone, I had to go. I felt as surely as I felt my parents' reluctance that Israel would give me another piece of the puzzle, that living there would help explain why no matter how successful and accepted I was in school and with my friends, I felt somehow apart.

Like most of the first-born children of survivors I had spoken with, I had been an unusually active child and teenager. I had always felt invested with energy. My teachers had often remarked that I seemed to have more of it than I knew what to do with. I did well at school, where I organized clubs, wrote songs and our Senior Play, was captain of volleyball and basketball teams. After school, I went ice-skating, bicycle riding, to weekly piano lessons, or to work babysitting. I sang in choruses; I did volunteer work. When I was twelve, I had begun to structure my time, hour by hour, on a sheet of graph paper that hung on the bulletin board above my desk. The chart left hardly a half-hour a day unaccounted for. I moved from one activity to the next, unencumbered by introspection.

My parents did not encourage introspection and I thought

I understood why. Time had to be used to a purposeful end and introspection achieved no tangible end. "It's not good to think so much," my mother or father would tell me if they found me mulling over some problem I was having. They could not bear to see me brood. They could bear indecision no more than other survivors could abide "talk." There was a pragmatism and urgency to their lives that made every moment that was not used properly a waste of time. Moreover, they equated inactivity or too much thinking with unhappiness. Too often, when they found me looking out a window or disengaged from visible preoccupations, they would ask: "What's wrong? What happened?" and my father would coax me to give him a smile.

The fact was that beneath my facade of activity was a person who questioned the value of doing anything at all. The more I busied myself, the less I felt engaged. Like Al Singerman, I often wondered whether there wasn't something missing in my makeup that prevented my feeling the full range of emotions I read about in books and saw other people display. I seemed to possess extraordinarily slow reactions: events made themselves felt days and weeks after they had occurred, and my response to them was indistinct, muffled, often not there at all. My childhood nurse, Milena, the woman who had been my adopted grandmother and favorite adult, died slowly of cancer as I reached my mid-teens. I visited her and cooked for her with unflagging cheerfulness and when she finally died, I never cried. I did not mourn for her anymore than I had mourned for my real grandparents. One day she was simply gone and I was left with another photograph. I had grown up with a family that existed in photographs, with a gallery of images rather than a living, breathing clan. Now there was one more.

I did not feel anger when I looked at these pictures. At least I do not remember feeling anger. I felt numbness, an absence of feeling that seemed to carry over into other parts of my life as well. Anger seemed to me to be a privilege that my parents had earned and that I had not. One had to have suffered in order to be angry, I thought, and I had been told from the time I was small that I and the rest of the children I grew up with had not the slightest idea of what suffering was. We knew it second-hand, my parents said, and when they looked at the lives my brothers and I led, they weren't even sure about that. We had almost everything we wanted; we seemed oblivious to the possibilities of hunger, loss or imprisonment. Our lives were easy, and while my parents worked hard to make them that way, they could not help but remind us by their very presence and attitudes, that we their children enjoyed opportunities that they had irrevocably lost.

Whenever I felt angry at my parents—for saying no, for embarrassing me, for any of the reasons children feel angry at their parents—I swallowed the feeling whole and pushed it down far away. How could I presume to be angry at them? They had enough to contend with. During the sixties, a time when adolescent rebellion became something of a national style and teen-agers were busy throwing their parents' values out the window, I, like many of my peers, tried to measure myself by my parents' standards. I studied my parents: I *took on* their values and I wanted to imitate their experience. Like almost all of the children of survivors I had interviewed, I was put off by the insouciance of the middle-class society in which I lived. I grew restless at parties and dances. I was scornful of my friends who could spend an entire day doing nothing, or going to an amusement park, or lying on a beach. In high school, where most of my friends dreamed of marrying well, or making a successful career, or having the money to buy fancy wardrobes, I dreamed of finding ways to suffer, to confront, feel and vanquish pain.

My preoccupation grew stronger at a time when my family was finally beginning to live more or less like the other families in the neighborhood. By the time I was thirteen, my father had become a unionized cutter in the garment center

255

and was assured of year-round employment. My mother's dressmaking business was also doing well. She employed three helpers, could afford to tell off troublesome clients, and even had enough income to allow for vacations in the Berkshires during the summer. My mother's chronic depressions had subsided; my father's anger had mellowed somewhat. Fifteen years after they had been liberated from concentration camps, they had achieved a modicum of security.

In 1960, when my mother was forty and my father fifty-six, my mother unexpectedly became pregnant for a third time, and this event seemed a symbol of their change in circumstances. Her doctors warned of the risks she would incur in having a third child. Her back was badly damaged: she had spent weeks at a time in traction and had had trouble with almost every organ in her body but her heart. Abortion was illegal in New York at the time but they offered her the option of a hospital procedure, on the grounds that having another child would endanger her life.

Despite their recommendations and despite the financial strain of a new baby, my parents decided to go ahead. I sensed that they could not bring themselves to cut off a new life when so many other lives in their families had been cut off. My baby brother David would be the newest leaf on our family tree, another member of the small society that was our family.

Taking care of David became yet another one of my activities. When he was two and three months old, I plastered his carriage with posters of John F. Kennedy and distributed campaign leaflets as I walked him in the park after school. President Kennedy appeared to my parents a younger, more vital incarnation of Franklin D. Roosevelt, the man they thought responsible for bringing an end to the Second World War. Kennedy and the group of young Americans he brought to the White House seemed proof of all the good the United States had to offer, proof that they had chosen the right place to rear their children. Even a year later, when the Eichmann trial was televised and my parents sat riveted in our living room listening to testimony with impassive faces, there was always the laughter, the first steps and words of my baby brother to offset the hold of past memory. My parents reveled in their newborn child; they seemed to grow younger and more carefree.

In 1964, yet another unexpected discovery enlarged our family. My mother, as was her habit, was reading *The New York Times Book Review* one Sunday morning when she came across a review of a book by an Austrian author named Ilse Aichinger. The book, *Herod's Children,* had just been published in English. My mother puzzled over the review. It seemed to her that she recognized the plot of the novel without having read it. She called the public library and when my father brought the book home, she read it in one sitting, until two in the morning. The novel was about children in Vienna during the war and as my mother read it, she realized that the characters were barely disguised relatives her father had told her about when she was a child. With an excitement I had never seen her display, my mother sent off a letter to the author and promptly received an astonishing reply. The family in Austria, Ilse Aichinger wrote, had assumed that my mother had died in Auschwitz twenty years before, when they had not found her name on any of the lists of survivors.

It was as if a weight had been lifted off my mother's life, and that lessening of her burden made itself felt in our household. Much later, I was told that my mother had completed three years of psychoanalysis, that she was one of the relatively few survivors who recognized that she needed professional help. Then, I did not realize that she had spent four mornings each week lying on a couch trying to come to grips with her past. All I knew was that my mother, who had always seemed so alone in the world, now had a family that extended beyond me and my brothers into a network of people who were like her. The pieces of a puzzle I had only dimly known existed began to fall into place.

I had always wondered where my mother's passion for music came from, whether there were any other people in the family so interested in books, whether my mother reflected her family's tastes or had rebelled against them. When physicians asked me for information about family tendencies toward a specific disease, I had never been able to supply medical information because I did not know what diseases members of my family had ever had. When friends asked me which branch of the family I took after, I also had scant information, particularly on my mother's side. Now, with the discovery of family, my mother suddenly began to talk about the Rabinek side of the family as she never had talked before.

Her grandfather, engineer Rabinek, she explained to me, had built the railroad from Vienna into Serbia. Each of his five children was born in a different town along the route. They were raised in the Austro-Hungarian monarchy of Franz Josef. They lived in the Vienna of Freud, Schnitzler and Mahler, my mother said proudly. Her eldest uncle Leo had died of sunstroke while sitting in a Viennese café. Her uncle Gustav was poisoned to death on a riverboat in the Belgian Congo. He had been an ivory trader there, a man who got along so well with the Africans that the Belgians found it necessary to kill him. Her aunt Gisela had died in a concentration camp and her aunt Gabi, along with all her cousins, had fled Vienna in 1938 and gone to England.

The Viennese branch of the Rabinek family now had outposts in Berkeley, California; London, England; Salzburg, Austria; Belfast, Northern Ireland; and Woodstock, New York. Its members were a composer, a writer, an artist, a physician, a pharmacologist, a biophysics professor and assorted other intellectuals. All had left their Jewish identities behind in Vienna, and lived as Christians in their new locations. My mother's favorite aunt, Gabi, had for seven

258

years lived six blocks away from us in Manhattan and the two women had never crossed paths. She had died in 1955, never knowing that her niece lived in the same neighborhood.

An international correspondence was set into motion, followed by a series of visits in which the outlines of my mother's story were fleshed out by faces, voices, real people instead of characters in stories. My mother looked like her relatives. She talked the same mixture of English laced with German expressions. She cooked the same sort of food and read the same books. For once I saw my mother not as a solitary adult but as the youngest cousin in a large family. She became respectful as well as girlish with our relatives. I began to catch glimpses of what she might have been like before the war.

At about the same time that my mother discovered her relatives, the German government's restitution authorities finally saw fit, after a prolonged correspondence, to award my mother a pension for damages she had sustained during her internment in concentration camps. They refused to acknowledge that she had incurred any physical disabilities but a series of psychiatrists had arrived at the conclusion that she was 30 percent manic depressive, and thus entitled to payment. My father and mother, unlike some survivors, felt no compunction about receiving the money. On the contrary, they took the pension gladly and quickly put it to good use. My mother set off on the first trip abroad she had made since her arrival in the United States. She flew to Prague, to visit her cousin Kitty; to Salzburg to visit Ilse Aichinger, and to Jerusalem, to visit Margot, the woman to whom she gave the credit for keeping her alive in Terezin during the war.

When she returned from her trip, full of stories, I was ready to go. I was a Junior in high school then, chafing to get out into the world. Although in school I knew people like myself, Jews whose parents had left Europe before or after the war, I felt somehow at odds with my surroundings.

I and my friends grew up in that peculiar version of America that was the West Side of New York City. The teachers in our schools, the men behind the delicatessen counters, the writers and musicians who lived in our neighborhood were overwhelmingly Jewish. But unlike the Jews in Boro Park, Brooklyn or Downsview, Toronto, whose lives were circumscribed by religion, the Jews in my neighborhood took a certain pride in dissociating themselves from religion. If they attended synagogue, it was a gesture toward community rather than an act of faith. At school, if my friends were asked whether they were Jewish, their stock response was: "My parents are."

The community of Jewish refugees in which I grew up was extremely ambivalent about its Jewish identity. It had kept the cultural traditions of Central European Jewish life: its members attended New York City's finest concerts, opera, theater; they kept up with the latest books; and urged their children on to professional goals. They instilled in their children a pride in European things but gave them very little in the way of Jewish pride. Many of them seemed reluctant to point out to their children that they in fact had a Jewish heritage. They relinquished their role of helping to shape a transplanted Jewish tradition to the religious Jews or to those interested in Zionism. The assimilationist stream of Judaism that had flourished in Germany, Czechoslovakia and Austria seemed to have evaporated in the passage to America. Its premise, that Jews could participate freely in Christian society while retaining their cultural affiliation, had been dealt a blow by Nazism. Those many survivors who had lost their faith in the war did not know what to pass on to their children. The Holocaust had become the touchstone of their identities as Jews and it became a touchstone for their children as well. The trouble was that while it conferred an identity, it provided no structure, no clue to a way of life.

This was one reason I felt attracted to Israel. There, at least, Jews seemed to have grappled with history and arrived at a new definition of Jewish identity. Beneath all the superficialities I disliked about Zionism was a cogent, compelling argument: that the Holocaust was but the last of a horrible history of persecutions; and that after one-third of the world's Jewish population had been murdered, a Jewish state was established as a bulwark against homelessness and helplessness.

Like Yehudah Cohen, I did not see this state as a refuge. Rather, it seemed to me one of the very few places which offered an option, a possibility of living in a community where there were people like myself, where the experience of death and displacement was the rule rather than the exception. Perhaps too, I wanted to emulate the emigration of my parents. I set off for Israel with few possessions, determined to learn a new language, Hebrew, as my parents had learned English; to learn to live in a new country with a new climate, new set of laws, new foods, new kinds of people. I arrived in Israel ready to join the army if need be, ready to renounce my American citizenship and start from scratch.

The Israel I found in 1967 was an open, wildly optimistic country filled with the euphoria of having won a short, decisive war. The barbed wire which had for years pinched its frontiers had been torn up. Israelis were busy traveling to places they had never thought to see in their lifetime. The country was teeming with young people from abroad who, like Yehudah, had volunteered to work in the places of men who had gone to war. They had flown in from Europe, South America, North America and Australia, drawn by the conviction that their presence in Israel would make a tangible difference, drawn also by the chance to test their mettle. Not all of them were children of survivors, but over the next three years I discovered many who were. In them I found the first peer group I had ever known.

We stood, sunburned and blinking in the cloudless summer light, at the sides of the highways linking Jerusalem, Tel Aviv and Haifa, self-conscious, unaccustomed to the dust and the hot, dry wind that sucked the sweat off our faces before it had time to collect, awkwardly trying to thumb rides. The *mitnadvim,* or "volunteers" as we were quickly termed by the press, always stood a bit farther down the road from the soldiers who stood hitch-hiking. Our hair was longer and more unruly than that of the soldiers; our bodies were softer; and instead of army uniforms we wore cut-off jeans and T-shirts. Most of us were university students whose closest exposure to war had been in movie theaters; many of the boys had done their best to avoid military conscription back home. For us, the army had always been something to avoid. Now, we saw it as a mark of honor. We glanced secretly and enviously at the young men in uniform, whose guns hung casually from their shoulders, as casually as tourist cameras. Their faces were as young as our own; their features were familiar. A great many of them were the sons and daughters of European Jews who had arrived in Palestine just before or just after the Second World War. But for a few twists of family history, I thought, the two groups standing at the side of the highways might have been standing in each other's places.

I was nineteen that summer and eager for experience, eager to be part of a national community. I felt that my life until then had been an easy one, devoid of hardship. My face was smooth, unlined and rather bland. Often when I looked in the mirror, I wished for it to show some sign of character, which meant, to me, some sign of experience, some trace of pain. I had grown up protected. The very action of standing in the heat by the side of the highway seemed to me a first step in rectifying that condition. I felt honored when a soldier looked at me and deferential when one of them deigned to initiate conversation. I saw in those soldiers everything I wished my parents and their friends could have been: fighters who might be risking death but would die on their own terms.

Despite all my protestations against Zionism and sentimental folklore, I would turn to jelly when a car finally stopped for me and we would begin the long climb up the mountains from Tel Aviv to Jerusalem. The cars were packed with hitch-hikers at that time. It seemed that everyone who owned a vehicle felt an obligation to share it with other travelers. We hummed accompaniments to the songs on the radio and exchanged stories about the places from which we came. We passed groves of orange trees whose scent seeped in through the car windows. Then there were long, snaking jets of water irrigating green fields of crops. Then, as the land began to rise toward the mountains, crumbled, skull-like boulders and rusting armored cars lined the sides of the Jerusalem Highway in memory of the Israeli War of Independence.

Each time I rode the road to Jerusalem, I was flooded with inchoate feelings of pride, wonder and a strange comfort. To the names of Rabin, Dayan, Sharon and Gur that were repeated over the radio, I added the names I had so obstinately refused to remember in Sunday school: Gideon and Deborah, Joshua, David and Jonathan. History came to life for me on the road to Jerusalem. The air seemed full of the spirit of battles and pilgrimages. For the first time, I felt part of a history that extended far back before the Holocaust to an era when Jews had fought as equals, army against army.

The Hills of Judea were unlike any mountains I had ever seen. Bent and broken with age, their sinews swelled out one from the other like the muscles of an old man's back. They seemed not only indestructible but also infinitely fertile, able to nourish new growth even after centuries of erosion. Whole new forests had been planted in the gray, powdery ground and those woods of young trees touched off in me memories of bringing dimes to Sunday school and receiving a stamp imprinted with a leaf for each dime. We had a large poster of a tree in our classroom—that was one of the few things I remembered of those Sunday mornings—and, one by one, we children would lick our stamps and stick them on the empty branches until the tree was green and lush with leaves. Our dimes went to plant a tree in Israel, we were told then, and when I saw the forests rising out of the mountainsides, it was as if I saw my own family tree magically restored and growing.

I lived in Jerusalem for three years. During that time Martin Luther King, Robert Kennedy and students at Kent State University were murdered; the war in Vietnam intensified; the newspapers recorded marches of blacks, women, homosexuals, and hippies as well as the rock concerts, riots and other mass events of the late sixties. In Europe, university students were forming political alliances with workers and barricading themselves in the streets against police.

In Israel, it was quiet. The university population was busy making up for the time lost during the war. The campus in Jerusalem was tranquil; it bore more resemblance to a stately national archive than to a college. There were no demonstrations. Students prepared for the degrees that would bring them livelihoods.

In August of 1967, I and hundreds of other foreign students were working six hours a day, six days a week, trying to gain enough fluency in Hebrew to understand the lectures that would begin two months later. From eight in the morning until two every afternoon, we read, wrote and spoke Hebrew. We read excerpts from the Bible, from the newspapers, from the short stories of Peretz and Agnon, from the poetry of Bialik, Tschernikovsky and Rachel. The syllables I had found so ugly when they were chanted in synagogue in New York now seemed to me the most musical of sounds. I rolled them over my tongue and held them in my mouth like exquisite chocolates. Like my father, who had steeped himself in *Reader's Digest* condensed books when he arrived in New York, and had repeated "Early to bed; early to rise," until it became an incantation, I walked the streets of Jerusalem reciting proverbs under my breath. I had learned from my parents that language was the key to a culture and I was determined to transform myself into an Israeli as quickly as possible.

When I asked directions on the street, I did not permit myself to ask in English, or even to request that the informant speak slowly. I tried to grasp the gist of what was being said and only after wandering and getting even more lost than before would I ask again. In Hebrew. I stumbled upon obscure neighborhoods in this way and was often late for appointments, but within a few months I spoke fluent Hebrew with hardly a trace of an American accent.

That was a matter of pride with me. I did not want to be identified as an "Anglo-Saxon," a curious term that collected Australians, Americans, South Africans, Canadians and British in Israel, and connoted wealth, education and a comfortable station in life. All the opportunities for which my parents had emigrated to America now seemed to me luxuries that I had not earned. I would have liked, if I could, to deny the fact that I had spent almost all my life in the United States. I was Czech, I told people. I had been born in Prague. And pretty soon, people began to detect what they thought was a Czech accent to my Hebrew. They remarked on the ways I was different from other American students, unaware of how hard I was working to make them think so.

I imitated the mannerisms, expressions and tastes of the Israelis in my dormitory and avoided the company of Americans. I threw out my worn New York City sneakers and replaced them with the heavy, functional sandals that were the footgear of the kibbutz. I began to wear my wristwatch with its face on the inside of my wrist, like a soldier. I pulled back my hair, which I had formerly let hang loose and wild like the coffeehouse folksingers of Greenwich Village, into a neat, conventional pony tail. I took a part-time job as a mother's helper, cleaning and cooking for four young Israeli boys ranging in age from seven to seventeen. I needed spending money, but more than that I wanted to integrate as much as possible into my surroundings. I wanted to be part of Israel. I wanted to make my life there.

At first, the transition went smoothly. I liked rising at seven in the morning, when the air was fresh and cool on the skin, and the hills of Jerusalem looked as obdurate as the hills in a medieval painting. I learned to slow down and move to the rhythm of the city, where shops closed every day for two hours in the afternoon and where, on the Sabbath, the roads were quiet, the cafés and movie houses dark. *For the first time, I had a sense of context,* another child of survivors told me about his first few months in Jerusalem. *The days were connected. Eating was a meaningful thing. My needs came from inside out rather than from outside in. I stopped doing things because I thought they were expected of me and started doing them because I needed to. Israel made me normal. There was no one incident or revelation. It was more a working out of some kind of meaningful way to live, of creating a sensibility. Israel was the answer for me.*

In Israel, it seemed, all the troublesome questions of Jewish identity were resolved. On Chanukah, menorahs glowed on the tops of public buildings as well as in the windows of private homes. One did not have to think about Christmas presents. Christmas and New Year's Eve passed almost unnoticed like any other days of the week. Jews were normal in Israel. That is to say, they worked as garbagemen, bus drivers, construction workers, hairdressers, cops *and* robbers in addition to the traditionally middle-class professions that the great bulk of Jews had moved into in the United States. Most startling of all to me was that Jews in Israel now patrolled occupied territory. They were administrators of land they had won in war. The Military Government which administered law in the West Bank of Jordan, the Gaza

266

Strip, the Sinai Peninsula and the Golan Heights was regarded as the oppressor by a group of people who saw Jews not as Holocaust survivors, not even as the victims of millennium-long persecution, but simply as powerful and sometimes ruthless invaders.

This new version of the Jews impressed me deeply and made me more uncomfortable the longer I lived in Israel. It was inescapable. When my friends and I, clad in our shorts and sandals, drove down to the Dead Sea, we passed the abandoned refugee camp outside of Jericho where displaced Arabs had lived nine to a room before fleeing again. In East Jerusalem, in the Arab sector, old men and barefoot urchins hawked keychains and postcards bearing photographs of Israel's generals with so complete a disregard for their own pride and culture that it made me wince in shame. We volunteers were warned to avoid the Gaza Strip and Arab towns like Hebron and Nablus because anti-Israeli feeling was so high, and although the press made much of the humanity of the military authorities, it was far easier for me to feel the pain and humiliation of the conquered than to identify with the conquerors.

Rationally, I could not support my feelings. After all, the Six-Day War had been a defensive war. Egypt, Syria, Iraq and Jordan had built up their troops on the borders of Israel; Egypt had requested the United Nations Peacekeeping Forces to leave their positions in the buffer zone; Egypt had closed the Straits of Tiran in a blockade of Israeli shipping. Israel had not started the war. It had not set out to conquer people or territory. The fact that it had happened that way was cause for rejoicing rather than the ambiguous, uneasy reactions I was having.

"I don't understand you," my Israeli friends would say when I tried to talk about this. "Would you rather we had lost the war? Do you think any of us would be alive to talk about our feelings? We would all be dead." I understood what they were telling me and I wanted to be able to speak

267

as unequivocally as they did, but the longer I lived in Israel, the more I realized the extent of the gap that existed between my concerns, my way of thinking and that of my *sabra* classmates. Our sensibilities were different. We had been formed by different experiences. In my literature and musicology seminars, most of the Israelis were silent. They took notes; they were interested in getting the subject matter straight and knowing the right answer. I did not believe there was a right answer. Everything I had seen or heard in my life had shown me otherwise. Where they were dogmatic, I was reflective; where they were certain I was not so sure.

Their lives had been highly structured from the time they were children, and ruled by what was good for the group rather than by what was good for the individual. They had moved in groups from the time they were toddlers: first in kindergarten; then in the youth movement; then in the army. They were as integrated into their society as I was alienated from mine and, although I wished I could be like them at times, I found I could not. I had too many doubts and too many questions. They ignored the few Arabs studying at the Hebrew University; I talked to them. They accepted the assumption and practices of our professors; I challenged them. They appeared uninterested in exploring the history which had resulted in their growing up in a Jewish State; I was passionately interested in trying to make sense of it. The Holocaust was implicit in the monuments, the lifestyles, and the faces of the people I lived with in Israel, yet it was a subject that was rarely broached. *Deep down Israelis think of themselves as Lot's wife,* a young lawyer I had interviewed in New York had remarked to me. *They're afraid if they turn around and look back at the Holocaust, they'll turn into a pillar of salt.*

By the time I began my second year at the Hebrew University, I had come to the same conclusion and that conclusion disappointed me. One major reason I had chosen to study in Jerusalem was to straighten out the strands of recent Jewish history, but instead of finding a dialogue in which to participate, I found reluctance to open the subject at all. As I had first dissociated myself from the Americans in my surroundings, I now began to move away from the Israelis I had tried so hard to emulate. We were at cross purposes. I wanted to open doors that they had shut firmly behind them. Their sights were set on obtaining the staples of middle-class American life that I was rejecting.

I moved into the loose circle of volunteers who had stayed in Israel. Most of them were the first generation of their families to be born in their respective countries. When their Hebrew faltered, they spoke French, Spanish, German or English. They had all grown up speaking at least two languages, one foot planted in the traditions of Central or Eastern Europe and the other in the culture of the Western countries. They were all hybrids like me who had come to Israel hoping to find a context. We did not speak of this quest directly. We rarely tried to analyze exactly what we were looking for. But the stories we told each other over coffee, between classes and late into the night were all variations on the same theme. The journeys each of us had made to Jerusalem had something of the character of pilgrimages, and although at the time I did not know that I would one day put the stories of those pilgrimages together, I began to write them down.

"I have a story and no language in which to tell it," began a young man late one night in the student quarters in Jerusalem. He was from Czechoslovakia and spoke some Russian but no Hebrew or English. Since I was the only person present who spoke Czech as well as English and Hebrew, I began a simultaneous translation of what he had to say.

Tomas had been born in Prague in 1946 into a family that had been severed by the war. His father had been sent to concentration camps because he was a Jew. His mother, a Christian, had worked with the underground. When his father was liberated, in 1945, he returned to Prague and tried to resume the life he had led before. The Nazi regime had, however, made him a Zionist. He rushed off to Palestine in 1947 to fight for the Jewish State. "Until I came to Israel this year," Tomas said, "I do not remember seeing my father face to face. As far as I know, he had intended to come back to Czechoslovakia but after the War of Independence he settled in Israel. He married another Czech refugee he met there and soon after their daughter was born. He never divorced my mother."

Tomas talked rapidly, as if he had been bottled up for months. He was short and thin, his hair and eyes pale, the skin of his face stretched tautly over high cheekbones. He was feeling especially tense that night because he had decided to return to Czechoslovakia. He had traveled to Israel legally during the time when Alexander Dubcek's liberal government gave travel visas out freely. Then, the Russian invasion had put an end to "Socialism with a human face" and stringent travel restrictions were again put into effect. Tomas knew that if he returned to Czechoslovakia he would, in all likelihood, never again be able to leave. That, he explained, made the telling of his story so important.

"I was told about my father in bits and pieces. First he wrote my mother that he intended to stay in Israel. Then, when he remarried, he asked her to keep their marriage and my existence a secret. He wrote letters to me too and I wrote back to an address that was not his home. When I was a child, I dreamed about sailing to Israel and bringing my father back. My mother never remarried. Her life was centered around me and her work. She never became a member of the Communist party even though she came under much pressure to join. She always read Western newspapers and magazines. She was never afraid of the authorities."

Tomas had grown up in Czechoslovakia knowing little about what had happened to the Jews during the war. He had received a Communist education. The Soviet Union was

270

the liberator that had driven the Nazis from the country and put an end to the decadence of capitalist influence there. The extermination of the Jews was not mentioned. He had never believed what he learned in school because his mother told him otherwise. Particularly, he did not believe the official party line on Israel. He had grown up with the notion of Israel as a land of heroes, a place where his father had gone to be free. His mother had always told him that his father had been compelled to fight for his people, that he had had good reason to abandon his family. As Tomas grew up, he began to understand. There were very few Jews left in Czechoslovakia. The Jewish Community Center in Prague, once a bustling, active organization, was dark and empty. Old men gathered there at lunchtime for hot, kosher meals. The synagogue which was one of the oldest in Europe was also empty. On its walls, in letters less than one inch high, were the names of the 80,000 Czech Jews, including both sets of my grandparents and one set of his, who had been murdered in the war.

"I was in high school when my sister suddenly found out about me," Tomas continued. "She was not a happy child. Maybe she sensed that when my father looked at her, he remembered that he had left another child behind. She was an only child. She was lonely. One day when my father was out, she looked through his desk and found one of my letters. She did not tell my father she had found the letter, but she wrote me. She wanted an explanation."

Tomas passed his hand through his hair and began to pace around the room. The rest of us—there were about seven or eight people sitting in the dimly lit room—kept quiet. I went on translating from the Czech into English, feeling as though I was transmitting blood. Had my parents not emigrated to America, I kept thinking, I might have gone to school with Tomas. We might have lived in the same neighborhood. We might have been friends.

"So my sister and I started a correspondence," he continued. "I was a fairly aimless student. I did not know what I wanted to do. I drank a lot. I listened to Western music on the radio. I listened to Joan Baez and Bob Dylan, records that relatives and friends of friends had brought in to the country. I decided to go to art school. I did not work very hard. I found no incentive. It was the bohemia of Prague. We drank. We slept around. The letters I received from my sister seemed to come from a different planet. We wrote to each other for a couple of years and I enjoyed the correspondence. Her letters could never have been described as lukewarm but as time went on they became so full of feeling that a stranger who did not know our relation would have called them love letters."

In 1968, when Tomas was twenty-two, the government of Alexander Dubcek began to liberalize the policies of Czechoslovakia in what the press was to call "The Prague Spring." Travel restrictions on Czechoslovak citizens were lifted and when this became known outside the country, Tomas' father and sister both wrote, urging him to visit. Tomas had, as he grew older, taken an increasing interest in the events transpiring in the Middle East. During the Six-Day War, he had followed the official Czechoslovak news broadcasts carefully, comparing them to the reports he listened to with his mother at night on the channels of Radio Free Europe. He wanted to see Israel. He wanted to travel anywhere outside Czechoslovakia. Most of all, he wanted to see the phantom of his imagination that his father had become.

"My mother encouraged me to go," Tomas said. "In all those years she had never allowed herself to become bitter about my father. She would manage, she told me. She thought I needed to go. *I* was the one who couldn't make up my mind. It was as if I sensed what was going to happen. I thought maybe it would be better not to try to change the way things were, not to ever know who my father was. But in the end, my curiosity was stronger than anything else, so I came."

272

It was midnight in Jerusalem and all of us sat in the room of one of the student hostels wide awake. Tomas stopped his pacing to drink a cup of tea and then resumed. My throat was dry. Occasionally, a shiver would run down my spine. Tomas' story was both strange and yet recognizable to me. I felt as if I could fill in all the details he was leaving out. I had made a journey to Prague the previous summer. I had seen the Jewish Community Center and the synagogue with my family's names printed on the walls. It was the only place in the world where their presence on earth had been noted. The synagogue had been closed for reconstruction that month. Someone had discovered evidence of Roman ruins in the ground beneath it. I had bribed the custodian to let me in and I had stood, surrounded by the walls of names alone, sobbing, letting out years of dammed-up tears, all the tears I had never let free when I listened to my parents talk about the war or their dead families. The custodian had left me there for five minutes. Then he came back to tell me I would have to leave. There was no place to leave a stone or a flower or anything else. I touched the few inches of the wall that had my grandparents' and uncles' names written on it. Then I left.

All the feelings I had had then, walking in the rain through the cobblestoned streets of Prague came back to me as Tomas talked. He talked angrily now. He gestured with his arms and his thin, sharp features tensed into an expression of tremendous anxiety.

"I did not feel good here, from the moment I landed at the airport. I was used to Prague. I was used to beauty. All I saw when I came here was dust and sand. The sands of Africa, I kept thinking. From the start when I saw my father I knew nothing would be explained. He was an Israeli now. He wanted to show me everything about the country he had fought for. He showed me off to his friends. He showed off his son. He gave me money. He wanted me to learn Hebrew and to stay in Israel. To join the army. To work in his business. He is a very busy man. He works hard. He does not like to talk very much. Not about the past. He was happy that my sister had someone to spend time with now. She was a troublesome child, he said. She had always had problems.

"I was very pleased with my half-sister. We could talk together. She spoke Czech. She showed me around. We had wonderful times together. We went to record stores and bought all the records I had wanted in Czechoslovakia. We bought records of the Beatles and she taught me the English words. There was a song, 'Hey Jude' that we played over and over again until I knew it by heart. *Take a sad song and make it better.* That song was ours. I slept in the living room where the phonograph was and I listened to music. I walked around the city and I went to school to learn Hebrew but I had difficulty learning the language. I didn't like the people. I hated the climate. The heat. I missed Prague. I missed my mother.

"My sister was going out with a medical student. He took my sister to parties and to the beach. Sometimes he sat with us in the living room listening to records. I understood that my father and my stepmother wanted her to be married. We went to the beach often. I had never seen the sea before and I would walk along it for hours wondering what I was doing in Palestine. My father and my sister refused to believe that I would return to Czechoslovakia. There was no future there, my father said, after the Russian invasion. The borders would be closed tight. If I went back, I would never be able to come out again. My father was pleased that my sister and I got along so well. I was learning Hebrew. I was his son. He expected me to decide to stay in Israel.

"That idea seems impossible to me," Tomas said, stopping in the middle of the room. "I was not raised as a Jew. This is not my country. These aren't the people I know. I can't speak the language. I don't like the food. I tried for the first few months to like it here. I tried to be what my father

274

wanted. All the time I've been in this country I've tried. But I can't do it. I can't make myself into something I'm not. The more I think about it, the more impossible the situation becomes. Completely apart from my relationship with my sister."

Tomas sighed and ran his hand through his disheveled hair.

"She came home from the beach one day crying. No one else was at home. She came and sat down beside me in the living room where I was listening to records and told me what happened. She had gone to the beach with her boyfriend. He wanted to go to bed with her and she was afraid. They argued. She didn't want to. He did. In the end, they slept together and that was why she was crying. It wasn't the way she imagined. It wasn't the way she had wanted it.

"I put on that record we both liked. The one with 'Hey Jude.' I tried to comfort her. I held her and told her it was like that sometimes the first time. I told her it would get better, that she would learn to like it. But she would not stop crying. She said it was all wrong, that it was a terrible way to lose her virginity and that she wanted to erase it. She wanted *me* to sleep with her. I wanted to help her. I felt for her. So I did."

I translated those last words and wanted to stop, to go back and ask him questions. But I was not an interviewer in this situation; I was a translator. Tomas went on talking and pacing and gesturing.

"So that's how it started. And then it continued. It continued for three months, all of us living in the same house and my father and my stepmother knowing nothing, suspecting nothing. My father even asked me to try to talk some sense into my sister. She took what I said to heart, my father told me. I was a good influence on her and I should make use of it. I should tell her to hurry up and marry the medical student before he changed his mind about her. He would say that my sister lived in a fantasy world, that she

275

thought her parents would always be there to take care of her. It was hard to make her understand that this was not the case, he said. Anything I would say would be a great help. And how was my Hebrew going? My father would exchange a few sentences with me in that horrible language. Then he would predict I would be ready to work in his business within a few months. That was the character of our conversation.

"My father does not spend a great deal of time thinking about what he is told or wondering about what people really feel. It did not occur to him that even if I stayed in Palestine, I would have little interest in his business. It did not occur to him that his daughter might not love the man he wanted her to marry. He was ignorant of anything going on between the two of us. My sister told him that I loved the sea, that she wanted to take me to Eilat and my father gave us enough money to stay in the best hotels.

"We camped out in Eilat. We rented a jeep and drove out into the desert. We rode the glass-bottomed boats over the coral reefs along with the American tourists. We smoked hashish with the beatniks on the beach. We imagined we were free. We talked about eloping, running away to someplace far off like New Zealand and adopting children. We swam and sat in the sun until our minds were dull. Then it was over and we took the bus home.

"She slept most of those eight hours, and I stared out the window. Some people write poetry about the desert; to me, it looked like an endless stretch of rubble. I thought about my father leaving the city of Prague, the church spires and the winding streets, the sloping roofs, the river. How could he have abandoned civilization for this? How could he have abandoned my mother and me? I thought also about my sister. That this was all a daydream that had to end. That the best solution for both of us was for me to go back to Prague and for her to marry the medical student. It was the only solution."

276

Shortly after the two returned from their vacation in Eilat, Tomas' father announced the engagement of his daughter. She would be married in a fancy hotel, where the American tourists stayed. Tomas thought daily about returning to Prague as soon as the wedding celebration was over, but he made no concrete plans. He would soon be twenty-three, not much younger than his father had been when he had left Czechoslovakia for Palestine. The father and son had never once discussed that decision. The father had not volunteered information and Tomas had not asked questions. The past hung between them like an invisible curtain which neither made a move to raise. The present too was something Tomas could not discuss with his father, so they made small talk. His father talked business and Tomas listened.

The wedding took place as planned. The newlyweds had moved into their apartment, and Tomas continued seeing his sister. The situation had become unbearable for him, he said. He had no desire to stay in Israel. His roots, his tastes, the parts of his family he felt closest to were in Czechoslovakia. His language was there. Here, he could barely make himself understood. He had not been raised to live in a Levantine country, he said. How could he suddenly transform himself into a Jew when all his life he had been unaware of religion or Jewish tradition? If his father had wanted a Jewish son, why had he left him in Prague? Why had he kept Tomas' life a secret from his sister? Things were a fine mess now. They could never be straightened out. The only solution was to leave and go back to Prague. That was where he belonged. What difference did it make if he would never again be allowed to leave Czechoslovakia? Where did he want to go? Where else was there for him to live? The only thing holding him in Israel now was his sister, and it would be best for all concerned if he went away.

"But I can't go," he said. "I just can't leave her here. I'm all she has. I'm her family. I'm the only one she trusts."

277

He stopped pacing and sat down, spent. No one said a word. No one moved, not for a long time.

That night, nearly ten years ago, Tomas had entrusted his story to me. I had been working as a reporter for the *Jerusalem Post* and in his mind that was enough to qualify me as a serious writer. "Promise me you'll write this down one day," he said. "I can't write. I don't speak English. You understand what I said. One day you can put it in a book."

A few months after that night, Tomas returned to Prague. His passport was revoked and although he wrote me letters, they arrived only sporadically and I thought that some had been intercepted by the Czechoslovak postal authorities. Tomas was not circumspect in his letters, as were my parents' friends who wrote from Czechoslovakia. He described the political situation there in concrete terms. He wrote of prominent people being jailed and of the arguments he had at work in a small printing shop. Some time later, he wrote that he had married, and later still, that he had left his wife. He found himself speaking up for Israel whenever conversation among his friends turned to the Middle East. He began to sign his letters in Hebrew characters. It was clear to me that he had become as much a Jew living in Czechoslovakia as he had been a Czech living in Israel. I worried about him.

For nearly ten years I carried his story around among my papers. It was something I had to grow into; something I had to wait to understand. At first, Tomas' story had awed me: it seemed like a Greek tragedy, stark, enigmatic, about one of the most ancient taboos. It was unusual in the extreme, I thought. It had no connection to me. But, over the years as I reread what I had recorded of his story, I began to view him in the context of other children of survivors I had met. Like the rest of us, he had grown up with an unexplained mystery about his past. He had been told that whatever happened had radicalized his father so powerfully that he had felt compelled to leave his family. Tomas had grown up without a father and had traveled to Israel to claim him. But his father had sealed off the past and Tomas' attempt to uncover it had failed.

Instead, Tomas had found a sister, who seemed to share his sense of abandonment even though she had grown up in the same house with their father. What had happened between them, I came to think, was less the result of physical attraction, or circumstances, or a desire to take revenge, but of a desire to heal. Their affair had begun as a kind of healing, as an attempt at repair. It was, I thought, a form of restitution.

SIXTEEN

I lived in Israel for three years, from the age of nineteen to twenty-two. It was a happy time for me. Students, like soldiers or kibbutzniks, were accorded a special status and respect in Israel. There were only six universities in the country then, and barely 40,000 students. We heard lectures in bright, freshly built lecture halls and studied in the National Library that stood at the center of the Hebrew University campus. Restaurants, bus lines, theaters and concert halls gave us special discounts. The country's most prominent figures came to our auditoriums to address us, for we were the nation's élite, the pool from which future leaders in a multitude of fields would be drawn.

I enjoyed that status and took advantage of the options that it offered. I spent long hours in the library and even longer ones in Jerusalem's many cafés, engaged in the elaborate, open-ended discussions that are a feature of student life all over the world. I had also, at the age of twenty, become a part-time reporter for the *Jerusalem Post,* the country's only English-language daily, and that work led me into neighborhoods and lifestyles that many other university students never saw. I was interested in the problems new immigrants had in Israel, in the problems they had finding housing and work, and in adapting to a new culture. I was interested in writing about the Oriental Jews, who comprised less than 5 percent of the university population at the time. Many of them lived in conditions far more Spartan than the poorest university student. I was interested in hardship.

"You kids have no idea what life is like for most people," my mother used to tell my brother and me when we were growing up, and I knew she was right. I thought it important that I should know. I wanted to know the way other girls I knew wanted to know about love or sex. Knowing danger or poverty or discrimination seemed to me the measure of adulthood. I was not overly concerned with professional success, or money, or property. My parents had none of these and yet led rich lives. What they did have, and what I wanted, was a sense of being able to survive any kind of catastrophe. They had a strength and resilience, as well as compassion, that I believed was the result of suffering.

"You don't have to look for it," my mother often told me as I was growing up, for even as a child I was drawn to poor people, unhappy people, people I thought I could help. "Life has a way of making you suffer whether you like it or not." But I was impatient. I sensed a double message coming from my parents. On the one hand, they wanted me to be trouble-free. On the other, they looked down on people who were complacent in their trouble-free lives. They did not fully respect them. I felt that people who had never been victims were not altogether human. There was something missing. Psychiatrists had observed that some survivors and their children identified strongly with the aggressor; others, like myself, could identify only with the victim. To be part of the oppression, even to be part of the Establishment, was

281

tantamount, in my mind, to being a Nazi. It was largely an unconscious association, but one that had influenced my choices all my life. In high school and in summer camp, on committees and teams and in organizations, I had consistently challenged authority and the exercise of power. Moreover, when I was given authority over others, I felt uncomfortable with it. The idea of authority in my mind was synonymous with inflicting pain.

After my first year at the Hebrew University, I had moved out of the modern, centrally-heated student dormitory and into a rented room on Shmuel HaNavi Street, in a near-slum of Russian, North African and Hungarian immigrants. My landlady was a Russian grandmother, Pani Sborovskaya, who talked to me in a mixture of Yiddish and Russian and often recalled hiding in her family's cellar during pogroms in Odessa. She lit Sabbath candles on Friday night, hovering over them in the center windowless room of her three-room apartment as if there were still hordes of potential enemies outside. She hoarded her possessions, monitored my use of hot water, and questioned me about the monetary value of everything visible in my room.

"*Skolko?*" How much? she would demand, pointing to my typewriter, my battery-operated phonograph, my radio, or to a coat my mother had made for me. I would do my best in Czech and newly-acquired Russian to explain how much these things cost in New York and Pani Sborovskaya would nod and cluck and marvel at the abundance of America. Her reactions often amused me but more often I felt a deep, gnawing guilt. Her tiny apartment, her incessant preoccupation with prices, the shabby, sack-like dresses and *babushka* she wore on her head were always a reminder that I was merely passing through and that I would go on to better things.

During the winter months, when the Jerusalem cold seeped into the stone buildings, Pani Sborovskaya's only source of heat for the entire apartment was an ancient kerosene stove. Its wick had to be soaked in kerosene and then lit with a match, causing great puffs of smoke to fill the room. The smoke and stench made it necessary to open the windows, defeating the purpose of the exercise, making the room even colder than it had been before. On cold nights, I typed letters to my parents wearing gloves on my hands and I wore sweaters and socks to bed. I took pride in my discomfort just as I took pride in living in a country that was in danger.

By 1969, the initial euphoria that had followed the victory of the Six-Day War was over. Now, newspapers carried accounts of the "War of Attrition," a less dramatic and constant war, a war of nerves. Radio newscasts reported frequent border skirmishes along the Suez Canal and international airline highjackings, along with incidents of sabotage within Israeli cities. In Jerusalem alone, the cafeteria of the Hebrew University, a central supermarket, and Machaneh Yehudah, the open-air market, had been rocked by explosions that injured dozens of civilians. At the university, an iron fence now enclosed the campus. Routine inspections of handbags and parcels were instituted at the university's entrance as well as in movie theaters, banks, the post office, and other public buildings.

The war against terrorism was unlike the wars shown on television. A bomb might be placed inside a student's briefcase, an explosive inside a paper bag left on a park bench. Schoolchildren were taught to identify the more common explosives. University students were instructed to report any unattended parcels in the library and in our classrooms. If some of us had come to Israel looking for danger, our mission was accomplished. Every few weeks there would be an explosion or the discovery of an explosive somewhere in Jerusalem. From our classrooms we would hear sirens, then the chopping of a helicopter taking the wounded to Hadassah Hospital. Later, on the green lawn in front of the National Library, students would gather around a transistor

283

radio to hear the details. If the sabotage was major, and likely to be reported on the American television networks, the American students would line up at the central post office to telephone or cable home that they were safe. The war had moved into our lives. Interspersed between our lectures and student parties were moments of shock and fear. None of us talked about feeling scared; it was considered bad form. But a certain strain became part of life in Jerusalem. Sabotage meant not only death but the prospect of being maimed or scarred for the rest of one's life. That prospect frightened me and I was ashamed of feeling frightened. I wanted to cure myself of that feeling. After all, my parents had lived with the threat of death for three years. On the border kibbutzim of Israel, farmers worked their fields under constant threat of artillery fire. At the time, my university was sending student volunteers to those border settlements in an effort to boost morale. I decided to go for a week, as a reporter as well as a volunteer.

On a clear April morning at 5:30, I waited at the university for the bus that would take me and some fifty other volunteers to the Beisan Valley. They looked sleepy, soft and exposed against the landscape, which was already brownish and dry with the approach of summer. They wore jeans and safari shirts. Two or three carried guitars. They were mostly "Anglo-Saxons" like me, students from the United States, England, South Africa and Canada who had the carefree look of vacationers off for a week in the country.

A few feet away from them, sitting on a boulder, was a man who looked different. His face was pale and thin, the nose beaked. His shirt and pants hung loosely from his slight frame. He looked like a ragamuffin watching a parade. It was the expression on his face, a curious blend of sarcasm and eagerness, that caught my attention.

The bus arrived then and the volunteers got on. They traded sandwiches and fruit. After a while they took their guitars out of their cases and began to sing the songs of the sixties, the American folk and protest songs that made their way around the world. I knew the words by heart; I had sung them several years earlier in Washington Square. I soon lost interest in singing. I was interested in the thin man who sat by himself at the front of the bus and soon asked if I could sit down beside him.

I explained I was a reporter writing an article about the students who had volunteered to spend their spring vacation working on a border kibbutz. He looked amused. I had the distinct impression, without his having said a word, that he thought my introduction, my assignment, and the whole busload of students slightly ridiculous.

"What do you study?" I asked him.

"I don't," he said. "Once I studied sociology."

"And now?"

"Now I don't study."

"How did you get on this bus then?"

"I said I was a student."

"But why?"

"I had my reasons," he said, and smiled.

Something in the quickness of that smile and in the seared quality of his face held my attention.

"Where are you from?"

"Warsaw," he said. "I was born in the Ghetto. When I was two years old, they smuggled me out. My parents died there. Do you really enjoy asking questions or is it some sort of game you play?"

I looked at him in surprise. It had not occurred to me before that anyone could have been *born* in the Warsaw Ghetto. I was silent. I did not know what to say.

"I'm sorry if I offended you," he said. "I'm just not accustomed to people asking me questions."

"You didn't offend me," I said slowly.

He had impressed me. I had always been impressed by men who looked as though they had suffered and Marc, with his sharp, tensile face and nervous smile, looked as though he had come through fire.

By the time we arrived at the border kibbutz, Marc had

told me that he had grown up on the outskirts of Warsaw and that he and a friend had played at journeying to Palestine since they were children. Even as a university student, Marc had retained that vision and before graduating he had made his way to Haifa.

Israel had been as much of a shock to him as it had been to Tomas when he arrived from Prague. Marc had imagined a country of farmer-philosophers living in a utopian society. He did not say what had led to his nervous breakdown, just that it had occurred shortly after his arrival nine years before. He said he had stowed away on the bus because he had spent his last welfare check and had no more friends from whom to borrow money. He liked the simplicity of kibbutz life, he said, and was happy to work six hours in exchange for food and lodging.

At the time, I did not really see the man who was talking to me. I saw history. I was too intrigued by where he had come from to understand his situation now. When I was eight years old, my parents had taken me to the theater to see *The Wall,* a play about the Warsaw Ghetto. The strains of melancholy tunes played on the concertina had remained in my ears. I imagined Marc as an infant, hidden in bunkers with a handkerchief pressed over his mouth to muffle any cries, and I imagined that he had been carried out of the Ghetto by a resistance fighter who knew his way through the sewers. The Warsaw Ghetto was an island in my imagination of the war. It was there that Jews had taken some of the enemy to death with them. The fact that Marc had been born there and that his parents had died there, attracted me the way good looks or good prospects attracted other girls to men. We spent time together that week and I hung on his words.

Every morning, the volunteers rose at five and waited for the mine sweepers to clear the banana fields. Then we went out among the plants, feeling brave as we glanced up toward the Jordanian hills, wondering if we would draw fire.

The kibbutz appeared idyllic in the early morning. Its flower beds, white cottages, lawns and rows of palm trees hardly advertised danger. The only signs of security precautions were the white, giraffe-like protrusions that rose from the lawns at regular intervals: the passages to the shelters.

The shelling came on the fourth morning, just as the sun was beginning to send light into the valley. The shells flew with a long, vacant whistle. When they landed, the sound was like dynamite inside a distant mine. It was rhythmic, the shelling: pop, long whistle, *boom!* pop, long whistle, *boom!* The rhythm pulled me out of sleep, into half-wakefulness. I listened for a while without realizing what it was.

"Wake up!" someone screamed in the next room, and the cottage came alive with voices and scrambled noise. The other girls rushed out the door and down the steps to the shelter. I stayed behind, pulling on my clothing slowly. I looked out the window for some visual confirmation of danger, but all I saw was the neat pattern of cottages and paths in the dawn light. Then a shell exploded which sounded close by, and I ran down into the shelter.

It was long, cool, narrow and clean, like the corridor of a well-maintained steamship. Wood benches lined the white walls and wooden bunks provided accommodation for sleeping. There were some twenty people inside sitting, reading, talking and eating the Jaffa oranges and sour candies that one woman passed around. Above us the shelling continued: pop, whistle, *boom!* pop, whistle, *boom!* The students imitated the casual manner of the kibbutzniks. It was difficult to know what they were thinking. I was thinking about Marc, wondering if he had childhood memories of the Warsaw Ghetto. After the shelling had stopped for a few minutes, we left the shelter and went to work in the banana fields. No one talked about the half-hour underground.

"You found enough material for your newspaper article?" Marc asked on the bus ride back to Jerusalem.

I told him I had and that I was glad to be returning to

the city. He was too. He said he lived in a valley filled with shacks like his own, pre-fab dwellings that had been built for the influx of new immigrants twenty years before. The people who had lived there then, he said, had long since moved away. Poor North African families lived there now. "People you don't read about in the newspapers," he said. "Certainly not in English, in the *Jerusalem Post*."

I told him that if ever I found myself in his neighborhood, I would drop in for tea. When we got to Jerusalem, we said good-bye.

Half a year later when I came home from the university, Pani Sborovskaya told me I had had a caller. "A drunkard," she said, giggling. "Like in Russia. A *real* drunkard. And he knew your name."

"I don't know any drunkards," I told her. "He must have been looking for someone else."

There was a knock at the door and when I opened it, I saw Marc standing against the stair railing.

"You never came to visit," he said. His words were slurred together. His thin cheeks were bright red.

"No. I was never in that part of ..." I stopped myself. "Would you like to come in?"

"Definitely. I definitely want to come in. I decided last week to come and see you."

He lurched past me and past Pani Sborovskaya who stood blocking the way to her part of the apartment, into my room, where he folded himself into a corner on the floor. "Can you give me a glass of brandy?" he asked.

"I don't have any," I said. "I don't drink."

He dug his hand into the pocket of his pants and held out some money. "Please buy me a bottle then."

I stared at him.

"I'll go down then," he said, moving to stand up.

"No, I'll go," I said.

I left him sitting on the floor and hurried out past Pani Sborovskaya who was sitting in her housecoat and *babushka*

288

at a vantage point from which she could observe whatever she could of this extraordinary visit.

"Where are you going?" she demanded. "He's going to stay in your room alone?"

"I'll be right back," I told her.

In Israel, liquor is sold in most grocery stores and I had no trouble finding a bottle of brandy. When I returned with it, Marc asked for two glasses and some orange juice. Then he threw the brandy down his throat.

"Why do you do it? It's so ugly," I said.

"Don't you know it's possible to be an optimist when you drink? No, you wouldn't know. You probably have never been drunk in your life."

"No, I haven't."

I sat down crosslegged on the narrow cot that was my bed. He remained sitting on the floor, leaning against the wall. His face was red, which made him look even more birdlike than before. His eyes were growing red-rimmed too. I wondered what would happen next. I wondered what had occasioned his visit.

"It seems we have mutual friends," he said. His speech was becoming hard to decipher even though his manner had grown more formal. "I was invited to dinner with some people and your name came up in the conversation. I asked for your address.

"I came here today to ask you if you would be interested in having an arrangement."

"An arrangement?" I asked. I had no idea what he was talking about.

"I came here to ask you to be my mistress. I will arrange for a place where we can meet. You need not worry. My situation now is better than it was at this time last year. I have some money. We could meet once a week at first. More often, if we found it desirable."

I said nothing. The situation was so exotic, so different from anything else I had ever experienced that I was speechless. I was accustomed to casual American boys who came on smoothly with well-practiced lines, or Israelis who practically knocked you over into bed. Certainly no one in my experience had ever turned up drunk and then formally proposed that I become his mistress. Even the word sounded peculiar, as if it had been taken from a nineteenth-century novel.

But before I had a chance to reply, Marc slumped against the wall and fell into a harsh, snoring sleep. I covered him with a blanket and then sat back down on my bed, listening to the rasp of his breath. I did not deliberate whether or not to accept the proposal. He was already there in my room. My acquiescence had little to do with love or sexual attraction. It was a test, a test of my endurance and a crash course in living on the underside of society.

When Marc woke up it was still bright outside. I brought him a mug of coffee and he drank it down without a word. I felt everything had been settled, a compact had been made.

We went out into the street. I took nothing with me but my keys. We had walked several blocks before Marc realized I had brought no money. He had used the last of his to buy the bottle of brandy.

"All we need is one bus fare," he said. "No problem." Then he told me to keep on walking down the street irrespective of what he did.

There were five or six street kids clustered around two motorcycles up the block, languid in their shiny pants and shoes. They were slum kids, the kind that started brawls in the balconies of movie theaters on Saturday nights and sprayed the floors of buses with chewed-up sunflower seeds. Marc stopped beside them and I kept walking. A few moments later he caught up with me and pressed bus fare into my palm.

"Did you *beg?*" I stopped moving.

"No, I found the money in the street."

"What are you going to use for bus fare?"

"Wait," he said, when we reached the bus stop.

He told me to enter the bus when it pulled up as if I were alone. When I got to the back of it, I should look to see if he was aboard and, if not, pull the wire signal and get off. I did what he said. From the back of the bus I could see him debating with the bus driver, his face sallow and unshaven, his thin arms gesticulating as he argued. Marc seemed untroubled by the rows of passengers watching him talk his way to a free bus ride. He was polite but determined. I cringed as I watched him. I felt humiliated.

"There are very few drivers who will refuse," Marc told me a few minutes later, when passengers had stopped turning their heads to see where he had sat down. "The advantage is always with the man who is asking. The guilt attaches to the man who can give but does not."

I said nothing, as was to become my habit with Marc. I was beginning to see the world from an entirely different angle than the one I was accustomed to. I had left my wallet with all proofs of my identity and privilege in the apartment of Pani Sborovskaya. I was suddenly without documents and in the company of a man I would have regarded as a bum in any other circumstance. Now, he had become my guide to a world where people lived on the charity of others.

We went first to the apartment of a friend of Marc, the first of a group of Polish emigré friends I was to meet who appeared to be living in a shared and somewhat sinister past. The woman who opened the door for us was Marc's age, near thirty, but she looked older. Behind her, the apartment spread out like an unfrequented pawn shop. Old clocks, framed photographs and wood boxes piled up against the walls, their tops gray with dust. It looked the way I had imagined my mother's apartment to have looked when she returned to Prague from the war. It had a feeling of desolation and tragedy, of time arrested in its flow.

The woman spoke in Polish to Marc and I could make out that they were arguing about money. We drank tea in glasses, and then the woman brought out a clay pipe and a small bag of hashish.

"Do you smoke?" She addressed me for the first time.

"She's an American," Marc said before I could answer.

That apparently meant that I was accustomed to drugs, that I took for granted a practice that in Israel was still associated with Arabs and the underclass of North African Jews who had emigrated to Israel. It also underscored my difference from the old, mildewed world of that room. I was fresh, unfettered by the past, naive, strong. An American. There was a mixture of envy and disdain in the way both of them pronounced the word.

I sat there quietly, taking the clay pipe when it was offered to me, taking in the atmosphere of that dark, heavy room. It was like a museum room reconstructed to resemble an original which had been destroyed in Europe. Certainly, one had no sense of being in Israel when sitting there. When we left and came out into the pink afternoon light, I felt as if I had been sitting in a movie theater.

We walked away from the massive concrete apartment complex to the crest of the hill on which the buildings stood. Across from us was another hill, with another set of new buildings, white, square and clean against the blue sky. Between the two hills was a valley filled with about one hundred asbestos shacks, the kind of vista that makes poverty look picturesque. From a distance, the shacks looked homey and far more human than the huge blocks of apartment buildings. A few of the inhabitants had marked off their tiny plots of ground with barbed wire and planted shrubs. Others had put together small sheds of corrugated iron and sheets of plastic. A narrow road coiled down to the bottom of the valley, empty of traffic.

"The grocery store is over there," Marc pointed out, as we walked down the road. "The bus stops there. Only once every forty minutes. Not like the bus in Rehavia. If you miss it and are in a hurry, you have to walk up those steps." He pointed to a pyramid-like set of steps that climbed toward the concrete blocks at the top of the other hill. Class lines were geographically clear here: the people in the valley lived looking up.

There was no sidewalk from the road to his shack. There were no sidewalks at all. We walked through the weedy yards of neighbors along a dirt trail. I lost my footing on a loose stone and wondered how people found their way around at night. There were no street lights. Up close, the shacks were flimsy, shabby, like matchboxes. Poorly dressed, dark-skinned children wandered outside them. I remembered a picture I had seen in *Life* magazine of *favelas* in Brazil.

"If you faint it's on your own time," Marc warned as he turned the key to his door. Then he pushed it open.

I saw green walls, the pea-green color of hospital corridors and neglected institutions. The floor was piled ankle-deep with wasted things: damp clothing, torn books, old shoes, empty bottles, pots and plates caked with the remains of food. The windows were small, closed and almost opaque. One light bulb hung from the ceiling. There was a dirty sink in one corner of the room, a wood desk strewn with papers in another. A metal cot piled with three distended mattresses, old magazines and blankets was pushed against a wall that had newspaper pages tacked over the cracks.

"Have a seat," Marc said, pushing the things on the mattress into a pile.

I sat down cautiously on the cot. A large brown stain ran across the mattress ticking where I had leaned my hand and I moved it quickly to my lap.

"You didn't expect this."

I shook my head.

I thought: How could anyone live like this? How could anyone let themselves be buried in the refuse of one's life? But while one part of me recoiled from the contents of the room I was sitting in, another part recognized in it a futility and despair that was not unfamiliar. It was the other side of my busyness. Already, I had become competent and efficient: I was thinking of ways to clean it up.

"Have you changed your mind?" Marc asked me. His voice was double-edged, sarcastic as well as anxious.

"What are you thinking?"

"Why you live here," I said.

"It never disappoints me." He rapped the thin walls with his knuckles. "It's about the only thing that doesn't. People, books. Even nature. They all disappoint you in one way or another. I've had too many disappointments."

My expression must have registered the note of self-pity in his words for suddenly Marc became brisk and cheerful. He began to kick the mess on the floor into a pile. "I want to throw most of this out," he said, picking out pieces of clothing that were dirty but worth saving. "We can make a fire outside and burn it."

"Burn it?"

"Why not? Do you see anything you want to keep?"

"No."

"Are you going to sit and watch?" He scooped up an armful of the pile on the floor and carried it outside. "Well? Are you going to help me?"

For a moment I thought: There's still time to walk away. I imagined what my parents and my friends would say if they saw the shack and the man who lived in it. "Are you crazy?" they would say. "What on earth are you doing here? What are you trying to prove?" I would not have known then what to answer. In retrospect, I know that I could not have truthfully told anyone what I was really doing, not Marc, not my parents, not myself. I was drawn to the idea of sinking to the bottom of society, to getting lost in it the same way Al Singerman had wanted to get lost in the American army. I wanted to feel connected to the experience my parents had undergone and Marc was a kind of vehicle for me to do so, an unwitting instrument I was using.

294

Only years later, when I came across a diary entry by Moses Leib Lilienblum, an early Zionist in Russia, did this become clear to me. "I am glad I have suffered," he wrote during the Odessa pogrom of 1881. "At least once in my life I have had the opportunity to feel what my ancestors felt every day of their lives. . . . I am their son, their suffering is dear to me and I am exalted by their glory."

Standing in the shack that afternoon with my arms full of refuse, I had no such clarity about what I was doing. All I knew was that I was acting on a deeply-felt impulse that had to be kept secret from everyone I knew, particularly Marc himself. He saw me as a happy, healthy, American girl whose strength and optimism he could tap. I wanted him to do that. I felt that I had strength and health to spare, and that it should be used to good purpose. But that too had to be kept a secret for Marc would not acknowledge that he needed help of any kind. He had been visited by a social worker at one time. "Once a week," he had told me, "she would come and talk. She asked me questions mostly. The only problem was that the questions she asked were irrelevant to me and everything she was writing in her reports had no relation to reality. She wasn't stupid. She was forced to admit that there was little she could do for me but provide company for an hour or two. And since she was so distressed at not being able to change anything, she was not very good company at that."

There was no need for talk at first with Marc; there were things to do. He had made a fire outside, on the small plot of dirt in front of the shack and as the sun set, we burned everything that could not be salvaged. A few neighborhood children came to watch the flames and smoke wondering, no doubt, what we were doing. A terrific feeling of setting things right, of cleaning up a mess, had come over us. We were beginning. We were like children constructing a toy house, making something out of nothing, participating on a minuscule scale in the national effort of rebuilding. There were so many details to consider, so many plans to make in regard to the house we were creating, that we had no time to consider the relation between ourselves.

I made lists of things to bring over from my apartment, things to borrow, things to buy, things we might find discarded in the street. Marc would collect all the empty bottles in the house and carry them up the steps to the supermarket at the top of the hill. With the money he received in exchange, he would pay part of the electric bill. Then he would gather up whatever linen had not been burned and take it to the laundry.

When the fire was reduced to a few glowing lumps in the ground and the floor of the shack was cleared, it had grown dark and chilly. There was nothing more to be done. I was cold and hungry. I wanted a bath and there was no tub, no hot water. "I don't want to stay here," I told Marc, "and you can't stay at my place." Marc nodded. "I have a friend."

We walked out into the darkness over the uneven ground and up the steps to the top of the hill, through empty streets to the building where his friend lived. The apartment where his friend lived was empty. There was food in the refrigerator, hot water in the bathroom and mattresses on which to sleep. We slept there that night. We sealed the terms of our contract and there was care but no current in our touch. I felt like a dead person making love. I felt no physical sensation, no sharing of blood. My thoughts zoomed in and out of the makeshift bed on the floor of a stranger's house: I was an accomplice, a sister, a partner perhaps, but not a lover. Our encounter was brief and it left me numb, lying awake with my eyes wide open, examining and re-examining the day's events while Marc slept alongside me. Once that day, he had given me a curious glance and said, "You think you're Florence Nightingale, don't you?" I had not answered him because to admit it would have been to end the affair before it began. Marc could haggle with bus drivers and beg for money in the streets but he clung to his dignity in personal affairs. My reasons for being with him would have to remain secret.

The next day and the days that followed it, I went off to university in the morning, leaving Marc to spend the day reading, walking, visiting friends. He had not held a job for some time. I did not know how long. Unlike the bulk of humanity, he said once, he did not require work to make life bearable. Now he had the task of assembling things for the shack. While I attended university lectures or interviewed people for the *Jerusalem Post*, he went out reclaiming articles he had once lent to friends, or bargaining with Arab vendors in the Old City for new items. Each time I took the long bus ride to the bottom of the valley and made my way through the weeds to Marc's shack, I found new additions to the interior. One day there was a small electric broiler on the counter beside the sink, an appliance that had belonged to him some years before. Another time there were new plates, then a teapot, a small lamp, and then some brushes and several cans of paint.

One weekend, we painted the green walls white. We cleaned the wood vegetable crates that friends had stolen for us from the supermarket in town, painted them and attached them to the walls for use as shelves. We obtained old mattresses from people who were buying a new bed and we piled them up in the newly white living room, covered with a blanket. The shack began to look bohemian instead of shabby: it began to have style. At night, when Marc brought out his brandy and proceeded to get drunk, I persuaded myself that this too would change, that his life could be reconstructed just like the shack. I sat with him as his eyes grew red and his speech grew garbled, trying to understand what drove him to do what he did. Marc, in turn, tried to pry out of me my reasons for being there with him. We spent whole evenings like that, coming no closer to understanding than we had been from the start.

Occasionally friends would come to the shack to visit. My friends came out of curiosity, to see where I had disappeared to. They came to the valley like tourists, looked around with dismay, found little to talk about with Marc and left wondering what I was doing there. They sensed I was involved in some sort of experiment that would not last long. Marc struck them as a pathetic, enigmatic figure, an oddity in a country which at the time had no counter-culture or alternative lifestyle. They saw he was very intelligent and they saw that his life had come apart at the seams, that he needed help. A few were drawn to him, the rest repelled. They waited for me to come to my senses, to resume the uncomplicated student life I had temporarily interrupted.

Marc's friends were different. They were older and although some held jobs, they seemed to live on the fringe of society. Most had lived in Israel for several years but their lives had not taken root there in any of the conventional ways. They had not married; they had not become part of Israeli society and yet they had no tight community of their own. Most had come from Eastern Europe by themselves and they led solitary lives, cut off from family or any group. They seemed separated from the fabric of any society past or present. They were people who did not fit in anywhere. Each of their lives seemed touched by tragedy and emotional instability and the explanation of it always had something to do with the war or immigration to Israel. They were cynical, mistrustful of strangers and their major interest in life seemed to be extensive, elaborate talk. Failure marked each of them: failure in work, failure in health, failure in forming ties to other people.

At first these people fascinated me. I would sit and watch them drink tea out of glasses and then brandy. I would try to follow their conversations about art and politics. A persistent melancholy informed their faces just as a persistent freshness and naiveté characterized the Americans living in Israel. That melancholy had been terribly attractive to me

298

the first day I had met Marc. I saw in it the melancholy of my mother and the melancholy I had always thought I carried inside me. But in Marc and his friends, this quality overshadowed all others. It ate into conversation and deadened laughter, corroding everything it touched. When I thought seriously about what little I knew of Marc's life, I no longer found it romantic but depressing. It frightened me. It was not something to play around with. I did not want to become like Marc or his friends. I could not even feel sure that I was helping him.

By the middle of my third year in Jerusalem, I had begun to feel a tug toward home. I had come to Israel to live as a Jew in a Jewish state, but also, I began to understand, to experience for myself the problems my parents had faced in emigrating from Czechoslovakia to the United States. I had managed well. I had learned to speak the language that had survived centuries of exile, dispersion, oppression and the Holocaust, a language that my grandfather had never known. I had, through my studies and simply by living in a Jewish society, become able to see beyond the Second World War, and back into a history that was rich, multiform and independent as well as marked by persecution. Israel had given me a Jewish education far better than any Sunday school and far broader than what my parents and their friends had given me. Living there had shown me that I could, if necessary, endure hardship and survive a war. I had seen, in that shelter on the border kibbutz and in my university classes where my fellow students had all been soldiers, people no different from myself. I saw that hardship had not necessarily conferred nobility of character or even compassion upon them, that its effects were as varied as human personality.

I had also found that I had my own history, separate from that of my parents. I had been raised in New York City, not Prague. My tastes, my values and my expectations of life had been shaped by America as surely as by my Central

European Jewish upbringing. I reread my parents' letters to me with a finer understanding. "I decided in 1948 to move to the United States so that you could grow up in freedom," my father had written to me. "We were a little tired after the war and, were it not for you, we probably would not have emigrated. Your mother knew it wouldn't be easy, especially for me, to start all over again at the age of forty-four. I understand your idealism about Israel. But as a 'survivor' I am above all interested in avoiding any further sacrifice of our family. I want my children to live in peace, in a country where they have the best opportunities."

In Israel, I saw a future of limited possibilities. I felt the constraint of hostile borders and began to understand the exhilaration my parents felt on Sunday mornings when they drove for miles into the country. I saw the limitations imposed by living in any small country, the professional and cultural limitations that induced many native-born Israelis to pursue careers abroad. Most of all, I began to feel the strain of living in a state of constant, low-grade tension, of expecting news of death or destruction as a matter of course. The stock response in Israel at the time was the slogan *Ein breira* or, "We have no choice." That continual state of exigency had its attractions. It removed the burden of making choices by eliminating them. It made reflection and doubt luxuries that could not be indulged and reduced the spectrum of life's colors to black or white. But I had choices. Like most young Americans, I had an abundance of choices, and I chose to go home.

Leaving Israel was not easy. Even strangers appeared to react to my decision as though it were a personal affront. Going home laid me open to accusations of abandoning a moral commitment for a life of convenience and friends did not hide their disappointment in me. "What have you got in America?" they asked me. "Don't you see people like you are needed here? Don't you know a Jew can never be secure in the Diaspora? How can someone like you, after all your parents went through, not understand that Israel is the only solution for the Jews?"

My parents' experience had taught me nothing of the sort. On the contrary, it had taught me to distrust ideologies and final solutions of any kind. It had engendered in me a deep-seated resistance to efforts at defining who I was or what I should be doing, even if those efforts came from other Jews. My parents' experience had taught me to be independent and extremely self-reliant and to follow my instincts. I had lived, studied and worked in Israel for three years, and had grown to love the country. But I wanted to put Marc, and war, and suffering behind me. I wanted to be in America again. I had been accepted at the Columbia University Graduate School of Journalism and, in the summer of 1970, I left Israel to go back home.

SEVENTEEN

"Suffer?"

Deborah Schwartz looked up at me with slow surprise. Even when she was startled, her face had a regal quality of perfect control. "Suffer?" she repeated. "No, I never wanted to suffer. Certainly not to establish a link with my parents or to prove myself. Why would anyone choose to suffer? I was sick and tired of suffering. If anything, I felt chosen to strive for a full life and to make up for my parents' losses. I felt an obligation to my family who perished and to my parents who survived but that obligation was to transform the past. I felt that my life wasn't entirely my own, and I wanted to make the most out of it that I could. Didn't you ever feel that they were all looking down on you from up there? Didn't you ever hope they felt they had not died in vain? I didn't want to let any of them down. I wanted them to be proud of me."

In the summer of 1970, as I was coming home from Israel,

Deborah was preparing in earnest for the Miss America Pageant that took place every September in Atlantic City. She was eighteen then: slender, vivacious, confident, and such a goody-goody that it was a wonder that her three younger siblings could bear her. Every morning Deborah performed a set of special exercises to streamline her body. Every day she lay motionless in the sun to obtain an even tan. For hours she played and replayed Frederic Chopin's *Revolutionary Etude* on her grand piano, trying to coax a maximum of drama and nuance from the phrases. Her performance would have to be striking, as striking as Deborah herself hoped to be, and if everybody in the Schwartz household could whistle the étude in their sleep by September, so what? It was a family effort.

For weeks, Deborah lived on diet sodas, salads without dressing and lean meat. "My parents watched me," she said. "My father would take cookies out of my mouth if he caught me eating them. There was lots of electricity in the house. Everyone was involved in every detail. I felt this great feeling of solidarity behind me. The whole city knew me: the gas station attendants, the mailmen, the people in the stores, the kids in the street. People would walk into my father's business all the time and ask, 'Are you Debbie's parents? We just know she's going to win. We want to let you know we're behind her all the way.'

"My parents were very happy. Very excited. And it felt good to be able to give them so much *nachas,* so much satisfaction. I thought I'd win. Not because I was so impressed with my looks, although I thought I had the basic exterior qualities to wear the crown. I was convinced I had a special story to tell. To win would be a victory for me, I thought, but also a victory over Hitler and Nazism, a victory for minorities who had been persecuted, and a victory for my parents who survived the Holocaust. For somebody of my background, whose mother was in Auschwitz at age sixteen, to become an American beauty queen was a great achievement. I valued being an American more than any other girl in Atlantic City. I didn't take it for granted."

Deborah Schwartz told me all of this in a cool, pleasant voice that did not falter or curl in embarrassment even when it carried a cliché. She was still, eight years after the pageant, unabashedly patriotic and likely to say the kinds of things about the United States that most young people associate with army recruitment posters, Daughters of the American Revolution, and the speeches of perennially optimistic politicians like the late Senator Hubert H. Humphrey. In fact, her ambitions had always been political. Even as a small child, she had often daydreamed about becoming a queen like Queen Esther in the Bible, who married the Persian King Ahasuerus and saved her people. Later, she had taken the daydream one step further: she imagined herself marrying an Arab leader like President Nasser of Egypt or Jordan's King Hussein and reconciling the warring parties in the Middle East. By the time she became a beauty queen, she was acting out the dream.

At Atlantic City, the press found her somewhat of a departure from traditional beauty queens. The press kits they received listed the honors, ambitions and favorite sports of each young woman. Miss Louisiana had been a "campus beauty" on the "pompom line." Miss Alabama had been an "athletic officer in her social sorority." Most of the state queens were intending to earn degrees in nursing, elementary school education, home economics and physical education when they graduated from college. When they took part in sports, they preferred water skiing, swimming and tennis. They had tame, rather childlike hobbies.

Deborah was different on several counts. She had been president of her regional branch of B'nai B'rith Youth Organization and had worked on a "Committee for Responsibility for War-Burned and War-Injured Vietnamese Children." She intended to major in political science and then go to law school. She listed chess and running track as her favorite

304

sports. But the most striking difference between Deborah and the forty-nine other state queens became apparent when the judges examined her application. *I am a first generation American,* she had written. *My parents, homeless and orphaned after surviving the Nazi concentration camps of World War II came to America in quest of a new life. I hope to be an ambassador to a foreign country, but first my mission is to tell a story about America to Americans. I want to tell it to my contemporaries, to their parents and to everyone I meet. I feel responsible to arouse Americans into participating in the "greatest experiment in human freedom and dignity ever attempted by man"—our country! Life is far too short to waste away in wars and petty misunderstandings.*

"Boy, was I ever idealistic," Deborah said now, and her finely etched, blue-gray eyes widened. Although she had been married for six years and now had two children, she still looked and talked very much like the slender, ambitious and idealistic girl who had planned to take Atlantic City by storm. There was an almost irritating quality of responsibleness about her, the unequivocal rectitude of an obedient first-born child who had made good on every single one of her parents' expectations.

This quality existed side by side with a hidden but persistent insecurity about the future. Since childhood, she had been plagued by nightmares of men chasing her and her family. She still had nightmares about members of her family dying or being killed. When she attended concerts or rallies, Deborah often wondered about the chances of someone having planted a bomb on the premises. When her husband had to be away overnight she lined up glass bottles in a row before the front door—an early warning system that would allow her time to escape.

"It's like your iron box," she told me. "I have a rock in my closet. I always think of what I would do if I needed to escape. Where are the exits? Who would I go to? Who would hide me and my family if I needed to be hid?" Although strangers were charmed by Deborah's slow, Southern manner and ready smile, she herself took her time opening up to people. She was careful and skeptical. She distrusted appearances. She had a strong measure of the street sense I had found common to all the children of survivors I had interviewed. It had taken her more than a year to decide that I could be trusted.

We had become friends, an unlikely pair of friends. To a casual observer, we seemed to have nothing in common. She was a conscientious wife and mother who also managed to give fifteen children piano lessons every week. Her family and household kept her so busy that she rarely found time to read a book through from beginning to end. I was a conscientious writer who spent most of my days alone, who had never been married, and who had always viewed the suburbs as a form of death. Yet I took the train out to the suburbs to visit her and she came downtown to see me. We enjoyed each other. We gave each other glimpses of the roads we had not chosen. The difference in the way we lived interested me because she and I had been very similar as children and teen-agers. We had both been extremely close to our parents and comfortable in the company of adults. We had both succeeded in school, at sports, at music lessons. People noticed and remembered us and our younger brothers hated it. When she talked about her childhood, I felt at times she could have been describing me.

"My father is the sole survivor of a family of nine people," she had learned to say in the same clear, dispassionate voice I adopted when talking about my father. "My mother's parents and baby brother and most of her family were also killed. These two people represent the links of a chain Hitler failed to break and I see myself as a further link in it. My parents never tried to hide the facts of suffering and loss from me, and I always had a desire to know even though it hurt. I always had a very hard lump in my throat when we talked about the subject but I never cried in front of them. I know they couldn't take it. They can't stand to see any of their children suffer. If one of us has the slightest headache, they get upset. If they were to see me unhappy or unhealthy, they would feel punished and I didn't want to punish them. I've always felt that my parents had more than their share of suffering and that I certainly did not want to add to it by not being good or respectful toward them."

Being a good child had been easy for her as it had been for me, even though, like her brother Joseph, she always felt different from everyone she knew. "In the South, families have roots that are generations deep," she told me. "People buy a piece of land and think: this is where the family will live. My parents didn't feel that way. They went south because there was a factory for sale. They had no social reasons for being there and I didn't either. I've never felt rooted anywhere. I grew up in a small town where not only were we different from the community but we were different from the other Jews in the community."

Her difference was something in which Deborah took pride, she told me, something that gave her strength and direction. At St. Catherine's school for girls, where she was the only Jewish girl in a class of thirty-five, she made a point of educating the people around her in aspects of Judaism. She taught her classmates and the nuns who instructed them whatever Hebrew words she knew; when it was her turn to lead prayers, she recited the *Sh'ma Yisrael.* As president of the student body, she wove references to the Holocaust into her speeches. Although she claimed never to have experienced an instance of anti-Semitism in school, I imagined that had such instances occurred, Deborah would have been far too proud to acknowledge them. A record of her high school career read like a résumé. Academically, she had always been among the top three students in school. She excelled in athletics and was usually the captain or best player on her baseball, basketball or track teams. She won awards from the National Federation of Music Clubs, from *Scholastic Magazine,* from the Soroptimist Club, and from the B'nai B'rith

Youth Organization. She wrote articles for the local newspaper's youth page. After school, she tutored black children and also volunteered to work with mentally retarded children. "I was never bored," Deborah told me. "I was always very busy and that was a good thing. I was very aware that my roots had been hacked away mercilessly in Europe and that no one had cared. For most of my adolescent life 'caring' about others, especially those persecuted or less fortunate than myself motivated me to help and to represent the good. I felt that, human nature being what it is, the past was likely to repeat itself sometime in the future. I thought people should be made aware of the past, so I talked about it."

The nuns at St. Catherine's encouraged Deborah's activity; her classmates at the Southern boarding school were less sympathetic. "They were the kinds of girls you saw in *Ingenue* and *Seventeen* magazines," she told me. "They wore Papagallo shoes and Villager clothes. Half of them were from out of town. They came from country club families. They played tennis and went horseback riding. When I got to be fifteen and sixteen, the age when you start going to parties, I wasn't invited to those parties. I'd hear about them from catty girls at school."

Deborah paused to consider her words and I was again struck by her carefulness and by the value she placed on dignity. She disliked dwelling on what she called "negative things" just as she disliked people who took pleasure in spreading bad news. She was not the kind of person who would ever admit to having been humiliated. She was also careful not to burn any bridges she might later need to cross.

"I was accepted at school," she said now, "and we would discuss things on the telephone the way most young girls do. But when it came to a social life, I didn't have one. I hardly went out with boys at all. I knew that I would hurt my parents terribly if I began to go out with non-Jewish boys. I would have had to do it behind their backs and I didn't want to do that. I felt very committed to my parents and I just couldn't see going out and deliberately disobeying them, bringing more heartache to what they had already experienced.

"I was always aware of their experience and particularly aware of it when we had a disagreement. When I did something bad, my mother would say, *How can you dare not respect me? How can you talk back? I wish I had my mother here.* Whenever she reprimanded us, she brought it up to give extra force to what she was saying, to impress it upon us. And you know something—it made an impression on me. What can you answer? There's nothing to say. If I wanted to spend the night at a girl friend's house and my mother didn't want me to, or if I wanted to go to the movies and she said no, I felt I had no right to object. The degree of your suffering has no relation to the degree of suffering that she experienced. I don't think she did it to make me feel guilty. I think she really believed: *How can you consider this thing so important that you're willing to talk back to me?* You know?"

I knew. Of course I knew. Almost every child of survivors I had spoken to had described the same pattern of behavior that was superimposed on family arguments. Whether the dispute concerned dinner, new shoes, a sleepover date, college, marriage or travel, talk would shift from the question at hand and become a question of relative suffering. *How can you cause me pain?* our parents asked, implicitly or explicitly. *How can you add to our suffering?* Some children of survivors I spoke with were simply baffled by this logic. "I didn't know what to think," one young doctor told me. "I mean, I hadn't done anything to them. I wasn't a German." Other children responded with an anger that grew until they could barely talk to their parents. "It was emotional blackmail—pure and simple," said a young dance company manager. "Everything they did, their bad temper, their nerves, their judgments—everything was justifiable because of the war. I was always accused of being ungrateful. I always felt that they wanted me to feel guilty and I refused to. Why should I feel guilty or ungrateful?"

Others, like Deborah and myself, had acceded to our parents' point of view, identifying with it to such a degree that their values and ambitions became indistinguishable from our own. We repaid the emotional investment in our lives with absolute loyalty to our parents. We saw ourselves, in part, as torchbearers whose success was not only personal but a vicarious one for them.

Deborah's interest in beauty pageants had, in fact, been kindled by her mother. Whenever she took Deborah to dancing lessons or to child photographers, Mrs. Schwartz had been told that her daughter had unusual charm, good looks and personality. In the South, a state's beauty queen was a public figure almost as well known as the state's governor. By the time Deborah was in high school, Mrs. Schwartz had made inquiries about the selection procedure, and had become convinced that her daughter could win. She saw the title of state queen as one of the highest honors a young girl in the South could aspire to and by the time she was a Junior in high school, Deborah thought so as well.

Deborah did not, however, talk about entering any beauty pageants with the people she knew. "Almost all my friends thought the pageant was worthless," she said. "They thought it was a cattle show. Not the kind of thing a Jewish girl did. I didn't feel that way at all. I liked standing up there in front of all those people. I won the swimsuit competition and I was proud of it. But more than that, I was very aware of the fact that the title gave me a platform. I admired Bess Myerson and I knew that being Miss America had helped her in her career. It was a way to catapult forward and it opened up all kinds of doors. Miss America wins a scholarship to the university of her choice, and I wanted to go to law school after college. Had I won the title, it would have paid for my education and it would have given me a calling card to go into politics. I thought Miss America was a position that was being underutilized. I was far more politically minded than other girls who went to Atlantic City and I've always thought that was a factor in my not winning."

Miss Texas, who had a pet crab, won that year in Atlantic City and Deborah went home disappointed. The pageant had, however, taught her more about people and politics than she had thought possible. She determined to use her year as state queen to its fullest advantage. She led a march, danced the hora and gave a keynote address protesting the treatment of Jews in the Soviet Union, provoking the local newspaper to print "Deborah Schwartz ... extremist?" under her photograph. She addressed the State House of Representatives and State Senate, discussing her background and urging action to alleviate the plight of political prisoners. Then she turned the microphone over to her mother who gave what was probably the only speech ever delivered by a Holocaust survivor to a Southern state legislature.

For a year, with her mother as her official chaperone, Deborah was busy attending state fairs, visiting hospitals, touring army and marine bases, and appearing at political rallies along with people like President Richard Nixon, Vice-President Spiro Agnew, and visiting notables like Mrs. Moshe Dayan. She met with city managers and mayors, becoming familiar with both administrative and political procedures. She grew sophisticated in her dealings with the press and lost a good deal of her naiveté. That year, she also became even closer to her mother.

"We drove all over the state together," Deborah said. "It was the first time she took time off from the business and from raising the kids and she really loved it. I always had the feeling that my mother put everyone else first, that she never took enough care of herself. That year, she looked better than she ever had before. It was good for her. She never told me that she was living out her fantasies but I knew that both of us were doing the kinds of things and meeting the kinds of people that she herself might have wanted when she was my age."

By the time her reign ended, in the summer of 1971, Deborah Schwartz was exhausted. For the first time in her life she slept late, stayed at home and did little but read. Her year as state queen had given her an overdose of exposure. She was tired of crowds and publicity. Her college education had been interrupted and she wanted to get on with it. Also, she wanted to leave the South. Various institutions and political groups were asking her to work on their behalf, but she put them off. She planned to finish her undergraduate work at UCLA and then apply to law school.

"At the time, I wasn't thinking much about marriage or boys," she recalled. "When I was nineteen, I didn't have much experience with them. I had never been out with the same boy more than three times. I had not dated in high school and there was no time for it when I was state queen. I had never been the kind of girl who sat around dreaming about boys. On Saturday nights, I would read or talk to my parents or talk to my friends. I didn't feel any pressure from my parents to get married. I thought that was in the future, that I would get married when I was about twenty-five."

The Schwartzes had both come from orthodox Jewish homes in Hungary and although they had grown casual about religious observance in America, they retained a conservative, traditional view about marrying off their children. Often when they came to New York on business, they would inquire about suitable young men for their daughter. They wanted a stable young man from a good family that was wealthy and Jewish. When they met parents of a likely candidate, they talked about their daughter and showed off her photographs. "At the time, I didn't think they were looking to get me married," Deborah remembered, "but now I see they were. When they suggested I meet someone, I didn't mind. I know some kids would have told their parents

312

it was none of their business, but I didn't have strong feelings about it. I wasn't going out with anyone. My parents weren't my enemies. They wanted what was best for me."

One day in August, Deborah's father told her he had invited a couple he had met at a *bar mitzvah* to Sunday brunch and would she please be at home. They were Hungarian Jews who had emigrated to Israel after the war, left, and finally settled in Canada. Their background was very similar to that of the Schwartzes and they had a son who was four years older than Deborah. "My father was always seeking out survivors," she told me. "When he goes to New York or comes to Toronto, he always looks up people who had similar experiences during the war and people who came from his hometown. My parents' closest friends were survivors; they were like family. So when this couple from Canada came for brunch and spoke Hungarian and talked about the war, I felt as if I was meeting relatives. They showed me pictures of their son * Joshua. My father started showing off my trophies and my crown. He gave Josh's father photographs to take home with him. Me and a jet plane. Me in the pageant.

"I was used to that sort of thing. Sometimes when people came over to the house, I'd sit down and play the piano. I was used to performing. Sometimes I felt a little bit like a monkey but I did it anyway. I was a good kid. I could tell that my father liked these people. He thought that their family had all the right ingredients. Joshua's father liked me very much. He wanted Josh to fly down and meet me the next weekend, but Josh wasn't about to fly anywhere for a girl. He had too much self-respect."

After the summer was over, Deborah returned to college for a single term at the University of Miami, where she had previously taken summer courses. By coincidence, Joshua's work-study program had placed him in Miami for three months and the two finally met when Deborah offered to help him find an apartment.

313

"He arrived with his parents," Deborah recalled, "and I remember kissing both of them and then shaking Josh's hand. I wasn't swept off my feet by him but I went out of my way to help him get settled because of the family. There's this close bond that I've always felt with survivors. You feel they're like your parents and like all the people who died. I associated all survivors with my parents and I was very simplistic in my view of them. My parents were good, generous people who were ethical in their business dealings and respected by their community. I thought that the war had made them that way, that being good was their way of conquering the evil of their experience, and that this was true of all survivors. And also, my parents were so warm when they met other Jews from Hungary. They set the pattern: you behave differently with survivors than with other people. You're more tolerant. You make allowances. It was only later that my father said, 'You think just because they survived the war, all of the survivors were good? There were bad people there too.' I never thought about that. I felt a bond with them, naturally. Maybe if I'd grown up in New York City or in Israel, it wouldn't have been such an event to meet someone like Josh. But where I had grown up it was like headlines to meet someone like myself. I felt this element of excitement about it."

Joshua found an apartment and called Deborah occasionally. Their dates were calm and dispassionate. Once, when the Schwartzes were in town visiting Deborah, Joshua came over with roses, but he did not hand them to her. He laid them down on a chair. The restrained quality of his attentions impressed Mrs. Schwartz and puzzled Deborah. She could not make Joshua out. He did not try to hold her hand or kiss her. He behaved like an old, close friend. "That was a different experience for me—especially with a boy," Deborah recalled. "I felt very secure, at ease and close to him. We talked about our backgrounds a lot. We went over the stories. How our parents came to leave Europe, where they were from, where they had been during the war. We talked about the people whom we were named for. We talked about not having had grandparents, how we both wanted to have children and how they had to have grandparents. We both felt that very strongly. We were driving somewhere and he started whistling 'Bells,' which was a song my father always whistled to us at bedtime. I thought: Here's someone who knows the same songs as my father; here's someone who's like me."

Joshua's parents came down to Miami from Canada to visit and the Schwartzes came too. They all went out to dinner together and Deborah felt as if everything had been decided, without any formal declarations. His parents had made clear their welcome. Her parents liked Josh. The two couples behaved like long-lost relations and yet nothing had been concluded between Deborah and Josh themselves. He planned to return to Canada when his work period was over; she planned to transfer to a university in Washington, D.C.

"I was twenty years old. I told you I didn't have much experience," Deborah said, and her eyes sparkled at the memory of what she was describing. "When I drove him to the airport, I told him I loved him. I mean, that's what I had seen in the movies. He didn't say anything back. I thought: This limb I've gone out on isn't that thick; I can't say that again. I told him I'd miss him. He said he was going to come back to Miami for a weekend now and then."

When Joshua left, Deborah found herself unable to concentrate on anything. She could not eat or sleep. For hours she listened to records. She wrote Joshua air mail, special delivery letters saying that she was coming to Toronto and was going to go to school there. It was difficult to get accepted at a Canadian university so she hit upon the idea of enrolling at the Conservatory. At the end of the semester, she flew home and told her parents that she had to move up to Toronto.

"They asked me if I was sure and I said yes," Deborah recalled. "My father had a letter in his pocket from a guy in England who wanted to meet me. A banking family. I wasn't interested. I drove up to Toronto in a blizzard. My mother came with me. I had no snow tires on my car and the weather was so bad we got stuck in Syracuse. But we finally got to Toronto and I found an apartment."

Several weeks later, the couple was engaged, and in June of 1972 they married. Both the mayor and city manager of her town were at the wedding, as well as Deborah's business manager from the state beauty pageant and several other officials. The entire congregation to which the Schwartzes belonged turned out for the celebration. But perhaps most striking in the crowd of people was the contingent of Hungarian Jews who had traveled from all over North America to attend the wedding.

"All my father's friends were there," Deborah recalled. There were about three hundred and fifty people, with a lot of talking and dancing. There weren't many people from our own families. The actual number of relatives was very small. That was part of the reason I would never have run off and eloped. We didn't have all that many people left in our families. We had to take advantage of every opportunity for celebration.

"At the wedding, my father made a long emotional speech. He said that it represented a victory over Hitler, that it was the one way of fighting back. It was like a hammer that came down on everything. Everyone was just silent and crying. I was proud. I felt sad and happy at the same time. I felt the wedding was a symbol also. My whole family had been killed and I was rebuilding; I was continuing the chain."

Deborah smiled and crossed her legs. Her back was straight in her chair and yet she looked perfectly comfortable. Her thick, dark hair fell over her shoulders gracefully; a stillness held her body. I thought, as I had dozens of times since I had first met Deborah, that she should be a public figure or at least on television reporting the news.

"So I never went to law school," she mused, "and I'm not an ambassador. I'm a mother with two children and I light candles every Friday night and I change diapers. I feel like I've accomplished everything I wanted to do. I have the rest of my life to do politics, and I think I'll probably do some form of politics when my children are older. But I wanted to have children right away. I didn't want to wait because I wanted to be sure they would have their grandparents. I love watching them play together. I feel as though I'm paying my parents back in a way for all they've given me."

EIGHTEEN

In June of 1972, Tom Reed was working as a researcher in New York City's Addiction Services Agency, evaluating municipal rehabilitation programs for drug addiction. He liked his job and did it well. He took pride in the fact that he had shied away from offers of job placement at the Woodrow Wilson School at Princeton University from which he had graduated the year before. "I wanted to find my own job without the old boy network," he told me. "I didn't want to join the team. A student at the Woodrow Wilson School would go right into major institutions of power: the foreign service; the World Bank; the United Nations. It was like a factory for future leaders: you name it and we'll put you there.

"I felt I had to make my own way without their help. To be my own boss. I didn't want to buy into the world of Princeton; I had been raised with a distrust of that world. I wanted to be competent, to prove I could do what I did well. But I felt a very strong ambivalence about success on their terms: I was afraid I'd lose contact with who I was."

In 1969, when Deborah Schwartz had won her first beauty pageant, Tom Reed had graduated from Yale *magna cum laude*. He spent that summer trying to decide where to attend graduate school. He had been accepted with generous financial assistance into the Yale School of Art and Architecture; the Yale doctoral program in American Studies; the University of Michigan doctoral program in Sociology; the City Planning programs of Harvard and Berkeley; and the Woodrow Wilson School at Princeton. The letters had arrived all at once and he had let them lie on his desk in New Haven feeling guilty, confused and overwhelmed by the realization that he did not want to accept any of them.

"I kept thinking: What's the matter with me? Why aren't I celebrating? They all want me. They're giving me money. They think I'm good. Why am I not responding to it?" Tom paused and his quick hazel eyes lost their twinkle. He began to expel deep breaths of air, huffing like a small steam engine as was his habit when agitated.

"Sometimes I feel imprisoned by admissions of difficulties," he admitted, "as though the admission itself creates a reality that otherwise wouldn't be there. I like to see myself as healthy and functioning. For me to say that I need help with this stuff now or that it has been there for so long is hard. I'd prefer to say it's over and done with, resolved. But the fact is that all my life I've always carried this sense of mission, this legacy, this torch. I knew it had to do with a part of my past that I had not examined adequately. I had to be strong because it involved running and not walking. It meant accomplishment, reclamation, vindication. It involved a high energy output. During one part of my life I reveled in it but there were other times, like that summer, when . I tripped up and stumbled over the legacy. I'm only trying to work through some of those things now. At the time, when I was trying to decide where to go to graduate school, I wasn't

319

at all sure whether I was doing it for myself, my mother, my grandfather, or for some kind of larger historical purpose. I felt I was running into a brick wall. I was like a football player who fumbled the pass. And it wasn't just being a torchbearer; it was hurting while I was doing it. I thought a part of the legacy was swallowing pain, feeling pain. I was very mixed up."

All four of Tom Reed's grandparents were alive at the time of his birth. He was the only child of survivors I had spoken to who was not named after some relative who had died in the war. But he had a name story to tell me just like everyone else. "My father had always loved the book *Tom Sawyer*," he said. "To my father, who had grown up in Breslau, Germany, Tom was a symbol of America and the new world. His family name was Rotholtz which means redwood tree and, it was always emphasized to me, it's a tree well known for its survival capacity. But my father wanted to sever all connections with his German roots. Recently I've come to suspect he also wanted to assimilate. At any rate, he thought of translating and shortening the name to Red but since he had never heard of any American named Red, he settled on Reed. I've thought of taking back the name Rotholtz although I'm quite content with Tom. I've always considered it fortunate that my father hadn't taken as much of a liking to *Huckleberry Finn*."

Tom's cheeks dimpled around his grin and I thought he looked very much as I had imagined Tom Sawyer. He was slim and mischievous, with long nimble fingers that tapped the knees of his jeans and a mass of thick dark-blond hair that would not consent to lie flat on his head. At thirty, he looked like a college boy, although he had been working for five years and had published papers in scholarly journals. It was only when his face clouded suddenly or his features sharpened in reflection that the long story he told me appeared to be his own. Tom had contacted me because he had heard I was researching children of survivors and he

320

thought it was time to stop sitting on questions he had ignored.

He had taken leave of absence from his job for one year. He and his girl friend Cathy who—like all the other girls he ever dated—was not Jewish, had split up. The family had learned that his mother was seriously ill. For Tom, all these things had created a hiatus in his life: "the Great Divide," as he liked to call it. He was using his year off to discover what his own needs and wishes were, quite apart from those of his family. He was attending classes at the New School in New York City and working on a children's book for which he had received a contract. And he was examining his family history as he had never done before.

Both sides of Tom's family had lived in Breslau before the war. His mother's family was well established in the city, prosperous and intellectual. His grandfather, Tom had been told since he was a child, had been a well-respected lawyer, and his grandmother was one of the first women in Germany to receive a doctorate in chemistry. His father's side of the family was not as highly educated and not nearly as conscious of their social position, he said. "They were merchants. There was a concentration on making ends meet. At least, this is what I felt about them. The saga—the story of the exodus from Germany—seemed to be more the province of my mother's family than my father's. I don't remember when my mother sat down and told it to me for the first time but I always harbored a knowledge that my family's history was unusual and that it bore a special message for me.

"Basically, the story was that at first my grandfather thought he could wait it out, that Hitler was an aberration, that he had fought for the Germans in the First World War and that his rightful place was in German society. My grandmother, who was in some ways more intuitive than my grandfather, urged rapid departure. My grandfather found out about this boat that was taking refugees to America, the

St. Louis, and the whole family booked passage on it. My father's parents booked passage on the *St. Louis* as well. At the time, they did not know my mother's family. My father had left Europe already. He had been studying at the Charles University in Prague when the university was closed by the Germans. He had come to the United States by himself, was drafted and sent to the Pacific. For the duration of the war he had no idea whether his parents were dead or alive.

"On this single boat then, were my mother's entire family and my father's parents. They had papers that allowed them to land and live in Cuba while they waited for their American quota number to come up. My mother was fifteen years old then. She always pointed out to me the contrast between the niceness of the voyage and the craziness of subsequent events. The *St. Louis* was a luxury liner. She was together with her family and they were all heading for something potentially very exciting. At the same time, there was a sense of the world gone chaotic. Men were proposing marriage to strange women on the gangplank because they had lost their families. They wanted to be part of a family and didn't particularly care which one anymore The norms of behavior had gone askew. My grandmother's chemistry training came in handy because the passengers were not allowed to take any currency or valuables out of Germany. She had melted down some gold to form a black compound which she hid in shoe polish containers. I always thought that was super-neat. That after the cargo of the *St. Louis* was confiscated, some German was unwittingly polishing his boots with gold."

Tom Reed chuckled. It was clear he took pride in the story. Pride in the capacity of his family to survive overrode any sense of humiliation or shame at being driven out of Germany, he told me. It was easy for him to recount the saga of the *St. Louis.* He told it as if it were an old folk tale.

"My mother remembers the trip over as pleasant, in a way seductively pleasant. People dressed up for dinner. They

322

adapted themselves to the atmosphere of an ocean cruise. The German crew treated the Jewish passengers very well. Then, chaos broke loose in Havana harbor. The Cuban government reversed itself and would not allow the *St. Louis* to land. The ship would have to return to Germany, which meant disaster to all on board. My mother remembers people running across the deck, slashing their wrists, jumping overboard. The boat meandered slowly back to sea while the captain and a passenger committee tried to work out a strategy of action. My grandfather was a member of that committee.

"My mother remembers seeing the lights of Miami on the horizon, of being *that* close to the United States. There was talk on board the ship of staging a deliberate shipwreck, because in that case the nearest country would be obliged to rescue the survivors. Even if some people drowned, it was argued, that was a fate better than for the majority to return to Germany. The United States Coast Guard made sure, however, that the *St. Louis* remained outside of United States coastal waters, too far away from shore to make a shipwreck feasible.

"So the *St. Louis* floundered around the Atlantic. Finally, four European countries agreed to divide up the passengers. My mother's family went to London; my father's parents to Brussels. London was obviously the better choice, and I always guessed that since my grandfather was on the passenger committee he could choose where his family would go. My father's parents had a very difficult time. Belgium was soon overrun by the Germans. They never talked about this period and I never asked them about it directly. I always heard that they survived 'underground' and when I was a kid I assumed that they had lived in a basement somewhere."

Eventually, Tom said—he was not sure of exact dates— both families arrived in New York. His mother's family came in 1940: they had been vouched for by the grand

323

American matriarch of the family, Aunt Minnie, who was comfortably established in America. When they arrived in New York, they did not contact Aunt Minnie until everyone in the family was employed. They worked at factory jobs. Tom's mother and her sister were in fact supporting the family before they were twenty years old. They brought in more money than their father, who had been such a formidable figure in Breslau.

"Aunt Minnie was very impressed that they had found employment so quickly," Tom told me, with a touch of irony in his voice. "She would retell the story each year at Thanksgiving, the only time we were invited to her home. She liked her German refugee cousins, but she also kept a certain social distance from us. For thirty years, we were invited to her home only once a year, and it was only later that I was invited more often. My acceptance at Yale was seen by her as a vindication of her good judgment in sponsoring my family's entry into this country."

His mother's family settled in the largely German-Jewish neighborhood of Washington Heights; his father's family lived on the Lower East Side. They spoke less English than his mother's side of the family; they were poorer; and Tom sensed that they had lived through something that his mother's family had not experienced. His father supported them and always behaved as though he had an obligation to make their lives as easy as possible. Tom did not fully understand why his father spent so much time with them. He did know, however, that his father's family had not mastered their fate the way his mother's family appeared to have mastered it. This sense drew him closer to his mother's side. Tom felt that they had a message for him, something for him to know.

Tom's parents had met at the Breslauer Club in New York City, where they had discovered the similarity in their backgrounds. They were married soon after and left New York City for Pearl River, New York, where Mr. Reed had found work as a chemist. "In many respects I was an apple-pie American boy," Tom told me. "I lived in a small town, went to a spanking new school and had young, pretty teachers. I loved Annette Funicello, Topper, Superman, and Ernie Kovacs. I loved things having to do with space travel. I flipped baseball cards and owned a hula hoop and remained intrigued with the eventual fate of the Edsel. My family was not religious at all. Being Jewish was, for me, always more connected with the immigration story, the war, and European roots than any Jewish law or ritual. On Passover, my father would tell the story of our own exodus in addition to the one in the Haggadah. The repetition of that story always made me feel like I was their anchor in the new world."

Tom began to expel huffs of air from his mouth and his puckish face turned serious. "We lived modestly. We really didn't fit into the Jewish community. Not in Pearl River and not in Trenton, New Jersey. I felt our family was different. It occurred to me that had things turned out just a bit differently, I might have been German or Cuban or English or Belgian. My being American seemed fortuitous. My family always behaves as if there were a lot to be grateful for, and my father made a point of distancing himself from everything German. When he met strangers, I remember occasions when he would deny that he had been born in Germany. He would not buy German goods and I was not to be taught German, which made it difficult for me to talk to my father's parents who spoke little English. But I don't remember any outright expressions of outrage directed toward the Germans. Stories of losses were told dispassionately. Occasionally someone would say 'That one was shot by the Nazis' or 'That one didn't make it.' The rage and pain remained beneath the surface, and as a result it has taken me a long time to connect with these things in a less than oblique fashion.

"Now, looking back, I think that the mythologizing of my

325

mother's family was a way of bolstering my grandfather's ego against the great losses he had suffered. It preserved a continuity with his past, which was marked by considerable accomplishment. His past stood in contrast to his present and the juncture was so great that it needed a supportive bridge. Even the modest economic activities of his later years were held up as indicative of his strength of character. He worked as a bank teller in New York City and did a number of other odd jobs. He worked as a kind of superintendent in the apartment house where he lived in Washington Heights. It was a refugee building and all their friends were refugees. The social order that prevailed there hearkened back to a world long gone, on something not in the present. I had a difficult time connecting the social life I saw them engage in and their workaday life. My grandmother worked in a factory for a while and I remember going to visit her there, having a glimpse into a life I was largely unaware of.

"I was also very aware of my mother's losses. The war had interrupted her education as well as her adolescence. It had catapulted her into an adult role prematurely and forced upon her a raw exposure to life from which she would otherwise have been buffered. She was blown out of a comfortable middle class home and in this country she had to attend first to the needs of her aging parents and then to the needs of her husband and children. These two activities cut severely into the time she needed for herself. She was forever a bright woman operating in environments that did not use her full capacities. As I was growing up, I sensed a pact between the two of us that was directed toward some goal of accomplishment for me. She was very supportive of me when I was a child. She was never delinquent to my needs. I felt big with her hopes. I felt a sense of importance.

"My grandfather died when I was nine. It was the first death I had known and there was much concern over how I would take it. My grandfather had asked for me on the day he died and the nurse would not let me in. In the days following his death I was told that I had been the apple of his eye, how much he had wanted to see me grow up, how he had calculated ahead to the year 1968 when I would be twenty-one, exactly on Election Day, and would therefore be able to vote. It was stressed to me how important a man my grandfather had been in Europe. How the captain of the *St. Louis* had recognized his merit. How Aunt Minnie had been impressed with him. How he had written articles for *Aufbau*, the German-Jewish newspaper in New York. All the women in the family began to swing their supportiveness to me, the way they had to my grandfather. My own father somehow remained outside all these legacy notions. They were all invested in me because I was the first-born son and I liked it. I liked having my mother and grandmother and aunt all there believing there were big things in store for me."

For a long time, Tom told me, these notions had not interfered with his life. Like Deborah and myself, he had been very successful in high school with a minimum of effort. He was first in his class academically, editor of his Senior Yearbook and popular with his classmates. He did unusually well on his college board tests and was accepted by Yale. In the autobiographical essay that was part of his college application, Tom had told the story of the *St. Louis*. He had presented himself as a first-generation American who had a sense of mission that grew out of his parents' war experience. But, he told me, the full reality of the historical themes he wrote about did not hit him until he had actually settled in at Yale.

"I was awed by being offered an entrée into this community and I was *scared*. I didn't know whether I could be up to it. Yale breathed history. Outside my dormitory window was a statue of Nathan Hale. I studied in the room where Eli Whitney, the man who had invented the cotton gin, had studied. Morse College was named after the Morse who invented Morse Code. Every plaque or building bore the name of great wealth or accomplishment, and suddenly I

327

was consciously struck by the importance of my own history. For a long time, it had been a backdrop, which only occasionally made me pause to think. Now, I had the feeling that it had to be reckoned with."

Tom Reed bit his lip and expelled some more air.

"Perhaps I also turned to my own history as a way of contending with all those WASPy prep school kids whose fathers and grandfathers had gone to Yale for generations. I wondered a lot why I had been accepted at Yale and I thought part of the reason was the *noblesse oblige* of the university toward a first-generation immigrant Jew with the Holocaust behind him. Yale was changing at that time. It was the middle sixties. The New England aristocracy was opening up to let in a few stragglers. I felt like I had elbowed into the social register, that my acceptance at Yale was a victory of sorts. That I had made it in Aunt Minnie's world.

"At Yale, I worked as I had never worked before. At the end of my first year I was ranked fourth in a class of one thousand freshmen. I got to shake the hand of Yale's illustrious President Kingman Brewster amid great pomp and circumstance and organ music playing away in Woolsey Hall: there was always something very ecclesiastical about Yale ceremonies. Brewster represented, to me, the pinnacle of New England aristocracy. The boat in *his* family was the *Mayflower,* and that made him even beyond Aunt Minnie! Brewster was dressed in academic robes and my parents were sitting up in the balcony while a brief biography of me and the other outstanding young freshmen was presented to the audience. I signed a ledger where there were signatures going back to the founder of Yale, and to my mind at that time, that was the height of delivering something. I knew these were the stellar reaches but I also lived with the knowledge that something was going to give. I just could not keep up that pace anymore. The legacy may have given me energy and support but it had not really given me direction.

328

Other needs were pressing. I was beginning to ask questions of myself that all my family's support could not answer.

"My sophomore year was very rocky, really the beginning of the Great Divide. I didn't know where I was going or why. I was having trouble. I had no focus. I think I would have dropped out of school then had dropping out been a live option. But the Vietnam War and the threat of the draft kept me in school. There was a lot going on at the time: assassinations, marches on Washington, coming to grips with one's position about the Vietnam War. Things were being shaken up and I saw Yale itself go through some big changes. People like Kingman Brewster and William Sloane Coffin became national figures. They called members of the Yale community to a historical consciousness and a higher purpose. Kingman Brewster was saying: Don't worry about what you choose to study; you can study truth and beauty; you don't have to study practical things because the world is yours; you'll graduate from Yale and jobs will throw themselves at you; you'll be ushered into positions of leadership."

Tom Reed's voice tapered off. Even though he had graduated from Yale with honors and had gone on to Princeton, he viewed this period in his life as the beginning of a failure to live up to what had been expected of him. Talking about it was painful: he wanted to gloss over it. "Maybe all of this has no bearing on my life at all," he said suddenly. "Maybe all this legacy stuff is just a big blown-up excuse for what happens to everybody else. Maybe it's all done and over with and is history. I wish I could just dump it. Leave it all on your lap like a big pile of shit. I'd like to forget it. It's over. I'd like to go on with my life."

From the time he was a child, Tom Reed's greatest pleasure was drawing. He had always loved art and his teachers had drawn attention to his talent. But he felt terribly guilty about spending several hours a day "just drawing." Kingman Brewster's call to study liberal arts struck a deep chord in him, yet it also intensified an ambivalence that Tom had felt all his life. "I didn't feel that jobs would be so easy to come by and I certainly didn't feel that the world was my oyster. I wasn't, after all, a full-fledged member of the Yale community. I had lingering debts to a different past.

"That first year at Yale, I thought seriously about studying medicine. But I couldn't make the commitment. I finally opted for an interdisciplinary major in American studies and focused on social history and immigration. I connected with that but I felt split, as if everything I had worked for up till then was going to come tumbling down. My mother kept saying, 'You can do it, Tom. You can do it. Don't worry so much, just keep going.' And I kept thinking: No, I'm in real trouble. I'm not a robot. I felt like I was letting the legacy go. Apparently, I wasn't going to deliver anymore. I wasn't going to become someone great. I wasn't even sure I'd be able to hold things together long enough to get my B.A. I felt I had betrayed my heritage. I felt I had broken something then that even now is still healing."

Tom graduated from Yale and went on to Princeton. At both universities, he felt compelled to prove his competence by their standards and after proving himself, opting out of the community, as if to say: "I'm good enough. I just don't want to do it your way." He felt split in half, and that split deepened after he left school and began to work for the Addiction Services Agency. He received promotions and regular raises in salary, but the trouble that had started when he was a sophomore at Yale did not go away. It embittered his dealings with his parents and began to interfere with the relationship he had with Cathy, who came from a non-Jewish, American family and was growing impatient with Tom's persistent difficulties with something he could not even identify. His mother's illness served to exacerbate even further Tom's conflicting feelings of obligation to the past and to the present. His younger brother was studying to

330

become a doctor and Tom often felt that the torch had been passed to him.

At twenty-nine, Tom finally did what he had wanted to do ten years before. He took time out. He left his job. He lived alone now and was working on cartoons, drawings and a children's book. He had put a lot of thought into the notion of trying to live out a legacy and had wanted to find people with whom to explore it. When he discovered I was writing a book about children of survivors, he was not surprised; he had wanted to write one himself, although his parents had never been in a concentration camp and his immediate family had remained intact.

"I wanted to help generate a community where before there was none," he said. "I didn't seem able to do it by myself. I wanted to work it out, let go of the legacy, so that I could get on with my own life."

NINETEEN

Community. That was the word repeated by every child of survivors I spoke with and the word which had never held reality for me. For seven years, from the time I returned from Israel to attend Columbia University until the cold March morning when I came to Toronto to interview Deborah Schwartz, I had alternately searched for it and tried to persuade myself that it did not exist. Maybe, I thought, there was no community there.

I tried, at those times, to pretend I did not feel the weight of my iron box, but its contents weighed more heavily with each passing year and became harder to disentangle. As soon as I began to examine a memory, even as concrete a one as my mother locking herself inside our bathroom when I was a child, some mechanism inside me set to work dissolving that memory, casting its authenticity into doubt, denying that it had ever occurred. I began to question not only my memory but the health everyone had always told me I possessed. When I went skiing in the mountains of New Mexico and in the evenings, blond vacationers sat in the chalet lounges drinking beer, I saw instead the Germans and Austrians my mother had told me about, the ones she had been among in 1938, in the Tyrolean Alps. In New York City, when the visit of a political celebrity or the calling of a mass rally brought out troops of uniformed policemen, my mind turned similar tricks and I saw troops of S.S. men instead of New York cops. Sometimes, in banks or in post offices, or any large bureaucratic institution, I would feel suddenly overwhelmed by helplessness or rage: the clerk processing my inquiry became a Gestapo agent and I his victim, with no rights at all. I was too old for this kind of paranoid fantasy, I told myself. My reality was different from that of my parents I had grown up in America a privileged child who had never once encountered an out-right incident of anti-Semitism. Like Tom Reed, I was loath to admit that I was in any kind of trouble, though. I wanted to straighten things out myself.

In those seven years, I did a lot of reading. Like many other children of survivors, I tried to find answers in history books. I read Churchill, Roosevelt, and Hitler. I read personal first-hand accounts of the concentration camps by former prisoners as well as by the soldiers who liberated them. I read psychiatric studies of Holocaust survivors. I reread James Baldwin and Ralph Ellison, who had both understood the effects of a history of persecution on personality. I read about the survivors of Hiroshima and their families after the Second World War. Analyses of the uprooting, deportation and slavery of black Americans and research into the destruction of Japanese communities after the explosion of the Atomic Bomb gave me some important keys to my own situation. I began to see that although "War is hell" had become a truism of American literature, few writers pursued the destruction that did not end with a peace treaty. Human lives were more subtly and permanently altered by violence. I began to understand why history books had always failed to bring me to an understanding of the times they purported to represent. Al Singerman had once told me, "Unless we start examining the Holocaust with our emotions, all we will pass on to future generations is numbers."

In 1974, in an effort to force myself to feel what I never could in the presence of my parents, I became a consultant to the William E. Wiener Oral History Library which had undertaken to record the life stories of two hundred Holocaust survivors who had emigrated to the United States. I was to interview both my parents as well as write the final report on the entire project.

The taped interviews I conducted with my mother and father were useful because, for the first time in my life, I heard their histories from start to finish in clear chronology instead of in bits and pieces. I now had a reliable source to refer to, a stable, unchanging record of my family history. But the tape recorder and the outline of questions I had been given by the Library only served to remove me farther from the feelings evoked by my parents' narrative. I was not, ostensibly, asking questions as a daughter but as an interviewer collecting data for posterity. My emotions were cut off; I was a professional. It was not very different from the time, twenty years before, when I was a child listening to my parents talk in our apartment kitchen about the years in camp. I felt a tightening in my chest and throat but I would not allow myself to cry while my parents could see. When my eyes betrayed me, I fiddled with the tape recorder or developed a sudden desire to fix something to eat. My attitude was cheerful. At twenty-six, I still felt the need to protect my parents from further pain.

They still felt the need to protect me as well. Neither one of them was enthusiastic about my taking on the oral history project. "When they put it all in the archives, you think someone will be interested to sit down and read what I tell you?" my father asked me. My mother, always the pessimist, did not ask. "This is all very nice but a little late," she said. "Nobody was interested in us when we were in camp and nobody is interested in us now. Hurry up and get it done, will you? All you'll get is a reputation as a Jewish writer for your trouble."

My parents did not understand what I was doing.

Like most survivors neither imagined how, over the years, I had stored their remarks, their glances, their silences inside me, how I had deposited them in my iron box like pennies in a piggy bank. They were unconscious of how much a child gleans from the absence of explanation as much as from words, of how much I learned from the old photographs hanging on our apartment walls or secreted away in the old yellow envelope below my father's desk. Like all people, they saw what they wanted to see and I did not, for the most part, contradict that vision. They had watched their daughter graduate from journalism school, publish articles in prestigious publications, become an assistant professor at New York University, enjoy many good friends, fall in love with a man they liked. They felt they had raised a relatively happy child into a happy adulthood. They could not figure out why I was "obsessed with this Holocaust business" as my mother put it. She wanted other people— Americans, Germans, all the Jews who had lived comfortably while she was in prison—to remember it. She would have liked my middle brother Tom, who had refused a *bar mitzvah*, refused to speak Czech and was now working as a ski instructor, to take more of an interest in his family's background. But she wished I would drop it. I would make myself sick, she said.

That, essentially, was what I proceeded to do. For an entire summer by a lake in the mountains of western Massachusetts, I read thousands of pages of personal testimony from concentration camp survivors who now lived in America, I read detailed descriptions of families in small towns in

Poland as well as the large cities of Germany, Czechoslovakia and Hungary. I read day-by-day accounts of survival in the forests, in attics and cellars, in Sobibor, Dachau, Terezin, Auschwitz and Maidanek. I read details of liberation and resettlement in Displaced Persons camps, and then of the passage to America, after which the case histories merged with my own memory.

By the time I wrote up the official report for the Wiener Oral History Library, I was saturated with the past and so filled with feeling that at times I could barely speak. The numbness I felt when I heard my own parents' stories disappeared when I read the accounts of others. I could take those in more readily. For the first time, I saw my parents' lives in the context of others. I could put them in perspective and measure them against a community. I had never known any family to place them in. Those survivors I had never met, whose lives I read about in transcript after transcript became a substitute for family. It was then that I realized I had to talk to their children.

"It was suddenly so obvious to me," a Tufts medical student later described to me the same revelation I had experienced then. "How could people go through an experience like that and *not* expect it to have a residual effect on their children? I kept thinking it had to be brought out in the open and that we had to do it ourselves. I kept thinking it was time for Elie Wiesel to move over. That there was another generation coming up behind him. I wanted to find and talk to those people."

By 1975, when I completed my report, the first wave of children of survivors was nearly thirty years old. Many of us were already working as physicians, psychiatrists, psychologists, social workers, educators, lawyers, in business and in the arts. Like most young professionals we were busy establishing our credentials, learning the ropes of working life and starting our own families. But in addition, several children of survivors began to apply their professional training to clarifying the issues that were troubling me. They too wanted to create a community, to make visible the peer group that had remained invisible and silent for so long.

Some began to write about children of survivors. "They are removed in place, time and culture from their parents' ordeal," wrote Toby Mostysser for the Jewish Student Press Service in 1975. "Many are ignorant of the specifics of what their parents went through. Yet the Holocaust is no more a set historical event locked away in textbooks and commemoration ceremonies than it is for their parents ... They possess as their own the emotions that grew out of their parents' uprooting, persecution and near extermination."

Others began to organize groups. In January of 1975, five New Yorkers associated with a small Jewish quarterly called *Response* sat down around a tape recorder to articulate their feelings about their families and the war. That group, which included a Legal Aid attorney, a social worker, a university administrator and two doctoral students, attempted nothing more than a conversation, yet the publication which printed it was passed from hand to hand, reaching well over the three thousand people on *Response's* subscription list.

In the spring of 1976, small notices reading *Groups Forming for Children of Holocaust Survivors—Call Eva* began to appear on Harvard, Brandeis, Boston University and Tufts University bulletin boards, in Cambridge bookstores, in kosher butcher shops, and in Boston's *The Real Paper*. Eva Fogelman and Bella Savran, both trained psychotherapists and children of survivors, had read *Response* and had decided to organize short-term awareness groups, centering around the issues that the five in New York had raised. After a year, they had talked to nearly one hundred children of survivors in the Boston area. Some had telephoned as soon as they saw the notice, spoke for an hour, rang off and were never heard from again. Others carried the notice in their wallets for months before deciding to call. More than half of the eighty students and young professionals the two women interviewed said they had no previous affiliation with any Jewish social, political, religious or cultural organization. A few said that the notice was the first indication they had ever had that they belonged to a group of peers.

In New York that same year, fifteen sons and daughters of Warsaw Ghetto survivors founded Second Generation, "a living testimonial to Jewish resistance during the Second World War," they said, and a vehicle for bringing members of the second generation together. Three of their original members appeared on WNET, the local educational television station, and within a few months they had more than two hundred people on their mailing list.

Meanwhile, unaware of any of these organizations, I had been trying to interest *The New York Times* in publishing an article on children of survivors, with no success. There was no indication that such a group existed, I was told. There was "no news peg," no event that made such an article "fit to print" in a newspaper. Then, early in 1977, an Israeli psychiatrist on sabbatical at the Stanford University Medical School gave a lecture on children of survivors. "The trauma of the Nazi concentration camps is re-experienced in the lives of the children and even the grandchildren of camp survivors," the university press release describing his findings began. "The effects of systematic dehumanization are being transmitted from one generation to the next through severe disturbances in the parent-child relationship."

A small item adapted from the release appeared in *Time* Magazine and shortly after it did, I received a telephone call from *The New York Times.*

For a full year after my article appeared in *The New York Times Magazine,* I received letters from children of survivors throughout the United States. The letters were long and intimate, like letters from long-lost relations. Some were written by teen-agers still in high school; others by professionals whose stationery bore impressive letterheads. Some wrote that they had read and reread what I had written for

338

several days in succession, unable to fathom how thoughts that they had believed to be so personal, so secret, so particular to themselves could be shared by others. Some wrote that they had not dared to read the article for weeks, but kept it beside their beds or desks like a touchstone or a lucky charm.

In the fall of 1977, I sat down in a room in New York City with ten other children of survivors who had been brought together by Al Singerman in the first of several small gatherings planned by the Group Project for Holocaust Survivors and Their Children. Al, together with Steve Schultz, a psychiatrist and also a child of survivors, and two volunteer psychologists, had drawn up a plan through which many such groups would begin to meet in the New York area. In Chicago, Detroit, Los Angeles, Toronto and Jerusalem, similar groups began to meet. Psychiatrists in the United States, Canada and Israel began to receive funding for research into the "long-term effects of persecution." Radio and television stations and newspapers in these countries began to take an interest in children of survivors.

In that room in New York City where eleven of us joined clinical psychologist Florence Volkman Pincus, there was a wonderful stillness. Ruth Alexander, small, pale, and more than a little nervous, sat across from Tom Reed, who was still not sure he wanted to "go public." Al Singerman and Steve Schultz glanced around the room with the pride of founding fathers. Lillian Weisberger, an auburn-haired fund raiser, sat beside Miriam Singerman, who taught children with learning disabilities. Jeff Benkoe, a newspaper reporter, sat between Edie Jarolim, a doctoral student in English, and Richard Lichtenstein, an artist and blacksmith. After we had settled down, Jeanette Wasserstein, a training psychologist rushed in, like Tom, still ambivalent about her participation.

We examined each others' faces in silence. The eleven of us were children of parents who had fled Austria, Hungary,

Czechoslovakia, Poland, Russia and Germany. Among us we had lost hundreds of relatives. Our parents had lived out multiple variations of survival. We ourselves, I thought as I looked around the room, were strikingly different people, people who would not have met under ordinary circumstances. I felt a tension in the air, a great sense of expectancy, as well as great reluctance, fear, anger, sorrow, embarrassment, hope and strength.

"Well? Shall we start?" said Florence Volkman Pincus.

The community I had spent so much time looking for had finally emerged.

EPILOGUE

The apartment on Riverside Drive where I grew up is quiet now. My mother lives there with my younger brother David, alone since my father died three years ago. He died of a heart attack which struck as he was walking in the sunshine down the street near the building where we lived. Strangers who saw him fall to the ground placed a pillow under his head. He never opened his eyes again.

My father had not wanted a rabbi to speak at his funeral. The service was brief. There was no eulogy. Instead, the Czechoslovak national anthem was played on a phonograph. Despite the concentration camps and the years in America, my father had never stopped thinking of himself as a former officer in the Czechoslovak Army, and a sportsman who had represented his country in two Olympic Games.

The small group of mourners in the Riverside Memorial Chapel seemed to understand this. All belonged to the dwindling community of Central European refugees who spoke

German or Czech better than English and who still met on walks in the country north of the city or during intermission in concert halls. They were the human bridge that linked my father's life in Europe to the one he had started, at the age of forty-four, in America.

A skeleton of family stood among the mourners. My father's wealthy first cousin was there, our version of Tom Reed's Aunt Minnie, who had vouched for my parents when they came to New York and who had provided their first bread and board. My mother's first cousin Peter, whom we children had always called Uncle and who had lost his entire family in the war stood beside my mother, my two brothers and myself. There were three other relatives.

My father did not like monuments any more than speeches. He had told us for years that when he died he wanted to be cremated. He wanted to be part of life, the water, the fresh air that were as precious to him as family. He wanted us to think of him when we went swimming or skiing. It was only infrequently, when he examined the strong, American faces of his children, that he voiced his hope that we would remember to say Kaddish.

One wet foggy day we buried his ashes at the top of the tallest mountain in western Massachusetts where, my mother said, they would eventually merge with the soil to help things grow. My father had always loved the Berkshires. They reminded him of the Czech countryside of his childhood. He also liked the New Englanders who listened to his odd accented speech with unfailing courtesy and who took such pains to keep their communities beautiful and clean. My father saw these people as the best in America, the people to whom he owed his life and the well-being of his children. "These last thirty years were a gift," my mother said when we left his ashes there. "By all laws of probability he should have died then when Mengele told him to go one way and then changed his mind and sent him on the other line. All the rest, all that time afterwards, was a great gift."

In the weeks and months that followed my father's death, my mother began to talk to me with a candor and a warmth that had somehow become unglued from the stiff, emotionless casement that had constricted her words before. "The night of the Communist *putsch* in Prague," she said, "when those factory workers were marching, armed, in the street, and your father decided we had to get out, I was terribly scared. I had a newborn baby. I realized that your father was forty-three years old and overly optimistic. I hated the idea of being someone's poor relation in America. That goes so against my grain. And I knew we would have to be dependent in the beginning. There was no way out of that. He had the idea he would become a water polo coach in New York and although I didn't know what coaches were paid in America I knew it would not be enough to keep us all above water. But your father was like a rock for me. If he said so, **we** were going.

"You were too little to understand what it was like. Daddy couldn't find a place for himself. He had jobs where on every Friday he could be told that he would be laid off. Sometimes for three days. Sometimes for two months. The insecurity drove me crazy, and I couldn't say anything. I couldn't reproach him because I knew he was doing what he could. But he was in my way at home. He helped with the dishwashing and the diapers but the apartment was tiny and I was working there.

"I got those terrible broodings. I thought that we were always going to be in this awful pinch. Both of us worked in seasonal businesses and there were times when neither of us made money, when we were living on unemployment insurance and then the first of the month came and all those bills had to be paid. You and Tommy weren't the calmest of children. You needed attention. I was working and cooking and cleaning the house, and I began to think that it all wasn't worth it. There were times when I thought there was no way out. I felt trapped. I wanted to kill myself. I wanted to kill you and Tommy too. That's what finally sent me to Dr. Rabinowitz. I was slapping the two of you and it was like I was slapping myself. You don't remember in the morning I would go to the doctor before I started working? Don't you remember?"

I did not remember my mother going into analysis just as I did not remember her taking my brother and me and a picnic hamper every day in the hot August weather on the subway and then the train and then in a taxi to Silverpoint Beach so that we could breathe the sea air. But it did not matter that I could not remember. What mattered was that a silence between us had been broken, the constraint that had muted our conversation was gone.

My mother still works as a dressmaker in what should be the master bedroom of her apartment. She still chain smokes cigarettes and the small blue tattoo on her forearm still makes strangers avert their eyes. She still has bouts of anxiety about her children and occasionally she will fall into one of those deep, seemingly bottomless depressions that terrified me when I was a child. But my mother seems to have inherited the vitality my father left like a legacy to us. Her laugh, which she had always claimed to have lost in the war, is strong and happy. She still works and listens to music with an intensity that I have rarely seen in other people. Lately she has learned to relax a bit, to have a good time, and sometimes I catch glimpses of the girl she must have been before the war, a girl with sparkling, flirtatious eyes who loved to dance.

I am thirty now and, like my two brothers, almost as tall as my father. Both my brothers are skiers, as avid for the mountains and the winter snow as my father was for the water. My brother Tom lives in a small town in Vermont and spends his days on the slopes teaching people how to ski. My brother David, who has just graduated from high school, spends a great deal of time watching television and studies electronics. They do not give much thought to his-

344

tory and neither of them care much for books. But when we are together with my mother at home, we feel a bond so strong that our differences melt away. None of us is frightened anymore when our mother succumbs to exhaustion or depression. Instead, we have learned to tell her that she is one of the strongest persons we have ever known, that she has survived far worse, and that she most probably needs a rest. My mother, in turn, has learned that her children cannot always be happy, healthy and free of pain. She worries less.

My brothers, like many other children of survivors, have lately begun for the first time to ask my mother questions about our grandparents, the relatives we never knew, and exactly where and how our parents survived the war. Like Al Singerman, who at the age of thirty-one, has begun to talk to his father, like Ruth Alexander and Tom Reed my brothers are often astonished at what they hear—and filled with pride. In 1978, when a series of nationally televised programs was aired on the Holocaust, my youngest brother arrived at school surprised to find his classmates discussing the subject he had never heard them talk about before. "It was just weird," he said, laconic as always. Then he added, "I told them that my parents were there."

Bibliography on Children of Survivors

1966 Rakoff, Vivian: "Long Term Effects of the Concentration Camp Experience," *Viewpoints* Magazine, March, 1966

1967 Rakoff, Sigal, and Epstein: "Children and Families of Concentration Camp Survivors," *Canada Mental Health,* Volume 14

1968 Trossman, Bernard: "Adolescent Children of Concentration Camp Survivors," *Canadian Psychiatric Association Journal,* Volume 13

Krystal, Henry: *Massive Psychic Trauma,* International Universities Press

1971 Sigal, John, and Rakoff, Vivian: "A Pilot Study of Effects on the Second Generation," *Canadian Psychiatric Association Journal,* Volume 16

Sigal, John: *Second-Generation Effects of Massive Psychic Trauma, Psychic Traumatization,* Little, Brown

1972 Kestenberg, Judith: "Psychoanalytic Contributions to the Problem of Children of Survivors from Nazi Persecution," *Israel Annals of Psychiatry and Related Disciplines,* Volume 10, Number 4

Rustin, Stanley and Lipsig, Florence: "Psychotherapy with the Adolescent Children of Concentration Camp Survivors," *Journal of Contemporary Psychotherapy,* Volume 4, Number 2

1973 Sigal, John, Rakoff, Vivian, Silver and Ellin: "Some Second-Generation Effects of Survival of the Nazi Persecution," *American Journal of Orthopsychiatry,* April, 1973

Barocas, H., and C.: "Manifestations of Concentration Camp Effects on the Second Generation," *American Journal of Psychiatry,* Volume 130, Number 7

Lipkowitz, M.: "The Child of Survivors: A Report on an Unsuccessful Therapy," *Israel Annals of Psychiatry and Related Disciplines,* Volume 2, Number 2

The Child in His Family (Yearbook of the International Association for Child Psychiatry and Allied Professions), edited by E. James Anthony and Cyrille Koupernik, John Wylie & Sons

"Children of the Holocaust" section includes articles by Judith S. Kestenberg, Moses Laufer, L. Rosenberger, Erna Furman, Dov Aleksandrowicz, Hillel Klein and John Sigal

Karr, Stephen David: "Second-Generation Effects of the Nazi Holocaust," unpublished doctoral dissertation, California School of Professional Psychology, San Francisco

1975 Personal communication, Henry Shaw, Melbourne, Australia

1977 Personal communication, D. Heroma Meilink, Amsterdam, Holland

1978 Personal communication, William G. Niederland

Savran, Bella, and Fogelman, Eva: *"Therapeutic Groups for Children of Holocaust Survivors,"* paper unpublished at time of this writing

In 1975, *Response* Magazine devoted an entire issue to children of survivors. That issue has been reprinted in paperback and is available as:

Living After the Holocaust, edited by Lucy Y. Steinitz with David M. Szony, Bloch, New York, 1977